Career Strategies

Planning for Personal Achievement

Career Strategies

Planning for
Personal Achievement

Andrew H. Souerwine

amacom

A Division of American Management Associations

The chapter-opening quotes from Sydney Harris's column
on "winners and losers" are reprinted by permission of
Sydney J. Harris and the *Chicago Daily News*.

Library of Congress Cataloging in Publication Data

Souerwine, Andrew H.
   Career strategies.

   Bibliography: p.
   Includes index.
   1. Vocational guidance. 2. Job satisfaction.
I. Title.
HF5381.S6469   650'.14   77-28087
ISBN 0-8144-5454-2

First Printing

To

About the Author

Andrew H. Souerwine is professor, Department of
Management and Administrative Science at the
Graduate School of the University of Connecticut.
He is a management consultant in management
development to several large organizations. Dr.
Souerwine is a member of several societies includ-
ing the American Psychological Association and the
American Society of Training and Development. He
is listed in American Men of Science; Who's Who in
the East, 1971; Who's Who in Consulting;, and
Community Leaders of America.

Preface

OVER a decade ago, when I was working with a Fortune 500 company on matters related to human resources planning and development, we became acutely aware of high turnover among career employees who had been with the company three to five years. A closer analysis as to why so many were leaving led, among other things, to the observation that these young people had no sense of identification with the corporation. They remarked that while the company had focused considerably on the kind of training that would make them technically sound in their present jobs, it had done very little to help them prepare for future jobs and to assist them in developing the career mobility that is so much needed in today's business world.

In an attempt to reduce the turnover, the company embarked on a variety of projects, one of which was the initiation of some formal training for these newer employees. At the outset, our mission was to prepare a developmental experience that would cut across departmental lines—that is, cover subject matters of value to all participants, regardless of technological or departmental affiliations—and that would prepare them for future jobs in their career path.

As we pondered the content of such a project and discussed the matter with individuals who might be part of this experience, we became aware that to these highly capable young people, "career mobility" did not necessarily mean "movement into management." They were still wrestling with some fundamental career questions: How far is "up" for me? Do I want a career in management or do I want to remain in the more technical aspects of this business? How much time do I want to devote to a job? How do I resolve the potential conflicts between job and family? How can I be effective with a boss who. . .? Should I compete with my fellow colleagues? Is this the place or the industry for me to make my career?

In fact, as we tried various designs of the program, we learned that most of these young people had not done much thinking about their careers and had not formulated a broad career plan, even for the short term. This led us into a design that focused on providing people with opportunities (1) to generate data about themselves for all aspects of their careers (not only the job as such) and (2) to have private, confidential discussions with professionals who understood the company and the kind of data that these people were generating.

The first point of our program gave these young people an opportunity, often for the first time, to sit back and do some concentrated and guided thinking about their careers. The second was even more important and to us became the "added ingredient" that made the experience such a meaningful one for the participants: the opportunity to get a second party's objective viewpoint on one's own personal data.

The conferees were prepared for those private sessions by being exposed to concepts about people and their careers, and then by learning how to apply these concepts to the evaluation of special case data developed for this program. We gave the conferees experience with trying to apply concepts to the analysis of other data before they turned to examining their personal data. This was done prior to their private session with the professional.

This book covers many, but not all, of the subjects discussed in these conferences. It covers what I consider to be some basic concepts that must be understood and accepted before a specific career plan can be formulated. Even if it is not possible to cover all the specific situations in which an individual might find himself, he will have a better chance of developing a successful career strategy once he understands the concepts underlying what he is trying to do.

In this sense, this book is different from many of the how-to texts on the market. I've tried to take the reader through some concept building, with concrete examples to bring the concepts to life, and with a genuine interest in giving the reader a reason for following my suggestions on implementing a career strategy.

Nevertheless, the book does not ignore practice. Throughout, I have tried to provide real-life examples and situations, specific recommendations on what to do, and some exercises that may help the reader to bridge the gap between concept and practice. When all is said and done, nothing much can happen unless the reader is willing and able to follow through and act on what he has read.

The book is written primarily for the individual with some business experience. Most of the examples are drawn from that perspective and will therefore be meaningful to that experienced group. Nevertheless, those about to embark on a business career can gain much from this volume by paying heed to the planning process and its potential barriers both inside and outside the organization.

Those previous references to "he" are, of course, in the generic sense only. They are not meant to exclude women or to suggest that women should not be considered in any discussion of careers. This book can be of equal value to men and women in the pursuit of fuller and richer careers.

Because the book is so much a result of experiences with young people currently in business, I must express a great sense of gratitude to the more than one thousand young people who were willing to talk with me confidentially about their careers. They are the living laboratory for career planning.

To my professional colleagues who worked with me on developing the content of the seminars and who were willing sounding boards for new ideas and approaches—in particular, to Drs. William N. Goodwin, Herbert Spirer, Boris Yavitz, and James Healey—I wish to express my appreciation for their willing hours of discussion and counsel. Special thanks go to David Phillips for his valuable help, not only in the seminars, but in reading and in assisting with portions of this manuscript.

And, of course, where would all this be without the careful typing and editing necessary? I am particularly grateful to The Travelers Corporation for providing me with excellent secretarial expertise, in great part from Miss Gladys Hewitt, who suffered through my sloppy handwriting and unorganized manuscripts, and occasionally from Ms. Lee Tworek. I must also thank my own secretary, Mrs. Dorothy Wolinski, and Mrs. Grace Adams, Mrs. Sally Bonjour, and my son, Drew, for their timely help when deadlines were imminent.

With any activity, it is a matter of choosing. When the writing had to be done, other choices suffered. My wife, Jane, understood the joys and sorrows of making those choices; that is why she is so much a part of my own career.

Andrew H. Souerwine

Contents

1

Why Develop a Career Strategy?

Some Implications from the Current Scene

GEORGE Richards, a young and outstanding management trainee with the Levy Real Estate and Urban Development Corporation, was just offered an opportunity to transfer to the Atlanta office as assistant general manager. To the great bewilderment but resigned attitude of his boss ("I can't understand kids these days!"), George refused the transfer. George indicated his appreciation for Levy's expression of confidence suggested by the offer, but expressed greater satisfaction for the lifestyle his wife and he are enjoying on their New England farm near Springfield, Massachusetts. George knows that this puts Levy Development in a bind and is willing to resign if the company so desires.

A recent article in *Business Week* by Arch Patton points out that "the chief officer of a company can no longer think of himself as standing at the head of a monolithic management corps. Instead, he will find that management below the top level is *increasingly con-*

1

cerned with what it wants for itself rather than what the company wants of it."* (Italics mine.)

An advertisement in *The Wall Street Journal* reads:

> Mrs. Robinson just may throw you a curve. Luisa Robinson used to grin and bear it when that "large economy size" turned out to be neither large—nor economical. And when she passed a belching factory smokestack—well, she just held a hanky to her nose. Not anymore.
>
> Nobody knows better than you do how far the Mr. & Mrs. Robinsons of this world will go, these days, to get their point across. They'll go to their local newspaper, for instance. Or their congressman. Or Ralph Nader. They'll even stop traffic with a picket line, if necessary. . . .†

Jim Turner works for General Motors Corporation. His job is to mold clay models of the new car designs being considered for manufacture five years hence. About his job, Jim says: "It's okay. Actually it keeps the wolf from the door and really keeps me in enough money to do those things I really like to do. Every evening I rush home from work and spend time—sometimes until 2 A.M.—in my studio over the garage. I hope some day to have a one-man show of my sculptures."

An article in *Fortune* states:

> Until just recently, research into the causes of aging produced such confusing and fragmented results that there seemed to be little hope of understanding this truly universal affliction, much less doing anything to counteract it. . . . Now, a dramatic turnaround is evident . . . the scientists have closed in on two related sets of bodily functions, the endocrine and the immune systems, where they are beginning to detect coherent mechanisms of senescence.
>
> What's more, the scientists are beginning to manipulate these controls of aging in laboratory animals. Their goal, it should be emphasized, is not to create a society that would be overwhelmed by the senile old, but rather to prolong the healthy middle years of

---

* Arch Patton, "Ideas and Trends—The Boom in Executive Self-Interest," *Business Week*, May 24, 1975, pp. 16–20.
† *The Wall Street Journal*, October 2, 1975, advertisement for *Reader's Digest*.

life. As that becomes possible, the life span intrinsic to the species will be stretched—for the first time in history.*

Business Week reports:

> The flexitime concept gets a wider test. . . . Although the concept of allowing employees a degree of flexibility in setting their own working hours has been discussed for years, the so-called flexitime system received its biggest boost last week when the House of Representatives voted by a wide margin for a major federal experiment under the direction of the U.S. Civil Service Commission. . . . Representative Bella Abzug (D-N.Y.) says that while both men and women benefit from "the greater degree of control . . . over one's work and lifestyle," she agrees with a recent foundation report that "flexibility in work schedules is a critical step toward equal opportunity for women." †

This list of incidents could be expanded tenfold. Similar ones are occurring every day. But the above items are examples of the dramatic shifts that are taking place in the quality of the working life and in the attitudes and value systems of workers. You—we—are caught up in these changes, changes that have impacts on how we look at our jobs, the decisions we make about our careers, the lifestyles we follow and to which we aspire.

These dramatic cultural events provide, in fact, an insightful backdrop to a rationale for thinking seriously about our personal career strategies. Indeed, they emphasize the growing importance for individuals to do more on their own in the shaping of their careers rather than to rely solely on the organizations of society— companies, clubs, municipalities—for direction and control.

In the following, I list some of the more telling of those factors.

Cultural Shifts

People in our society are becoming more educated. I do not mean by this that they are becoming brighter or more intelligent. Nor do I suggest that their education is "better." It's simply a fact that more people are being exposed to more experiences. They

---

* Gene Bylinsky, "Science Is on the Trail of the Fountain of Youth," *Fortune*, July 1976, p. 134.

† *Business Week*, May 24, 1976, pp. 37–38.

know more; they are learning more. Whether what they are learning is "good" for them is not the point.

Adult education is already "big business," and it's destined to become even bigger as more individuals see the necessity to learn more, not only to keep up with the technical and professional demands of their jobs but also to learn about the many activities and projects which, when entered into, help to lead to "the better life."

Classes in arts and crafts, music, literature, and business are booming; travel, sports, and leisure time activities are legitimately planned as a necessary part of the lifestyle of a growing number of individuals from all socioeconomic classes. These resources are no longer reserved for the fortunate few.

We are becoming more concerned with achievement for the sake of expressing ourselves as individuals rather than achievement for its own sake. In the language of the behavioral scientist, we are more concerned today with self-actualization. Our fathers and forefathers were caught up in a socialization process in business organizations that imposed job titles and responsibilities beyond the training of individuals, their interests, and, in some cases, their capabilities.

It led to the Peter Principle—the observation that people were promoted to their level of incompetence. It led to individuals becoming terribly ineffective in their jobs because the jobs did not respond to their strengths or interests, although they did provide some monetary rewards and status in the organization.

It led also to adjustment problems, with the increasing incidence of typical psychosomatic disorders and rising frustrations and conflicts in dealing with others, both off and on the job. It led, in short, to the inevitable problems that people feel when they are forced to change their interests in order to pursue their jobs.

This is gradually changing. Although it is true that organizations tend to socialize their employees so that the organization's goals are assured of accomplishment, people and organizations are beginning to see that perhaps both the individual and the organization can be served and that it is no longer an either/or matter. Workers are beginning to voice a concern—either through their unions or individually as did George Richards and Luisa Robinson at the beginning of this chapter—for the priority of their interests and values. In contrast to those before them, they are saying, "I will not change my interests in order to pursue your job. Better that I change jobs in order to pursue my interests." The need and concern for full employment is giving way to the need and concern for full living.

And so it can be. Our society has done much to fulfill the so-called basic needs of its members. Social security systems, portable and vested pensions, unemployment and welfare programs, fringe benefits of unions and corporations all make it possible for the vast majority of us to live at some marginal or higher level of existence if we so choose.

That is one of the messages of *The Greening of America* by Charles Reich.* The recent severe recession of the mid-seventies bore this out as well. Lack of employment did not deter the worker from his desire for a winter vacation in Florida. Neither did it have any positive impact on absenteeism or productivity or quality of work.

The fear of losing one's job—especially one that is not satisfying, not responsive to self-actualization—is no longer the fear that it once was. People now have options that make achievement stamped with one's own sense of self more probable. If they can't get it on the job, they know they have a reasonable chance of obtaining it off the job, in their extracurricular activities, as did Jim Turner in one of the items cited earlier. This, as you might expect, has led to a different way of looking at jobs.

The concept of job is shifting from one of singularity to one with serial and/or multiple dimensions. Let me explain. As I've indicated previously, a worker would join a company and do all he could to stay with it for his working life. Gold watches and forty-year pins were marks of achievement. That concept of loyalty is fading, primarily because of the concern for greater self-actualization on the job.

The younger worker entering a job is thinking more in terms of a series of jobs during his or her life span. "I'll work as a systems analyst until I'm about 30; then I'll see what happens. I have interests in other areas, and I think I'd like to get involved directly with the sales operations and try that out. Hopefully, by the time I'm 50 or 55 I can think of leaving all of this and maybe go into teaching or perhaps open up my own small business. We'll see how things develop."

That kind of scenario is not uncommon. And as the healthy middle years of life expand, as our article on the Fountain of Youth suggests, greater opportunities arise for a varied and longer career. Because there are more options, workers tend to think more in terms of keeping those options open. While some are thinking about it as a

* New York: Random House, 1970.

sequence of activities or careers over a life span, others develop the complexity of careers at a given moment in time. Because their interests are varied and they do not want to choose one priority at the sacrifice of others, they create career styles that permit involvement in two careers at the same time.

It is becoming more common to read of the young worker who during the day pursues an active career at work and, after hours, runs his own business or pursues social and/or political activities that satisfy a different, yet dominant, set of interests. Indeed, companies are responding to this, for example, by paying half an employee's salary while he attends activities that satisfy a specific individual and company need; and the other half of the salary may be picked up by the local Chamber of Commerce or the local university to serve still a different dimension of the worker's and the employer's interests.

Flexibility in planning careers is more realistic today than it was a generation ago. As options increase in number and as workers see a greater probability of being able to respond to those options, yet another shift in worker behavior will result.

Individuals are expressing their concerns more openly. Self-control, "biting the bullet," is giving way to an era of rising entitlements, to consumerism, to pressure groups, to attempts to shift the power base so that it serves individual concerns. Our item on Luisa Robinson exemplifies that; so does the one on George Richards. And so do many of the legal cases against big business regarding affirmative action.

As people become more vocal, companies and governments are trying to provide systems that are set up to listen and respond to expressed feelings. When people know what their concerns are, when they are able to express their feelings accurately, and when they know what they think ought to be done to alleviate those feelings, then the systems can respond, and usually do. The problem, of course, is immeasurably larger and more complex when neither the agency nor the one who voices his concerns knows precisely what needs to be done.

In the area of career management, situations like the following are commonplace. The disenchantment of the well-educated, underutilized management trainee is a recognized phenomenon in today's business. After a few years (at most) of training and orientation to the company and to the business, many young people experience a letdown, a feeling that they are not growing, that their work is no longer challenging, and that they do not have a sense of accomplishment.

It is relatively easy to voice those feelings to a boss. But somehow, hearing about those feelings must be translated by the boss into a course of action that, hopefully, will reduce those feelings in the younger worker. When the boss counters with: "I appreciate how you feel, and we want to help. What kind of an assignment are you looking for? What kinds of new responsibilities would you like?" it now becomes the responsibility of the worker to respond in some way that will ultimately lead to *specifics* in the definition of new assignments.

Unfortunately, our experience has been that the young worker does not support his complaint with a carefully thought-out idea of how he'd like his job—present or future—to be structured, except for reiterating the glowing generalities of wanting "more challenge, more responsibility, more opportunity to grow."

You can readily see that we are making a case for some carefully structured thinking about career strategy *before* such feelings are expressed. The frequency of opportunities for workers to express their concerns about their jobs is increasing dramatically. But the opportunity should be linked with a responsibility for developing an action plan that meets your own sense of priorities within the context of the realities of the environments in which you function.

Partial Sum-Up: Cultural Shifts

American lifestyles and value systems are going through some changes that have a profound effect on careers. More importantly, the changes are opening up opportunities for individuals to reap the rewards of an effective career strategy. Because most of our lower-level needs are basically satisfied, most people in our society are experiencing greater opportunities to seek "the better life." They are becoming more concerned with striving for a kind of career that permits them to be themselves, "to do their thing." They seek jobs that respond to their interests, values, and needs; they express a disenchantment with jobs that do not provide opportunities for growth and for using one's own resources. And if they can't get those satisfactions on the job, then they are willing to move or to do things off the job that will support that growth need.

The problem, of course, is complicated by the fact that most people are quite hazy about what they want. And the more ambiguous that picture, the more unlikely it is that they will be able to respond in positive ways to these opportunities. Opportunities can be grasped only when they are perceived, and they are perceived within a context of knowing what is wanted and how to go about getting it.

Organizational Concerns

The shifts in society's value systems are reflected in what is happening internally in many American corporations. These events produce another series of arguments in support of personal career management.

1. *There is an increased interest in goal-setting activities.* This takes its most usual form through MBO—management by objectives. While the interest is there, the competence for implementing it is usually lacking. The process typically takes the form of concern for setting and achieving organizational goals, with little regard for how those goals fit into personal career objectives.

There is little question that the organization's goals must be served if it is to survive. There is more of a question whether those goals must be served at the expense of individuals. Indeed, our earlier discussion of shifts in worker values indicates that workers find it increasingly difficult to endure a manager-subordinate relationship that is one-sided—concerned with the manager's goals but not with the personal plans of the subordinate.

The companies, of course, are aware of this trend. They are responding with flexible scheduling hours—that is, they give workers a choice of when to arrive in the morning and when to leave in the afternoon, insisting only that the required number of hours be spent at work in a given day or week. They are experimenting with four-day work weeks. They are providing more fringe benefits that provide more and more opportunities to workers to make choices about the amount and quality of their leisure time.

They think they are responding to it, also, through a simple addition to the MBO process. We are finding an increasing number of organizations that now include as a part of the process of objective-setting a portion reserved for the employee's personal goals. Subordinates may experience it almost as an afterthought. The boss says, "Tell me, subordinate, now that we've agreed on your job goals for next year, what are your own personal plans? What do you look forward to doing in the next five years?" (Almost as if it's possible to separate job goals from the personal life of the worker.)

Usually that conversation doesn't go very well, primarily for the reasons discussed in the remainder of this section.

2. *Managers are usually ill equipped in the skills necessary to carry off a counseling relationship.* The result is that the conversation between manager and subordinate is limited in scope, often does not probe the significance of career planning, and may contribute little to resolving the complex of conflicts that inevitably arise among company, personal, and family goals.

When managers are asked to work with subordinates on developing company goals, they frequently see this as a difficult chore, albeit one that is within the realm of their skills and their understanding. But when they are asked to probe less familiar territory, to become more "personal" with subordinates and discuss something other than "the job" or "the business," the very ambiguity of the situation, coupled with a lack of understanding of the psychology of such counseling, leads to a shallowness of discussion and a feeling of frustration on both sides. Or in an attempt to keep the discussion structured and less ambiguous, the manager clings to what he knows—the career paths laid down by the company for individuals in his function—and recites a litany of steps to the top that may be only tangentially related to the personal career concerns of the subordinate. The result: another unfulfilling conversation for the subordinate.

Even if managers had the skills, such conversations would probably not take place for another reason:

3. *Most organizations do not reward managers for helping subordinates to develop personal career plans.* Of course, most organizations would deny this. They say that they urge their managers to develop their subordinates and that they encourage training programs of all types. They say they urge subordinates to take on greater responsibility, to "learn the business," to "grow." But managers are paid for results, results that are *directly* related to the business *today*, not a year or five years from now. The emphasis is on performance related to achieving this year's goals of the company.

So be it! But the end result of this is that it takes a sophisticated manager to get to the point where he or she realizes that time spent on personal career counseling of subordinates today may have a greater payoff in subordinate performance next year than time spent on this year's company goals. Most companies simply do not reward managers for that kind of future-oriented activity. Until such time as managers are evaluated and able to get "brownie points" for the longer-range development of their subordinates, they will stick to the more immediate, more tangible, activities of doing today's job today.

The manager is not alone in this quandary. Subordinates have their problems with this as well, which is another reason for lack of effectiveness in most career planning efforts in companies.

4. *Subordinates themselves have not given much thought to their careers and don't know how to go about managing their careers.* That's a bold statement, but not far off the mark. We are very socialized products of the environments in which we must work and play. We begin to develop ideas of what we want to be, in some part, at least, on the basis of what it is we think society (the company) wants us to be. We mouth these "should be's" in general terms such as "I want to be a vice president some day"—and end up in that corner office, knowing eventually that the position is wrong for us. We develop all sorts of myths (which we'll take up in the next chapter) about what is needed to make a success of a career, and we build a career structure on these groundless foundations.

But even when we give a lot of thought to planning our careers, we tend to simplify the process (human beings do so much want to make things easier for themselves!) by looking at what's available, by stating the goal first before we really know whether it makes sense in terms of our total resources and probabilities of attaining it. We rarely go through the exercise of trying to find out exactly who we are, what we really want, what our priorities are, or whether reality is *really* what we think it is.

So when the boss suddenly confronts us with the question "What are your plans?" we usually parrot back some institutionalized response that may be close to what the boss would like to hear but far from what would be best for us and the organization.

Here is a case in point. A young woman, with her MBA and over five years of successful experience as a systems analyst, came to me recently for some guidance. She was upset with herself.

"I'm so mad at myself! I really blew it! The company has just initiated an MBO program, and the other day I had my goal-setting session with my boss. At the close of the session he asked me what my career plans were over the next few years. I honestly was taken aback. I didn't know exactly what to say. I had some ideas, but they seemed too vague and too personal, and certainly not the thing to say to my boss.

"So I heard myself saying some inane thing like 'I'd like to be a product manager and then move into general management some day,' only because it sounded right and I knew he'd be pleased. As I think about it, I'm not sure that's what I want at all. I'd like to talk to you about it. How do I go about setting meaningful career goals, and how do I go about communicating these things to my boss?"

I didn't dare tell her to wait until this book is published to find the answers to her questions! We talked—and I'm sure she'll be ready for the next conversation she has with her boss about her career plans.

Rationale for Planning

We have seen that a shift in attitudes and values is providing more of a rationale for the development of personal career plans. Secondly, we have seen that companies, while seeing the need for such emphasis, have not provided either the managers or the subordinates with the knowledge and skills necessary to implement career planning. A third rationale centers around a series of concepts related to individual development and change. What do these concepts tell us that may be valuable for understanding why personal career planning has some real payoff for those who engage in it?

1. *Individuals change best when the motivation for change comes from within the person rather than from outside.* The psychologists use the term "internalized motive" to refer to that inside motive; "externalized motives" is used to refer to those outside.

For example, when you say, "There's not much that I can do about my career until my boss shapes up and does something," you are relying on an *external* force to make change happen. Now, you may be correct; maybe the boss must do something in order for something to happen to or for you. But our experience indicates that even when such is the case, you can, if you wish, do things yourself that may hasten the boss's doing something. The waiting game rarely provides optimum payoff to the person who is doing the waiting!

Or you might say, "Things would be different for me if only my wife (husband) were to behave differently." Again, the motive for change is externalized. Change occurs more effectively when you say, in essence: "Things must be changed, and I am the one who must initiate the change. I must, in fact, change myself first. There are things that I can do which will have the desired payoff for me." This is an expression of an internalized motive. The "I" is feeling the responsibility for change.

When we shift from an attitude that suggests that the company, the boss, the spouse, or the children are responsible for what happens to us in our careers to an attitude that embraces the idea that we are responsible for our careers, career planning will be initiated more rapidly and change occur more effectively.

No doubt about it, that change in attitude to an "I" attitude is a difficult transition. We frequently believe that the control for our careers is in others' hands (again, see the next chapter on mythology). But, if you think about it hard, you have a lot more control than casual thinking would suggest. You really set many priorities on your job; you really decide in many ways what you'll get excited about and what you won't, when you'll agree with your boss and when you won't, when you'll stay a few extra hours and when you'll take a longer lunch or leave a bit earlier. In conscious and unconscious ways we set our priorities. We can rely on ourselves to give direction to our careers if we want to. Our chapter on motivation explores these ideas more fully.

2. *Individuals change best when their objectives are specific rather than general.* We'll have a lot more to say about objective setting in another chapter. Here we want to emphasize what appears to be obvious: we do more when we have purposeful direction. Once we have a specific purpose, we see change occurring more readily than when that purpose is general. Why? Specific objectives permit us to seek specific feedback on how we're doing. General objectives give only ambiguous information about how we're doing.

Here are some examples: "I don't worry about my career. I take things as they come. That way there are no surprises—no disappointments, no big events. Things just happen." Indeed they do. This is, of course, an expression of a reactive career. Under this set of conditions, an individual doesn't know when he's succeeding or failing, because he has set no goal criterion. As has been said in many ways: "When you don't know where you're going, any road will get you there."

Not too different is an objective stated in general terms: "All I know is that I want to get ahead; someday I want to be somebody."

Or, "I really want to do a better job." We're getting closer here, but the objectives still are lacking in specificity.

"To get ahead," "a better job"—these are relative terms that have different meanings for different people. Our experience has been that frequently the user of the phrase really doesn't understand what he means and finds it difficult to translate it into specifics. "Well, you know, a better job. A job that—uh, well, does more for me than the one I now have, one that's more exciting, more interesting." The problem is to get the individual to pinpoint this even more in terms of what specifically is exciting and interesting; this is when the objectives provide more direction.

More about this later; but for the moment, let us emphasize that putting performance measurements, time limitations, job titles, and actual rewards into the statement of a career objective makes it more specific, easier to determine whether it's achieved or not, and, therefore, easier to provide information to you about whether or not change is really occurring. And knowing that the desired change is happening provides considerable personal satisfaction.

3. *When people know that they are changing in a desired direction, there is a feeling of satisfaction.* That satisfaction provides for heightened self-esteem, and that increase in self-esteem leads to desire for more personal growth.

It's a happy cycle of events. We set our own goals, having decided that we can do something about change (internalized motivation). We make certain that we can measure our degree of success in the accomplishment of our purpose (specificity of goals). And then we see that we are actually accomplishing what we wanted to do.

It makes us feel good ("Look what I did!"); it gives us more confidence in our own ability to do things ("I have skills and abilities that help me achieve"); it all provides us with an awareness of who we are and how we fit into the scheme of the larger society (self-esteem, a sense of personal identity and worth). And all of this encourages us to try out other of our resources in other areas of accomplishment. ("If that worked for me, maybe this will, too!") Hence change occurs best when individuals have had some prior successes with attempted change.

But what happens when there is failure? That's not all bad. Failure certainly lets us know what our limitations are under the conditions in which failure occurred. More importantly, insofar as failure gives us an opportunity to learn without loss of self-esteem, it can be a very maturing experience. It gives us clues as to our limitations, what we need for further growth, what areas of our behavior need attention. That's why you'll be reading later that certain aspects of a career plan should be tested initially in environments that minimize the potential for psychological failure—the loss of self-esteem.

4. *Individuals change best when there is a personal commitment.* What is becoming apparent is that individuals don't change in a vacuum. They need feedback. The more specific that feedback is, and the more directly related to one's own behavior and specific personal objectives, the more informative it is; but more than this: it has an emotional characteristic that is lacking when the feedback is more general.

For example, note the degrees of emotional commitment in these steps in the training of managers in interviewing techniques. Step 1 (low personal emotional involvement): read literature on effective interviewing techniques. Step 2 (moderate involvement): be able to identify from videotapes good and poor interviewing techniques in others. Step 3 (heightened emotional involvement): have your own interviewing techniques videotaped and review them with direct feedback from a professional. In the first step, there is no real desire for change since one's own self is hardly involved. As your own self becomes emotionally more involved, commitment to change becomes stronger.

5. *Individuals change best when changes are timely and gradual rather than dramatic and revolutionary.* Change takes time. Individual change takes patience and time. A career change decided today can usually not be achieved by tomorrow. Most changes require a series of events to occur in some evolving way. Granted, we can help some or all of those events occur; but even then, the magnitude and complexity of career goals demand shifts in attitudes, values, policies, and procedures—and that takes time and careful planning.

Summary

Why, then, start on a venture of developing and implementing a career strategy? We've suggested here a rationale based on certain aspects of the changing American scene. First, the working group is becoming more educated and aware of the increasing number of options available to them. Second, there is greater concern for achievement through self-actualization. Third, more people show an interest in a series of jobs over a lifetime or in a job with multiple career dimensions. Fourth, there are greater opportunities today for self-expression and openness.

While many corporations now pay greater attention to goal-setting activities, there are certain manager-subordinate factors that stand in the way of successful career development programs. These include (1) a lack of managerial skills necessary to implement an effective counseling relationship; (2) a lack of a reward system for helping subordinates to develop personal career plans; and (3) a lack of thought and know-how about career strategies on the part of subordinates. As we have seen, individual development is most likely to take place when certain conditions are met; in particular, there is a need for internalized rather than external motivation, specific rather than general objectives, higher rather than lower self-esteem, personal and emotional rather than impersonal and unemotional commitment, and a slower, more steady, and planned change of events rather than a revolutionary, dramatic change.

There are, of course, many other ideas that might be listed as reasons for doing some serious thinking about one's career. Whatever they are, the fact remains that evidence is growing for the value of developing carefully thought-out career plans. We are now in a position to take a closer look at the important elements in formulating and implementing a career strategy.

We start with some "old bromides," some typical responses to the question: What's important for a successful career?

A winner has a healthy appreciation
of his abilities and a keen awareness
of his limitations; a loser is oblivious
both of his true abilities and his true
limitations. *Sydney Harris*

2

A Mythology
of Career Growth

Some Questionable Virtues for
Winning

I'VE worked all my life to get to this corner office—and I hate the job!" "There are so many things that I'd like to do, but I just can't find the time." "I'm on a treadmill. Every day there seems to be more and more to do; the list just keeps getting longer." "I'm boxed in; this company and my boss have me over a barrel."

Comments like these reflect the speakers' frustrations and anxieties about doing more with their careers and lives. And the people making them represent the entire range from the young in business to those with seniority, from clerks and management trainees to seasoned executives, from those in manufacturing, retailing, finance, and insurance to those in private ventures, from those who have no special desire to change jobs or move ahead to those who aspire to the heights of an organization.

In their struggles to cope with their careers, many people do some planning—perhaps more to the point, many do some dreaming. Although usually not written down or even well thought out, their plans and dreams are built on assumptions about people, bosses, organizations, and self that influence the individual's thinking and behavior. But such assumptions are the framework for the formation and implementation of career strategy. If they are reasonably correct, the strategy has a chance of being efficient and effective; if they are questionable, the strategy will be questionable.

Experience of working with hundreds of men and women in various organizations suggests that people develop a kind of mythology about the sorts of behaviors that they think are necessary for growth in a career. Their "rules to live by" emerge from a set of personal experiences, reinforced by social mores and recitations by bosses, parents, and teachers—people in perceived positions of influence. Because the behavior related to those rules seems to work, we find it difficult to question them, to break away from them, or to find out whether other guidelines would be more—or less—productive.

After all, we are creatures of habit: we cling to those behaviors that seem to work. Why trust our luck to the unknown? The result is that over the years we develop a mythology which, when tested against the data of human and organizational behavior, lacks real support. The myths persist because they "sound right"; they seem to possess "common sense" and "fit" into our perspective of what constitutes the road to career growth.

Because so much of a person's life is spent on the job and because most individuals think about careers in terms of vocational choices, the following examples of career myths pertain primarily to business organizations and jobs. However, careers extend beyond the world of work to one's family and community and, indeed, to one's self. These myths, therefore, apply equally to other aspects of a person's career. When an example refers to the boss, it could just as readily be wife, husband, committee chairman, or someone in a power position; and reference to subordinate could mean wife, husband, children, committee members, or anyone in a subordinate role.

Myth 1:   *The virtue of hard work, or "All good things come to those who work long hard hours."*

Our changing social values are beginning to raise questions about this principle. Nonetheless, it is particularly prevalent in the thinking and actions of people early in their careers. Those in power positions often fan the belief that long hours of devotion to the job are a necessary prerequisite for the next move, whether upward or laterally. People guided by this myth feel driven to put in 10 to 15 hours a day, six days a week, hoping to impress their bosses with their devotion to duty and assuring themselves and their families that "this is all necessary if I want to grow" and rationalizing that "I'll be able to do other things later on."

This keep-on-working compulsion raises some questions, however. First, a large body of data indicates that bosses and subordinates, teachers and students, and parents and children often have significantly different concepts of what the job to be accomplished really is. Just for starters, then, we can imagine the wasted energy when an individual works hard on what he thinks his job is, not realizing that his boss has a different idea as to what constitutes the dimensions of the position. The boss's perspective is that the subordinate is working hard on the wrong things: "He spends so much time on irrelevant matters; he really has no sense of the important responsibilities in his job."

To avoid this kind of confusion, organizations have initiated programs that encourage open discussion about the job between the subordinate and the boss. If and when those conversations occur, they typically seem to follow the line of: "You're doing a good job. Keep up the good work. You're one of us, and you're bound to grow if you just keep doing what you're doing." (Parents say: "You're such a good boy! Mommie's so proud of you!")

Spurred on by the general feedback, many people hypothesize: "What I'm doing is putting in long hours; at least I can't stop doing that and maintain the same image. Therefore, I'll keep working long hours." So that's what they do, putting in many hours at activities that (1) may have little or no relation to what the boss considers necessary, (2) have little or no relevance to the individual's effectiveness on the job, and (3) most important, have little or no relevance to their longer-range career growth.

While hard work may do little for an individual's progress in his career, it is often its own reward. Apparently, people like to work, to keep busy; most, given a choice, would choose to work rather than remain idle. Nevertheless, while keeping busy provides some satisfaction, something more is needed to sustain an individual's interest. Work should provide a sense of growth, achievement, self-esteem, and adequacy. Teachers, parents, and bosses who develop environments designed just to "keep the person busy" ignore that element of personal motivation.

Take, for example, what typically happens to most new employees in business. Despite their uniquenesses, they are frequently all exposed to the same training programs. "After all," says management, "there's a body of information that has to be learned, and there's an ideal, logical sequence for learning it. Since we find it difficult to differentiate among our people early in their careers, we'll treat you all alike."

The result: the same faces are seen in a sequence of training exposures, and there are no significant differences in compensation early in careers—all seem to get that first promotion at about the same time. Significant differences among workers are more likely to occur later. Not surprisingly, then, the hard-work myth persists on the assumption that it will pay off later.

Myth 2:   *The virtue of good work, or "All good things come to those who perform well."*

There is a growing belief among many in business that performance is what counts. Do a good job and you're bound to move along in your career. There is no question that doing an acceptable job is important, but we again run up against that problem of knowing what a "good acceptable job" is, as defined by the manager who seemingly controls career direction.

The situation appears to call for setting mutual goals by boss and subordinate so that each knows the direction and purpose of the other's behavior. This response is fine if the goals are indeed mutual and related equally to the concerns of both. But that is the rub! It is difficult for most bosses to be concerned with the longer-range concerns of their subordinates unless there is a payoff for them. The boss has a job to do, and his concerns for his subordinates are primarily related to their getting that job done. Building time and activities into a subordinate's job that will take away from the boss's immediate goals, even though it might serve the longer-range goals of both, sets up a value system that is difficult to impart to operating managers. Unfortunately, only a few companies put that kind of emphasis into the accountability and reward system of the line manager's job.

Thus, when the subordinate does a good job, it may not necessarily be "good" as far as his or her career growth is concerned. Individuals who are overly concerned about doing a job well in order to satisfy the boss, without regard for how that fits into their own career strategies, will find themselves with fewer options and more dependent on the boss and the power structure. Doing the present job well will lead to career and personal growth only when it encourages some activities that are more future-oriented. However, the subordinate must be clear in his own mind what that future should be. The impetus, in short, is really with the subordinate, not with the boss.

Myth 3:   *The virtue of the good boss, or "Growth in a career is largely a function of the kind of boss you have."*

This myth grows out of the assumption that career growth is something that "happens" to a person or that a person is somehow helpless to grow if the climate is "wrong." While we cannot deny the value of a helpful and supportive environment in enhancing one's career, we can question the defensive behavior of those who resign their fate to the quality of their bosses. Such a passive role denies the importance of one's own actions in lending direction and purpose to a career.

The realities of life suggest that rarely, if ever, are personal needs met without overcoming barriers. We just don't have perfect spouses, perfect subordinates, or perfect bosses. But the imperfections in our lives should not lead us to abandon goals that are dear to us. Rather, we have to struggle with the flaws in our lives and try to find ways to overcome or minimize them.

And yet, when it comes to considering possible strategies for careers in business, an amazingly large number of people tend to resign themselves to the imperfections of the organizational structure. Such a passive response may in fact be defensive ("If I can blame someone else for my lack of growth, I remain unscathed"), or it may be facing up to reality ("I indeed have an impossible boss"). This kind of thinking leads some subordinates to believe that the best they can do is to respond to what the boss wants and "keep my nose clean." They believe they can't do certain things because "my boss wouldn't like it" or "it's not in my job description."

The truth is, however, that probably not one of us does everything in his job description, and practically all of us do things on the job that are not a part of it. We create our own jobs; we tend to pick and choose, delay, ignore, add, and subtract from our jobs in accordance with our desires. We decide how much we'll really produce and figure out ways to tell the boss what he wants to know about what we do on our jobs. We do, in fact, have more control than we wish to admit over our daily activities. But how much more comfortable it is to blame our actions on "the other guy"!

The same passive acceptance of imperfections of the organization leads others to say, "Look around for the comers and attach yourself to their star; ride your own growth on their progress." As long as the "comer" keeps going, that strategy may work. But "comers" come and go; power structures change, and as they do, those associated with them may be affected.

To establish a career on what one hopes someone else will do is to create a dependency that denies the development of the mature adult. It places one in a passive role that implies that the direction for change comes from something outside the individual, that the subordinate behaves and changes primarily as a result of direction from his superior. A quick glance at that premise will bare its shallowness. External motivational factors are effective only when the subordinate perceives their value for the things that are important to him.

Myth 4: *The virtue of "They," or "When my manager cares about me, my career will grow. The little guy can't do much on his own."*

Somehow we conjure up an image of the manager as a sacrificial lamb, someone who toils without regard for himself and his needs, but with untiring and unquestioning dedication to the needs of those who work for him. Such managers do exist, but they are rare. Nonetheless, organizational policies on managerial responsibility for organizational development lead many to believe that every manager has a deep and abiding concern for employee development.

A problem arises when this concept is translated to mean: "They (the organization) tell me that my boss cares about me. Therefore, the onus is on my boss. C'mon, boss, show me that you care!" The wait for this to happen can be a long one.

The problem, of course, is that "they" are really "we." The issue of caring has to start with "us." In the process of career growth, we are inevitably led to consider the motivating forces from within one's self—the values, attitudes, beliefs, needs, wants, and desires that give direction to careers and to lives.

Myth 5: *The virtue of the perfect figure, or "If you really want to achieve in this world, you've got to determine what your weaknesses are and then work hard to correct them."*

In comments to executives regarding decisions on corporate strategy, Philip Selznick suggests that corporations will increase their probabilities of achieving if their strategies are based on effective utilization of their "distinctive competencies"—that is, the things they do uncommonly well, better than their competition. Corporate strategy is based on strengths.

The same can be said of personal career strategy. The people who succeed in achieving career objectives are those who base their directions on what they do uncommonly well. Rather than strive to overcome weaknesses, they build their careers on their strengths and then strive to improve the deficiencies in what they already do well.

Myth 6:   *The virtue of uniform quality, or "Whatever you do, always do your best."*

This, of course, is a corollary to the virtue of the perfect figure. There are those who would argue that since a person puts time into a project or activity, he should perform that activity as best he can. Those who follow that advice are usually scrambling to do more, frustrated by their seeming level of incompetence, anxious about their lack of accomplishments.

Such advice ignores the complexity of a career strategy and the necessity to put objectives into priority order, with different standards of performance for each. Which should be done to the very best of one's abilities? Those duties with the highest priorities; those tasks for which the performance standards demand the best from the person.

And which should be done at something less than one's best? Assignments that can be accomplished at something less than the highest standards of performance.

We've all had the experience of having to do a job that we know has to get done but that doesn't rank high in our scheme of things. These are the jobs that "get done," but with a minimum of concern for our best efforts. The situation, our priorities, and our goals simply don't demand any more.

Myth 7:   *The virtue of action, or "Doing something is better than doing nothing, and doing more of something is better than doing less of something."*

We learn by doing, so there are those who would say that if we want to learn, we've got to act. There is indeed virtue in action, because without it we lack the feedback that tells us whether we are making progress toward our goals. The greater problem, however, is knowing when to act and knowing the quality demanded of the act.

Because timing is an important ingredient, action taken when the situation does not provide the opportunity for proper feedback will not lead to efficient learning. In fact, it may "teach" the person something the teacher does not wish to convey.

A case in point is the young woman who returned to work after two weeks at a management seminar, all fired up and ready to do the new things she had learned at the seminar. Her enthusiasm pushed her into her boss's office with ideas that the boss wasn't quite sure he understood, and at a time when he had been waiting for her to return to complete a key project.

In a situation like this, the boss doesn't necessarily care or understand, and his behavior may show it. The young woman can easily conclude that because the boss is not interested in her ideas, he really should have gone to the management seminar instead of her.

But the same new idea, presented about a week or so after the boss's needs are taken care of, may win a more enthusiastic reception. Delay in doing something can, in many cases, be better than action.

When people decide to act, they somehow feel that doing more is better than doing less. Spending more time on the job is not necessarily better than spending less time, except that it may make people feel less guilty or help them avoid even greater frustrations off the job. Quality, not quantity, of the time spent provides the necessary payoffs.

This question of time frequently comes up in the career planning of young people in business. They get caught up in the conflict of deciding how much time to spend with their families and how much to spend on the job. They set up a goal "to spend more time with the family" and believe that if they've been spending an hour a day with the children, ninety minutes would be better. If they're not careful, more time with the family will create conflict for the family.

Myth 8:   *The virtue of apartheid, or "It's important to keep your home life and work life separated."*

"My wife (husband) and I just don't talk shop at home. It's far more important for us and the kids to have a life apart from our office chores, so we've made a pact not to talk or think work once we see each other at home." "My wife really doesn't like my job, but that's her hangup. It doesn't pay for us to talk about my job and the future; it just leads to some kind of hassle."

These and similar feelings reject the idea that man is whole, integrated in his actions, feelings, and thoughts, in his physical, psychological, and spiritual well-being. Optimum expression of what a person is results from a careful meshing of all these ingredients. We can't separate out and choose only those experiences that we wish to have an impact on us.

As adults, we must still live with the experiences of childhood. Our roles as husbands and wives are present in us as workers. Our feelings as workers are intertwined with our lives as fathers and mothers. Making career plans without considering the total person and how all our cogs interact to produce a slice of life guarantees the production of an inferior product. Failure to recognize what the individual contributes to his own career leads to senseless mobility in pursuit of jobs and careers.

Myth 9: *The virtue of upward mobility, or "I know that I'm succeeding; I've just been promoted!"*

The search for success is frequently reinforced by a series of events that lead people to believe that a promotion is synonymous with career and, therefore, life success.

Organizations spark this flame by communicating directly or indirectly to people from the very first recruiting contact that they're "looking for people who want to grow into management" or that they "believe in providing opportunities for people to grow and therefore have established a very carefully planned set of career steps that will help people to monitor their progress."

Individuals want to grow, of course. But is upward movement into management synonymous with growth in the eyes of the individual? Growth means *personal* growth—development of a sense of competency. Vertical mobility in companies does not necessarily test one's competency; neither is it necessarily a reward for past competency. As such, it does little for the feeling of career satisfaction.

Peer groups also fan the flame of this myth. Because they have grown up in a competitive society, they believe that competition is good. Because they are human, they tend to behave in such a way as to prove their own personal worth. As a result, it is unlikely that somebody who has moved to another job because it "is a much better opportunity" will voice a feeling that he made the wrong move. Rather, we tend to hear that "the decision was the smartest one I ever made. I'm making more money and learning a lot."

The probabilities are high that, indeed, his salary has increased and that, indeed, he is learning. New jobs tend to force that. But those things are temporary, and ultimately the individual is forced to face the issue of meshing himself with the job. When there's congruence, all is fine. When there's dissonance, however, the individual must reckon with the conflict. In fact, then, "How far is up?" is a question that the individual should answer for himself long before the company does it for him.

Myth 10:   *The virtue of a better fertilizer, or "Your lawn looks beautiful, neighbor. What kind of fertilizer do you use?"*

When conditions are tough and the lawn looks its worst, we often lean over the fence and look longingly at the neighbor's grass. We envy the person who with seemingly carefree abandon has a lush, thick carpet of green. It's only after we talk to him that we find we use the same brand of fertilizer. He just seems to spend more time than we have (or care to spend) working at keeping his lawn healthy.

Young people treat careers in the same way. Their cycle starts with that new job, when the company and the new employees are on a honeymoon. There is much concern for training, for learning, for orienting, and for professionalism on the job. But by the end of three or four years (sometimes sooner), the honeymoon's rosy tint is often lost.

That's when the employee looks across the fence to the neighbor's yard. Job hunting starts because, from a distance, the lawn next door appears to have no crabgrass. So the employee changes jobs and starts to play on the new employer's lawn. It looks good at first (there's that honeymoon period again); but as the employee digs into the job, he soon discovers that crabgrass grows there as well. Thus he learns that there are no perfect bosses, organizations, or jobs.

Just how many moves a person must make before he faces this reality seems to be a function of maturity and the extent to which he is willing to take a closer look inward and rely on his own initiative. Some of us spend a lifetime never realizing this and end up with less-than-satisfying growth in our careers. But if and when such awareness comes, people give new direction and strength to their careers. Our experience has been that when such awareness comes early in a career, people tend to remain in that organization where awareness originated and do what needs to be done there to optimize career growth. Withdrawal to new situations does little for the individual if he takes the same old attitudes, values, and habits with him without an awareness either that they exist or how they influence his career. The payoff comes when he begins to be aware of himself and what influence he has on his career direction.

A Time for Realism

We are inevitably led to a viewpoint that, unfortunately, is perceived by many as not very realistic. It sounds too pat. Nevertheless, it is basic and unquestionably the one virtue for sound career growth:

> *The virtue of self-awareness, or "If I become aware of what's important to me and how to optimize my strengths within the confines of reality, then I have a sense of direction that leads to purposeful action."*

Our concept of ourselves influences our behavior, much of what we see, hear, say, feel. What we perceive as reality is a function of what our own self-concept wishes us to perceive. We literally "create" reality to blend with our self-concept.

However, as we become more aware of how we see ourselves and how others see us, what our strengths truly are, and what our priorities are in a job and in private life, we become more aware of how we give direction to our lives. It is then that we realize we don't need to *let* things happen to us. We can *make* them happen for us. This is the essence of career growth.

Autobiographies of people in growth careers time and again reflect the fact that "luck" and "opportunity" are not the keys to their growth. Luck and opportunity can be used only when one is aware that they are present. How frequently opportunity knocks and we don't hear! An opportunity can be perceived as such only when we know what it is we want. Successful people know this and have a keen awareness of their strengths and how they relate to their personal career objectives.

A winner looks ahead, but not too far;
a loser looks back, but not far
enough. *Sydney Harris*

3

Characteristics of Career Strategy

Requirements for Winning

HOW does one go about the process of developing a viable strategy for one's career? And once that strategy is formulated, what must a person consider in order to implement that strategy? The answers to these questions go to the heart of successful career growth. If a strategy is realistically formulated on the basis of careful consideration of the important variables, then it will have a strong validity. But something more is needed; a beautifully formulated strategy is of no avail if the processes used to implement it are inadequate or poorly utilized. Both formulation and implementation are essential.

Let us take a look, then, at the key requirements for a sound career strategy.

Flexibility

A career strategy involves two tasks: establishing our goals and deploying our resources for achieving those goals. These two aspects are not independent but, on the contrary, have considerable impact on each other. When we implement a strategy, we receive feedback on how good the initial formulation was, thus letting us know what part of the plan needs changing. In short, a career strategy must be dynamic.

For example, a person can set a goal based on an evaluation of his particular skills and talents and, in the act of trying to achieve this goal, may learn that his evaluation was inaccurate. Consider the case of a young woman whose objective is to serve society through the medical profession. She believes she has the necessary aptitudes in chemistry and the appropriate interest and motivation to take courses in, say, organic chemistry. If she passes that course, she gets a clue that, at least in this one area, she has the appropriate competence related to her objective.

But suppose she fails that course. Now the process of implementing her strategy raises questions: Is her strategy appropriate? Has she accurately evaluated her skills in chemistry? Should she change her objective or take different steps to develop her resources?

It's important to see that career strategy has a dynamic quality. It's not something that is formulated once, to be doggedly pursued without regard to experience. The information we get about our strengths and limitations, our value systems, and our needs permits us to raise questions about the validity of our strategy and to change it or not as we see fit. Overdedication to any given strategy without regard to reality may result in lost opportunities.

Purposeful Orientation

How many times have we come home after a week of being on a treadmill and asked: "What have I accomplished? What's all this about anyway?" And how many times have we asked whether all our hard work will pay off?

These questions imply that there must be more to work than the actual doing. Work must have purpose. As we become aware of that purpose, we experience a sense of accomplishment when we know that the purpose has been achieved. People who spend a lot of time doing things but never feeling that they are accomplishing anything usually are people without objectives. And if they don't have objectives, they can never really experience satisfaction in completing a task.

Clearly, then, a statement of career strategy must tell *what* the individual wants to accomplish and *why*. Career strategy is not a simple, single sentence. It is, rather, a phrasing of the complexities of what the individual expects to achieve as he interacts with the many environments in which he functions. It is a statement not only of what he will be achieving in his work organization—with bosses, peers, subordinates—but also of what he plans to accomplish in his family life, his community, and his personal life. A career strategy must answer the questions: Why am I doing what I am? What personal needs am I trying to satisfy?

Activity Orientation

Although there is nothing wrong with stating what we want, this in itself is not sufficient to guarantee progress. Such a statement gives no indication of what the individual or others must do to achieve the purpose. Translating purpose into action, then, becomes an essential ingredient of career strategy.

"What specific things must I *do* in order to get to the point where I'll be able to acquire a vacation home by the lake?" This can be answered by saying, "I'll have to earn a lot of money someday" or "I'll have to inherit a lot of money someday." But such answers still don't tell you what you have to do; they simply tell you what must happen *to* you.

Translating purpose into action is an exercise that closes the link between strategy and personal competencies. Once the activity is defined, the individual can put it in relation to his available resources. Can he now *do* what is required of him? Or must he learn how to do what is required? And if he must learn it, what must he *do* in order to learn it? Or can he obtain the necessary resource from a friend, an expert, his family, or someone else? If so, in what activities must he engage in order to acquire the resource?

Role Orientation

Career strategy requires only secondarily a role orientation. "Someday I want to be a vice president," "I want to be a good husband," "I want to be the chairman of the town board of education"—these are all statements of what the person wants to *be*, what role he wants to play within his career. Too frequently, however, people use role identification rather than purpose and activity as the focal point of their career strategies. They seek out roles with no awareness of the purpose or the activities demanded by those roles. Purpose and activity must precede role identification.

Consider the case of salesman Pete Proctor. Pete was joyful the day he was promoted to vice president of sales. He had aspired to the position almost from the beginning of his work with the company. But six months after the promotion he was dejected. "Had I known just what this job was all about and what would be demanded of me," he said, "I never would have taken it, much less aspired to it. I don't enjoy the job, and, in fact, I don't do it very well. I'm a salesman. I miss the daily give-and-take of the client/salesman relationship."

He determined too late what activities were going to be demanded of him in his new role. Had he investigated earlier, he could easily have set a career strategy to seek out a role more in line with his personal resources.

To illustrate this point from another angle, try this exercise. Assume you have as an objective right now to make more money. List all of the possible activities in which you can engage to increase your daily income. This might include responses such as: "Get a second job." "Change jobs." "Ask for a raise." "Invest a lot of money." "Start a business on the side." Some might even say: "Embezzle funds." "Play the horses." "Make counterfeit money."

Note that in all of these cases, the purpose remains clear: to make more money. The roles, however, change. From moonlighter, job changer, or investor to embezzler, gambler, or counterfeiter. And as the roles change, the individuals planning them display varying levels of discomfort, depending on their own value systems, ethics, and morals. It can be seen, therefore, that:

■ Many different roles can achieve one purpose, and many different roles demand similar activities. Hence role selection should follow a careful delineation of what we want to *do* and what we will be trying to *achieve* by doing it.

■ The role(s) we select as possible choices in our career strategy are closely tied to our concept of self—what we see as our values, needs, beliefs, attitudes, strengths, and weaknesses. We reject some roles out of hand because they conflict with our concept of what's important; others sound reasonable because they tie in with what we think we are or can be and what we think society expects of us.

Future Orientation

By definition, having a career strategy implies that the achievement of an objective or purpose is in the future. Unfortunately for many, the future is the immediate tomorrow. These people work for today, assuming that tomorrow will take care of itself. But as so many of the futurists tell us, the rapidity of change in our modern world is such that tomorrow's reality is reaching us with ever-increasing speed, thus allowing us less and less time to prepare for it. And to make matters worse, they also tell us that the nature of that tomorrow may have only a slight resemblance or historical link with the past. The future will demand of us a different set of competencies from those that permit us to grow in today's environment.

This suggests that a dynamic career strategy should have a long-range perspective. But how long is "long"? One year? Five years? A lifetime? Surely, the further one projects that strategy into the future, the less precise it can be and the more ambiguously it will be stated. Nevertheless, there is much to be gained by constantly developing different scenarios that project you into later stages of your career. Such scenarios—even though they may be inaccurate and unrealistic at times—permit the development of alternative plans of action that are not available with a more limited perspective.

An example may clarify the point. A young man was trying to decide whether or not he should continue his graduate work leading to the doctorate. He reasoned: (1) doctorates were currently not in demand in business in his area of interest; (2) he was really tired of being a student and wanted to start earning some money; (3) he owed his wife some time away from the books.

The *immediate* environment and the *short-term* goals seemed to say: "Drop the idea of the doctorate. Get a job." But as he projected himself and his wife into mid-career and beyond, other values came to the fore: (1) he would probably have a multiplicity of careers in his lifetime since he couldn't see himself doing the same thing all his life; (2) he wanted the experience of business but wasn't really a "company man"; (3) he valued his freedom and time with his wife and, in the future, with his family.

Hence, even though he didn't need the doctorate now, and even though it detoured him from some immediate goals, he and his wife opted for more graduate study now. The doctorate, they reasoned, would provide greater options for the future. Clearly, his career strategy is long-range oriented. Of course, whether it will provide the appropriate payoffs only time and experience can tell.

Willingness to Take Risks

How much risk a person is willing to take is influenced by a wide variety of experiences that may or may not have built confidence in his or her ability to assess the risks in any situation. Take, for instance, someone who "risks" seeking a transfer into another function only to find out that his narrow-minded boss interprets that request as a lack of loyalty and departmental identification and therefore gives the person two weeks' notice. This victim of a vindictive manager probably will not be willing to take as great a risk in the future as someone who made a satisfying job change with the blessing of his former boss.

Nevertheless, as people are exposed to a variety of experiences and tune themselves into what those experiences tell them about their personal resources, they are more likely to establish objectives that have a moderate degree of risk. They are more likely to set goals that are challenging but realistically based, so that their chances of succeeding are good if they utilize their resources effectively. They will tend not to set low-risk goals that do not test their strengths; neither will they set strategic objectives with such high risks that accomplishing them rests mostly on chance. Their confidence in their own abilities will permit them to act on incomplete information; they are willing to run the risk of being wrong.

There are some qualitative measures that might be used to ascertain the degree of risk. Because strategy formulation is based on the availability of resources and the projection of their utilization at some time in the future, you can evaluate the degree of risk by taking a qualitative look at the demands on your time and resources.

In this regard, the first question you should ask yourself is this: *Over how long a period of time will I be required to commit my personal resources in order to achieve a strategic objective?*

Since any venture has some uncertainty attached to it, the longer you must wait for payoff, the greater the risk. Time brings changes in environment, and committing resources over a long time span makes the individual vulnerable to these changes. This is why any long-range goals must be anchored in a series of shorter-range objectives that, when accomplished, move the individual closer to the desired goal. These anchors also provide the individual with checkpoints along the way that help him judge whether the risk is worth a continuing effort.

The second question you should ask is: *How long will the necessary resources be available to me?*

The less time a resource is available, the greater degree of risk. Similarly, the more a given strategy is based on the assumption that the resource will be continuously available, the greater the degree of risk. Thus a career strategy based on having certain funds available for education over a period of years could be upset by a sudden change in environmental factors, such as a severe sickness in the family that drains these financial resources.

A more subtle resource is the kind of psychological support provided by a person's family as he or she pursues some career goal. If the achievement of that goal turns out to require continuing sacrifices well beyond those that the family is willing to make, then the risk of failure increases. This is why commitment of resources by others involved in the achievement of one's career strategy should be discussed seriously before the strategy is implemented.

The last question to be asked is: *How many of my resources must I commit to a given strategy objective?*

The greater the amount of your resources you commit, the greater the degree of risk. Although the payoffs may be larger, so are the consequences of failure if you do not meet the objective. Even so, where timing is essential to gaining some advantage, a total commitment of resources over some extended period of time may provide the optimum payoff.

For example, a young woman wonders whether she should drop her job for a two-year period and commit herself full-time to working for an MBA. Or should she stay on her job and extend her MBA work over a four-year span? Committing more resources for a shorter period may pay off if she finds that the MBA degree leads to the achievement of some immediate career objectives. But if her judgment was wrong and the degree brings no significantly different career advances, then the larger commitment of time and personal resources was needless.

Overall, this is the question of whether an individual should put all his eggs in one basket. The answer to such a question is not easily reached. After all, not committing oneself fully may be just as big a risk as committing oneself too much.

Conflict Resolution

As we become increasingly aware of the many different dimensions of a career, we are inevitably faced with conflict. Unless we wish to live with the inactivity and lack of accomplishment that come from indecision, we must resolve each conflict as it arises.

It is inevitable that we will struggle with conflicts between the demands of the job as required by our department and the job demands as we see them from a more corporate viewpoint. Even more apparent will be the conflicts we experience between the goals of the organization and our own personal goals or between what we want for our family and/or spouse and what they want for themselves. And, not least, there may be conflicts arising from our desire to fulfill many roles—for example, subordinate, spouse, and parent—effectively at the same time.

To attempt to implement a strategy that is known to have inherent conflict among its objectives is to flirt with frustration and potential failure. Therefore, some consideration must be given to ways to minimize conflicts among its various elements.

Conflict resolution is more readily achieved as we become aware of what is really important to us. A case in point involves a young man and his wife, who were very unhappy in their new transfer location; they longed to return to their friends and lifestyle of the Southwest. But they also liked the company and knew that the company regarded them highly. The husband was afraid, however, that his management would look unkindly on a request for a reverse transfer.

The conflict was not resolved until the couple made a value judgment and addressed the question of which was more important—living in the Southwest or remaining with the company. When they realized that where they lived had greater value for them, the request for transfer was easy to make because it no longer mattered greatly if the company reacted negatively. As it turned out, the company transferred them back to the Southwest, and they got the best of both worlds. The point is, however, that resolution of the conflict came only when the couple had given careful consideration to their values and placed them in order.

The existence of such conflicts provides opportunities to think through the important elements of a career strategy. Conflict, therefore, should be viewed as a means to gain a clearer understanding of who we are and what's important to us.

Reality Orientation

If we are not careful, we can deny the reality of experiences and events all around us and develop plans based more on fantasy than on fact. Capable, ambitious young people, who are impatient to reach executive positions in an organization, frequently fumble their chances because they try to achieve too much too fast.

A reality orientation permits a more responsible approach to planning. But it is not always easy to simply face up to reality and reject plans that are unrealistic. Here are some guidelines that may help in your efforts to get a more realistic perspective.

■ Plan activities that get you involved with other people who are in positions of responsibility. You can learn a great deal from others—how they approach problems, how they organize and plan to get a job done, and how willing they are to reject approaches where the payoff is limited.

■ Learn different ways to fulfill your needs within accepted social frames of reference. Needs to excel, to feel adequate, to be accepted, and to be yourself may be satisfied in a variety of ways. Holding on doggedly to only one approach when experiences suggest potential failure emphasizes the unrealistic aspects of your aspirations.

■ Use your experiences as a basis for self-diagnosis. Ask yourself: "What have I learned about myself from this experience? What does it tell me about my career plans—are they still realistic?" This is not to suggest that you should become overly introspective but only that a look back on your experiences will indicate trends and patterns that provide significant clues about yourself.

For example, whenever you have an exceptionally "good" day, reflect on it. What made it so good? What happened to you? Were particular people involved or particular kinds of activities required of you? Or did you accomplish something that you hadn't accomplished on other occasions? Your answers may give you clues about the things that are really important to you or turn you on, thereby assisting you greatly in developing career strategies that are realistic for you.

A Broad and Creative Perspective

The more a person learns, the better able he or she will be to bring different experiences to bear on new situations. Too frequently, young people, early in their careers with a company, confine themselves solely to the narrow technical aspects of the job, believing that growth in other areas will come later. While priorities may demand that learning the technicalities comes first, this activity must be placed in perspective with longer-range goals.

Bosses are often heard to complain, "Joe is such a fine technician, but he doesn't have a management perspective in his work." When individuals start to see their jobs in the broader perspectives of time and of their many relationships with company, family, and self, then they become aware of a whole new set of career possibilities.

This suggests, then, that the wise strategist makes time not only for his job and its technicalities but also for growing in nonprofessional areas. This means finding leisure time for the arts, books,

music, drama, sports, hobbies, family, friends, and new acquaintances so as to become a person with broader perspectives.

The necessity for a broad perspective to careers is stressed in a
report by AT&T, which summarizes some of the data concerning job
recruits who shared different degrees of success on the job. We
quote the relevant passages here:

> The enlarging life style is oriented toward the goals of innovation,
> change, and growth. The Enlarger moves away from tradition and
> places his emphasis on adaptation, self-development, and the ex-
> tension of influence outward, into the work and community
> spheres. The Enlarger looks for responsibility on the job and is
> likely also to seek and achieve a position of influence in service
> organizations. Self-development activities are stressed; thus En-
> largers are likely not only to read, attend the theatre, and keep up
> with current events, but they take night courses and even respond
> to the promptings of physical fitness and health food buffs. At the
> same time, their earlier ties to parents and formal religious prac-
> tices begin to weaken. The Enlarger finds that his values have
> changed so dramatically that he no longer enjoys the company of
> old friends in the neighborhoods of his childhood. Except for a
> certain nostalgia when he visits parents and relatives, he is not
> satisfied with the ties of yesterday . . . he makes every effort to see
> alternative points of view and to lend himself to new experiences
> of all varieties. . . .*

Tolerance for Ambiguity

Strategy requires a projection into the future, and the further we
project, the hazier the picture. But project we must if our various
activities are to have any purposeful direction, and if we hope to
influence the future environment in which we live and work. Some
people feel uneasy about such ambiguity, but this is just another
element of risk that the career strategist must accept.

A strategy unfolds; it does not reveal itself all at once. It is, by
definition, a series of events that, when added one to the other, have
a synergistic effect of providing a new whole. This means that even
when we tie some activity in the series to easily definable and
quantifiable measures and then see that activity actually completed,
we may still be left with the concern that completion of one of the

---

* Douglas W. Bray, Richard J. Campbell, and Donald L. Grant, *Formative Years in
Business* (New York: Wiley, 1974), p. 103.

series may not really lead to the ultimate strategic objective. Only time will answer this concern.

Suppose you've just completed a big project requiring a lot of extra work. You believe it will impress the boss and provide just another step toward that new assignment you want a year from now. But will it? Or perhaps you're taking courses in night school, sacrificing time with family and friends to learn something about computers. Not that you use computers on your present job, but you believe that tomorrow's managers are going to be linked more to computers, and you want to be ready. But will there be a payoff?

To go through with your plan with such questions on your mind, you must be willing to live with ambiguity. You need some faith in your overall strategy, some willingness to "wait and see" and accept those isolated key events that give you clues that you are on the right track.

Clarity and Specificity

At first glance, it may appear to contradict our point about ambiguity to state that a career strategy needs clarity and specificity. But whereas the former is concerned with being able to live with the potential ambiguity of results, this principle is more directly related to a personal commitment to communicating the strategy in words and practice so that you and others can respond specifically to it.

How many times have you heard someone say, "I really know where I want to go and when I want to be there. It's just that I can't express it in words."

If you can't put your strategy into words and practice, then the strategy probably doesn't exist. While a strategy must be flexible, it must also be specific enough to be clear in your mind and evident in your actions.

Writing down a strategy or talking about it to others helps clarify some of the murkier issues and explain things better to yourself. Putting a plan into words makes gaps in the thought process more apparent and helps identify the specific activities and objectives needed for the less definable longer-range goals.

Having a specific strategy also permits others involved in your plans to obtain a clearer picture of how they are involved. When a boss, an associate, or a spouse can read your plans or talk with you in specifics, he or she is in a better position to ask direct questions and help clarify various aspects of your strategy.

Finally, a specific strategy establishes a commitment to others. Individuals seem to be more committed when they write things down. Even more important, the commitment increases when they communicate their ideas to others. At that point, their self becomes involved, and there is a desire to gain acceptance and understanding of their ideas from others, particularly from those who are involved in the strategy. For instance, commitment about an aspect of job strategy to a boss who can play a vital role in the achievement of that strategy puts more pressure on a person to follow through. Conversely, a New Year's resolution never communicated to anyone can be easily forgotten and dismissed.

To live effectively is to live with
adequate information. *Norbert Wiener*

4

The Content of
Career Strategy

What to Study Before the Game

THE content of career strategy includes the identification and selection of objectives by the individual, the resources this individual will need to achieve those objectives, and the guidelines for achievement.* It includes four major components:

1. What are the things that I *might do?* This requires an identification of the opportunities made available by the many dimensions of the environments in which you function.

2. What are the things that I *can do?* This requires an identification of your competencies and the many resources available to you, including those you may have yourself (time, money, abilities) and those available from others (the skill and help of others who may deploy their resources on your behalf).

---

* There is a remarkable and understandable similarity between the process of formulating a strategy for a corporation and the process required by an individual developing a career strategy. Readers familiar with the process of corporate strategy will therefore recognize many of the concepts in this chapter.

3. What are the things that I *want to do?* This requires an identification by you of your personal values and aspirations. It dictates priorities for the many possibilities opened to you by your analysis of environments (see our first point above).

4. What are the things that I *should do?* This requires an identification of what you see as your obligations to the various societies in which you function. There is a difference between what society may expect you to do and what you think society expects of you. This element of career strategy simply identifies what *you* think you should do. If that is contrary to what society actually expects of you, then conflict may occur in the implementation of your strategy. These *should do* factors are an integral part of your total system of values.

Determining Challenges and Opportunities: What I Might Do

In the formulation of challenges and opportunities, a career strategy should take into account various environmental conditions and trends. The trend concept suggests not only that a historical perspective should be given to the analysis of these environments but also that some attempt should be made to project that environment into the future, when the strategy will be implemented.

In fact, as Peter F. Drucker suggests in *The Age of Discontinuity,** projection of history into the future will probably lead to false scenarios of what that future will actually be like. Because of the dramatic and rapid changes now going on in all environmental spheres, the future will have little or no resemblance to the past. Hence a more careful look at what the futurists are writing about probably brings us closer to an idea of what future opportunities will be like than relying on historical perspective could. History may provide us with lessons on how to behave, but probably not with insights into opportunities and challenges.

As we look at these environments, we should also keep in mind the massive complexity of the many specific environments in which we function. We can think of broader environments, such as government, economics, technology. But we also work in an environment of our peers, which is different from the environment we work in with our superiors, with our subordinates, or within a broader organization framework. Our family activities may be carried out in

* New York: Harper & Row, 1969.

an environment involving our spouse, which may be different from the environment involving our children. We also have environments related to our friends, our various community activities, our own personal lifestyles. Hence, when we project certain environmental conditions, they may take on different meanings for our career strategy, depending on the specific environments considered.

Take the case of Art Shoreham, who sees his vocational strengths as being primarily in the area of computer systems work. As he projects the economic trends, he estimates that companies will be increasingly caught in a cost squeeze that will force them to look for more economical ways to handle data and work flows. He assumes, therefore, that demand for systems people like him will increase.

Comparing himself with his peers, he sees himself in more demand than most of his peers, not only because of his technical qualifications, but also because of his advanced administrative/managerial talents and interests. He therefore projects rapid economic growth for himself if he moves into the systems/managerial career ladder.

But when Art projects these trends within the family environment, he perceives conflicts. For one thing, his wife wants him to spend more time at home; for another, he himself feels that his influence in the home is important now, as the children are growing up. The career path he envisaged, because of its demands on his personal time, may prevent that family need from being fulfilled. Hence, what appeared to be an opportunity viewed from the point of the peer environment becomes a threat when viewed from the perspective of the family.

It is within complexities such as these that we present various content elements of the many different environments that may signal opportunities for the individual. These environments include projections in technology, economics, government, and society generally.

Technological Environment

Technology and technological change may include a wide variety of factors. The impact of technological change is a focal point in many of the futurists' writings, and there appears to be no question of its influence on career growth and satisfaction. As Richard Hall states in *Occupations and the Social Structure:*

> From the professionals who are affected by the constant development of new knowledge, through managers and executives who

require new knowledge, and on through other white- and blue-collar workers, technological variations decrease or increase the amount and type of discretion that occupations enjoy or suffer. Similarly, technological change is important in terms of stratification and mobility as new occupations are created and find their niche in the stratification system and as others become obsolete or decline in their market and social value. The family system is affected by labor saving devices. The educational system must keep up with the changes.*

The host of books and articles on the future may well provide a framework for many of the ideas that can be developed in this area. Here are some examples, some perhaps more "far out" than others.

■ Will the medical technologies suggesting that man will live longer have any impact on the nature and quality of various stages of one's career? Will this have an impact on developing several career choices, each for different age periods in one's life?

■ Will the projected trends in the development of energy sources affect the nature and quality of family life? If so, what are the implications of potential energy shortages for individuals, in terms of employment opportunities, leisure activities, and the general quality of life?

■ Will the new technologies provide new businesses and different kinds of jobs? If so, what possible opportunities are opened up that one should consider? For example, the rapid changes that have taken place in data handling provide broadening opportunities for those with interests and abilities in mathematics, management science, computer science, and the like. Similarly, the shifts occurring in "word processing" will dictate changes in the demands and skills of those who now do "paper work."

■ Will the possibility of implanting a fertilized ovum in a "surrogate mother" provide opportunities for women who want a career as well as a family but do not want the personal experiences of pregnancy and childbirth? What impact might this have on the career strategy of a young woman trying to resolve the possible conflict between family and job?

The specific impacts of changes must be studied in relation to the key dimensions of your own career goals. For example, we may generalize the influence of automation on jobs by concluding that automation in plants has shifted the focus from manual to mental skills; new skills and a greater amount of judgment are now re-

---

* Englewood Cliffs, N.J.: Prentice-Hall, 1975, p. 314.

quired. In addition, advanced technology tends to increase the number of hierarchical levels in an organization and forces an organization to be more integrative in its operations. People with specialized knowledge gain power, and others become more dependent on them for their expertise.

This latter point led Daniel Bell to conclude that increased technology will give rise to the development of a "meritocracy"—a kind of professional model in which achievement and the rewards for that achievement are given to those who are proficient,* though whether this really will happen will probably in some respects be tempered by sociological, political, and economic forces.

As an example of the myriad of questions raised by futurists and their projections, consider the following passages from a report on frontier technologies in science and health, published by the Institute of Life Insurance under its Trend Analysis Program (TAP).

> But perhaps the most fundamental consideration of all is the role technology is to play in the future directions of the human race. Is it good and right to seek after a "super race" via computers, genetics and behavior modification? The eradication of illness used to involve means that were not so universal—they did not span generations as well as segments of the population. . . .
>
> How wisely will we use our knowledge of genetics, or how frivolously? Will we all seek to produce children who will be intellectual athletes? To whom will we turn to perform the more basic everyday jobs in the marketplace that machines cannot yet undertake? . . .
>
> To what extent could genetics be used for the suppression of one segment of the population by another, whether as a function of race, political belief, economic class, etc.? And who will decide the uses to which the new genetics will be put—the individual, the majority, special interest minorities, an elected body, a self-appointed panel of scientists?
>
> What have we done to realistically assess the consequences of our newly developing technologies? If sex preselection of offspring is perfected shortly, and the trend toward one-child families continues, will we find a vastly distorted ratio of males to females? . . . What would cloning mean to a society which has only treated the concept in science fiction?
>
> What are the legal considerations that will have to be dealt with? Are there legally three parents in an in-vitro birth process—the

* *The Coming of Post-Industrial Society*, New York: Basic Books, 1973.

female donor, the male donor and the doctor or laboratory which carries out the fertilization? *

All such projections have obvious implications for the number and type of future career opportunities—or threats. How can we anticipate technological change so that we are ready to respond to it when it arrives in force?

James R. Bright suggests that we can monitor the environment for clues.† He points out that "radical technological advance is made visible first in written words, then in increasingly refined, enlarged, and more effective material forms, long before it achieves widespread usage." According to Bright, the impact of innovation is evident years before it will affect society in any large degree, and such effects may be influenced abruptly by key individuals who control either the resources or the policies for application of the technology. He goes on to suggest that this monitoring is essential if we are to gain the long-term advantages that can come from planning in advance for the potential opportunities and challenges in the technology environment.

Economic Environment

The economic variables of the external environment certainly have an impact on the nature and implementation of career strategy. In this category we include those factors that influence the demand for your resources, the supply of those resources from other people in the environment, and the competition for those resources. In times of recession, for example, when jobs are difficult to find, individuals tend to stay put—or, if they must move, to move into areas where appropriate employment is probable. It is precisely in such times that a good career strategy has more of a payoff, because, if planned, the strategy provides options that those without plans do not have in economically tough times.

Hence, individuals reviewing the potential for the use of their resources should seek answers to certain key questions:

■ What kinds of resources (skills, values, attitudes, personality characteristics, abilities) are in demand in our economy these days? What is the extent of their demand—will they be used over a short or

---

* Trend Analysis Program, Trend Report No. 7, *The Employed.* American Council of Life Insurance, September 1973.

† "Evaluating Signals of Technological Change," *Harvard Business Review,* January–February 1970, p. 63.

over a longer period of time? When is the height of their demand likely to come?

■ What areas of our economy—manufacturing, industrial, financial, service, professional groups, community, government, church—are most likely to use these resources? Are they likely to use your resources separately or in conjunction with those of other people? For example, professional legal skills are likely to be used in all spheres of a society's work, and may be used independently or in conjunction with the services and skills of other lawyers or other professional or nonprofessional people. On the other hand, an individual with unique technological expertise in, say, highly complex computer software systems may have a more limited market for his services and may work independently of other skilled individuals in the market.

■ What is the ability of the economy to pay for your resources, now and in the future? Are there cycles in this ability to pay, or are there predictable trends in the availability of financial resources to support these resources? There was a time, for instance, when some individuals developed programmed learning skills and hoped to build a future on the utilization of those skills in corporate training programs. But the market leveled off rapidly, and new products evolved in the business of industrial training.

■ As you attempt to upgrade present strengths or develop new ones, what will be the cost factors related to that upgrading? Can we expect costs to rise or fall, and what are the implications for a potential return on time and money? Will the economy provide the opportunities for upgrading on a dependable basis (for instance, in the form of fellowships), or are such opportunities likely to be cyclical? This possibility of cyclical developments is too often ignored in trying to develop a career strategy. In good times, when their strengths are in demand, many people give little concern to building for the future, reaping the present rewards of the windfall. In poor times, when their resources are not in demand, they find themselves struggling to catch up by developing strengths that they should have developed earlier in anticipation of the downside of the cycle.

Political Environment

The government is becoming increasingly involved in activities that affect the nature and quality of our lifestyles. It is, therefore, essential when formulating a career strategy to be aware of the impact of politics and legislation—present, pending, and probable—on career decisions. When we consider the broad perspective of life and career, government touches all areas—job, family, personal property, and community involvement.

For example, legislation that permits employees to carry their pension contributions from one company to another will, in fact, provide individuals with an opportunity to explore new avenues of employment without risking loss of retirement benefits.

Tax legislation, too, has a great influence on many lifestyle decisions, such as purchase of personal property, acquisition of vacation homes, or ventures into private enterprise. (Many people rejected self-employment as an option because they had little basis for establishing pension funds. Through tax advantages, the new legislation now makes self-employment a financially attractive alternative.) Personal liability legislation is becoming a matter of concern for those who decide to run for the local board of education or to take a seat on a corporation's board of directors. Finally, legislation affecting social security, medicare, unemployment compensation, welfare, food stamps, and other benefits provides options for individuals to seek careers that are directed more at self-fulfillment than merely at survival and security.

Social/Cultural Environment

This category includes the entire spectrum of social mores, social morality, and value systems. As we become more aware of the trends in these areas, we are in a better position to formulate a strategy that takes into account the career opportunities or threats created by these environmental shifts.

Shifts in our social value systems are also providing new opportunities for women and minority groups, and this is not without consequences for the career strategies of those outside these groups. For example, husbands now consider their wives' careers as they review various strategies for their own. And many others who are considering career opportunities must take into account the fact that they have new competitors.

Similarly, concern about the quality of life has generated new attitudes and values regarding leisure, family, church, or community involvement. It has changed our view about stages in a career; more people now consider self-development a lifelong process rather than one restricted to the early portions of one's career. Hobbies after work are frequently attracting more of the individual's commitment and enthusiasm than the hours at work. And loyalty to a firm for a lifetime is giving way to mobility when interests are not being satisfied by the work situation.

Today, we find more husbands willing to stay home and do the housework and tend to the family while wives pursue a vocational career. Alternatively, both husband and wife may pursue their separate careers, delaying the start of a family temporarily or even permanently. We find people thinking about careers in terms of short periods—doing one thing for, say, ten years, with a deliberately planned move into a different career that taps different interests and resources for the next decade. And others pursue multiple careers simultaneously, planning their activities so that part of their day is spent in one kind of work, another part pursuing a different talent or skill.

The following scenario, taken from a report on the life cycle that was prepared by the Institute of Life Insurance, illustrates some of the possibilities that may face us in the future.*

THE LIFE OF JOHN SMITH: 1985–2070

Birthplace: Chicago   Status of Mother: Single, Age 27

Age 1 to 8:   Attended elementary school.

Age 8:   Traveled with a class of fifteen students. Visited a
                number of countries around the world. Learned
                several languages and cultures.

Age 10:   Returned to the U.S. and resumed formal studies.

Age 15:   Entered a rotating work-study program, electing to
                serve as an apprentice in three fields: architecture,
                social research, and communications science.

Age 18:   Went back to formal studies in the liberal arts. Also
                took advanced courses in architecture.

Age 19:   Spent three years abroad, studying comparative
                architecture.

Age 22:   Returned to U.S. and was employed as a draftsman.
                Lived for two years in an urban commune with
                nine other young professionals.

Age 24:   Moved into an apartment with three friends—two
                female and one male. They were all "married" to
                each other, and all income and properties were
                pooled.

* Trend Analysis Program, Trend Report No. 8, *The Life Cycle.* American Council of Life Insurance (undated).

Age 27:	Divorced himself from his living arrangements and married a woman who was also divorced. She had one child, aged 6. Took and passed his architectural exams.
Age 35:	He and his wife took two-year leaves from their jobs, took their 14-year-old son and went to live on Nantucket. There, the three of them jointly developed their interests in the arts: painting, sketching and sculpting.
Age 38:	Divorced his wife and lived by himself.
Age 50:	Set up house with two career women in their mid-forties. The relationship was economic and sexual, but not exclusive—he dated other women and they dated other men.
Age 60:	Left his job and residence, and went to teach communications science to students in a developing country.
Age 65:	Returned to the U.S. and resumed work part time. Also went back to school part time to update his formal education.
Age 67:	Remarried. His new wife had two children, both grown with children of their own.
Age 72:	Took a two-year leave and he, his wife, and one of their grandchildren traveled around the world. The 16-year-old grandchild remained with a family in London. He and his wife returned home.
Age 74:	Resumed work and school. Became interested in photography. Developed it as a full-time hobby and part-time income.
Age 80:	Took on a teaching position at a nearby university. His students ranged in age from 12 to 87. His topic was comparative architecture.
Age 85:	Died of sudden lung failure.

The More Immediate Environments

The general environments in which people work and play should also be viewed within the narrower confines of the more immediate environments in which career strategies are implemented. They generally include the organization in which one is employed, the family, the community, and groups in which a person functions socially or in a service capacity, such as the Rotary Club, the PTA, the country club, and so on.

Each of these groups functions within its own economic, political, technological, and social framework and therefore may define a different set of opportunities and threats for the individual. For instance, the economic conditions of the family environment may be quite different from the economic environment generally, and both must be considered in the formulation of a career strategy. Similarly, the social/cultural value systems of a particular company may be different from those of the general work environment outside, and again, any career strategy must take these differences into account.

The characteristics and trends of the various environments—general or specific, present or future—should be summarized in some systematic form to give you a clearer idea of the opportunities or threats arising from each. Such an analysis, even if it is sketchy, will provide an answer to your first question: "What are the things I might do?" Having some idea of possible challenges permits you to ponder the key factors required for availing yourself of these opportunities. And once those key factors are determined, you are in a better position to match them against your answers to our second major question: "What are the things I can do?"

Determining Strengths and Limitations: What I Can Do

This category includes not only the many resources you may already have but also resources available from others that may be necessary to the implementation of your career strategy. As the career strategy unfolds, the individual must continuously match up his repertoire of resources with those crucial factors needed for success in obtaining the best fit for himself and the society in which he functions.

Take the case of Mary Edwards. She perceives as one of her major assets her favorable social poise—her ability to meet people well and her tendency to social aggressiveness rather than social withdrawal. She is also an impatient person, wanting to achieve a position of power and prestige as quickly as possible; it's that impatience which gives her a high energy level and a strong drive to achieve.

As she views her various environments, she perceives an opportunity to grow in a sales staff position, working with salespeople and developing a good relationship with them. Her asset of social poise is an apparent strength. But growth in that area, although steady, is not as rapid as she would like. Here, her impatience to achieve status quickly proves a limitation.

She sees another opportunity to work in a product-development area, where the major issue is to get materials out fast. It is a job that requires concentrated effort, primarily by herself, on researching and developing new products. There is a fast road to a position of prestige if she does well. Here, her strong drive to achieve is an asset, but her strength in dealing with people is less useful to her, at least initially.

Weighing these opportunities and her resources, she decided to risk not using what she saw as her major asset for a period of time in order to meet her need to rise rapidly in the organization. She reasoned that ultimately her "people asset" would pay off in a position of authority.

Our purpose here is not so much to indicate how one should go about determining his or her strengths and limitations as to point out the key areas of concern that should be taken into account in struggling for a decision. Here are some of the issues and questions that need to be considered.

What You Have to Offer—Your Marketing Position

As you look back at your past performances and your present activities, ask yourself which are the key tasks that have had to be performed in order for you to succeed in the positions you held.

- At which of these tasks do you perform well? At which are you a mediocre performer? Which interest you and which turn you off?
- Which of these tasks do you perform better than other people? This answers the question: What are your "distinctive competencies"?
- What kind of reputation have you developed for your strengths? Is your image a positive one with those who have used or will use these competencies?
- Will future circumstances arise that will prevent you from competing effectively in your areas of competency? Will you be able to keep up with your competition?
- Can your strengths be transferred to a variety of situations, or are they so specific that they have value only in limited areas? Also, are you limiting yourself to specific geographical areas?

Too frequently, we take the things we do well for granted. They are done with such ease that we tend to lose sight of the fact that they are indeed strengths. Sometimes we are reminded of that when someone who observes us remarks, "You do that exceptionally well. I wish I had your ability in that area."

It is not a matter of being immodest to be able to look back and survey our work, education, and other experiences to determine just what we feel we have accomplished in our lifetime. There will be a pattern to those achievements that will reflect the skills responsible for our successes. That pattern should be brought into consciousness so that we can put our strengths to use over and over again as opportunities present themselves. Whether or not we will actually utilize our resources is, of course, another matter. Generally, it is a function not of what we *can* do but rather of what we *want* to do, as will be discussed shortly.

Maintaining and Developing Your Strengths—Your Production Position

To evaluate your production position, you must answer a series of questions relating to your strengths and distinctive competencies.

- Do they need continuing development, or are they presently at an optimum level?
- If they need further development, will the cost factors (time, money, effort) change the competitive edge with others? Are you flexible enough to want to keep upgrading what you presently do well?
- Do your competencies demand continuing efforts to make them available to others? If so, will you be able to keep up with the potential demand for your strengths? What are the limits to what you'll be able to produce?
- Do your strengths necessarily rely on the services or the work of others? If so, are those people going to be available to provide the necessary support? Can you develop other strengths so that you can function independently?

What becomes apparent as you provide answers to these questions is that there is no neat line differentiating these various positions. Indeed, some of your strengths (or weaknesses) may rest in your ability (or lack of it) to sustain an energy level to maximize other skills you have. Hence your very "production position" may in itself be a limitation to your "marketing position." That is why answers to these key questions should not be given in isolation from your answers in other areas.

The Ability for Change—Your Research and Development Position

Under this category, questions such as the following will need to be answered.

- Do you have the creative spirit and the flexibility to keep researching new ways to use your strengths? Or are you more apt to try to stick with "a good thing"?
- Are you willing and able to work on some of your limitations in order to develop them into unique advantages for you? To what extent do you rely on the ideas of others to utilize your major resources?
- Do you seek out new experiences and contacts with people who have similar competencies in order to stay on top of the things you do well and learn how to do them better?

Supportive Resources—Your "Capital" Position

Too often, we do not do all we can to enhance our "capital" position. We may be aware of our financial resources and even of our own inner resources, but we are frequently reluctant to consider the many resources of others around us, or we may not know how to use these outside resources. This is particularly true of our attitude toward our bosses, who are too often seen as sources of conflict rather than as resources that can be helpful in achieving our personal goals. But it also tends to be true of the view we take of our peers, whom we frequently see merely as sources of competition, thereby rejecting valuable opportunities to enhance our resources.

Here are some of the questions that should be asked to evaluate your "capital" position:

- Are other supportive resources necessary in order for you to meet your career strategy demands, or are your own resources sufficient to make things happen?
- To what extent do you have financial resources for developing and upgrading the skills and strengths necessary to implement your career strategy? Must you put a lot of time and effort into securing those financial resources or make sacrifices in other areas?

■ Are there some resources (skills, knowledge, contacts) that you don't have but that are available to you from other people? If so, is the price in time, effort, and money to attract and develop those resources worth the return to you? To what extent is involvement with others a deterrent to achieving your strategy?

How Well You Manage Yourself—Your Management Position

In the last analysis, an individual's development is really a function of what *he* does; all development is self-development. Indeed, how an individual manages himself may well be one of his "distinctive competencies," in which case the management position would be included in the person's marketing position.

There are two aspects to the problem of self-management: your ability to plan and organize, and your ability to control and measure. Here are some of the key questions relating to the first aspect:

■ What is your ability to set and achieve daily and weekly priorities related to longer-range goals that you have in mind? Can you ignore the nonessential, or do you frequently get bogged down in the nitty-gritty, to the detriment of the important things?

■ Are you familiar with the goals and objectives (and the planning process) of the organization(s) of which you are a part? Do you know what goals the company, the boss, the family, or others have and how you fit, or don't fit, into their plans?

■ Do you have an ability to determine what the future might bring and how this would affect the possible alternatives available to you?

■ Do you plan and organize activities that cover the broad spectrum of your life, or are they related to only one aspect of life, such as job or family?

■ Can you develop the kind of climate around you in which you can optimize the resources available to you from others? Do you know how to delegate tasks to achieve your objectives efficiently?

■ Do you have an ability to run meetings effectively? Can you develop team effort when necessary to achieve objectives?

■ Do you plan activities that will provide you with new experiences or skills that may be helpful in achieving some future

purpose? How innovative are you in developing and selling
ideas?

Some of the questions related to your ability to control and measure are:

- Do you set measurable standards of performance for your objectives? Do you provide ways to obtain feedback on how
  well you are doing?
- What techniques and skills do you have for influencing the
  behavior of others? Do they optimize the relationships?
- How good are you at bringing your activities back on course in
  the event of a setback? Are you willing to change course when
  the reality data suggest that? Are such decisions in your
  hands, or do you rely on others to make decisions for you?
- Are you able to control your time commitments? Are you able
  and willing to say no?
- Are you willing and able to face up to emotionally charged
  situations? Can you resolve them in ways that are not detrimental to you or to others? Do you have a sufficient energy
  level and drive to stick to situations and see them through?

Matching Opportunities with Competence

Your answers to the questions posed in the preceding
sections—*What I Might Do* and *What I Can Do*—provide a basis for
some strategy guidelines. They establish a broad framework of what
is possible and permit matching those environmental factors crucial
for success with personal strengths and limitations.

Up to this point, then, we can summarize the process of strategy
formulation as in Figure 1.

The model thus far does not clearly indicate what career strategy
you will ultimately select. However, it will provide you with many
different options to consider. Some alternatives will suggest a good
match between opportunities and competencies; others will indicate a poor match.

Relating Strategic Possibilities to Personal Values:
What I Want to Do

At first glance, it would appear that the career strategy alternative
that most people would select would be that which provides the

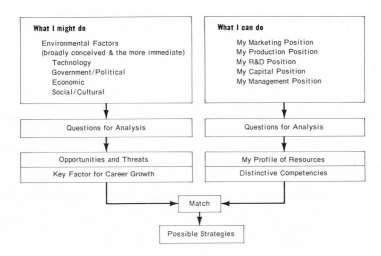

Figure 1. Matching opportunities with competence.

best match between opportunity and competence. This choice would, after all, provide a higher probability of success and potentially maximize the available opportunities with the least effort to the individual. When the match is a poor one, on the other hand, any strategy implemented on the basis of it is going to require the shoring up of needed strengths and demand more effort by the individual.

But the key in this process of matching is *you*, the individual who is deciding what is "best." Such a choice is not made on the basis of what the person *might* do or what he *can* do, but on the basis of what he feels he *wants* to do. These personal values and aspirations typically influence the choice of the career strategy finally selected.

Parents frequently experience this in their frustrated attempts to "motivate" their children. They reason that they know what their children can do; they believe they know what kinds of opportunities are out there waiting to be plucked by their son or daughter. But in making strategic choices for their children, parents frequently make the mistake of assuming that the children's value systems are identical with their own. "After all, that's what *I* would do if *I* were given the opportunity," is the typical response reflecting this attitude.

Bosses, too, are chagrined when a subordinate refuses an "opportunity" for promotion. They thought about it long and hard and finally decided that a certain subordinate should be offered the chance. But the chance must be perceived as such by the receiver before he seizes it.

The combination of values and aspirations that influence the ultimate strategy choice is extensive. They center around the individual's perception of himself—the things he thinks are important for him. "What do I mean by success; how do I measure it?" "Is it worth the effort?" "How much of a risk am I willing to take?" "What are the things I value—power, money, utility, people, esthetics?"

There have been several classifications of values suggested by behavioral scientists. Two that are frequently referred to are those measured by tests developed by Gordon W. Allport, Philip E. Vernon, and Gardner Lindzey* and by Donald Super.† Here we give modified versions of these classifications, beginning with six definitions based on Allport, Vernon, and Lindzey's work. They might stimulate your thinking about what values are important to you.

Theoretical Value. The dominant interest of the theoretical person is the discovery of truth. In the pursuit of this goal he characteristically looks for identities and differences and seeks only to observe and to reason. The interests of the theoretical man are empirical, critical, and rational, and his chief aim in life is to order and systematize his knowledge.

Economic Value. The economic person is characteristically interested in what is useful. His interest in utility develops to embrace the practical affairs of the business world—the production, marketing, and consumption of goods, the elaboration of credit, and the accumulation of tangible wealth. This type is thoroughly "practical" and conforms well to the prevailing stereotype of the average American businessperson.

The economic type wants education to be practical and regards unapplied knowledge as waste. Great feats of engineering and application result from the demands economic people make upon science. In his personal life, the economic type is likely to confuse luxury with beauty. In his relations with people, he is more likely to be interested in surpassing them in wealth than in dominating them (political attitude) or in serving them (social attitude).

Esthetic Value. The esthetic type sees his highest value in form and harmony. Each single experience is judged from the standpoint

* *Study of Values*, third edition, Boston: Houghton Mifflin, 1960, pp. 4–5. Copyright © 1931, 1951, 1960 by Houghton Mifflin.

† *Work Values Inventory*, Boston: Houghton Mifflin, 1970, pp. 8–10. Copyright © 1970 by Houghton Mifflin.

of grace, symmetry, or fitness. He regards life as a procession of events; each single impression is enjoyed for its own sake. He need not be a creative artist; he is esthetic if he finds his chief interest in the artistic episodes of life.

Social Value. The highest value for this type is love of people, with emphasis on the altruistic or philanthropic aspect of love. The social person prizes other individuals as ends and is therefore kind, sympathetic, and unselfish. He is likely to find the theoretical, economic, and esthetic attitudes cold and inhuman. In contrast to the political type, the social person regards love as the only suitable form of human relationship. Eduard Spranger adds that in its purest form, the social interest approaches being a religious attitude.*

Political Value. The political type is interested primarily in power. His activities are not necessarily within the narrow field of politics. Leaders in any field generally have high power value. Since competition and struggle play a large part in all life, many philosophers have seen power as the most universal and fundamental of motives.

Religious Value. The highest value of the religious type may be called unity. He is mystical and seeks to comprehend the cosmos as a whole, to relate himself to its embracing totality. Spranger defines the religious type as one "whose mental structure is permanently directed to the creation of the highest and absolutely satisfying value experience." Some people of this type are "immanent mystics," that is, they find their religious experience in the affirmation of life and in active participation therein.

Donald Super's classification is more directly related to values associated with the world of work. In his inventory, he includes the following work values:

Creativity: A value associated with "work which permits one to invent new things, design new products, or develop new ideas."

Management: Associated with "work which permits one to plan and lay out work for others to do."

Achievement: A value associated with "work which gives one a feeling of accomplishment in doing a job well."

Surroundings: A value associated with "work which is carried out under pleasant conditions—not too hot or too cold, noisy, dirty, etc."

* *Types of Men*, translated from the fifth German edition of *Lebensformen* by Paul J. W. Pigors (Halle: Max Niemeyer Verlag; American Agent: Stechert-Hofner, Inc., 31 East 10th Street, New York).

Supervisory relations: A value associated with "work which is carried out under a supervisor who is fair and with whom one can get along."

Way of life: Associated with the kind of work that "permits one to live the kind of life he chooses and to be the type of person he wishes to be."

Security: Associated with "work which provides one with the certainty of having a job even in hard times."

Associates: A value characterized by "work which brings one into contact with fellow workers whom he likes."

Esthetics: A value inherent in "work which permits one to make beautiful things and to contribute beauty to the world."

Prestige: Associated with "work which gives one standing in the eyes of others and evokes respect."

Independence: Associated with "work which permits one to work in his own way, as fast or as slowly as he wishes."

Variety: Associated with "work that provides an opportunity to do different types of jobs."

Economic return: A value or goal associated with "work which pays well and enables one to have the things he wants."

Altruism: A value or goal that is present in "work which enables one to contribute to the welfare of others."

Intellectual stimulation: Associated with "work which provides opportunity for independent thinking and for learning how and why things work."

Although the question *What should I do?* is discussed separately in the next section, it must also be dealt with under the heading of personal values. The answer to what we should do is of course directly and irrevocably linked with personal values. We might be aware of what society expects of us—how we should behave and what choices we should make—but ultimately, our decision will be based on what we think will best suit our value system. Hopefully, our value systems will take into account what society's needs are, and in that way, what is good for us is also good for society. But when conflict arises between personal values and social values, individuals make their choices on the basis of their own values.

That thought should not be disturbing to us. Conflict between what one wants to do and what could or should be done is an experience that should be accepted as a matter of course. What is more important is to be aware of such conflicts and to determine what might be done to resolve them. Too frequently, people feel that their decisions are being made objectively, without the slightest influence of their own personal values. The realization that choices are simply not made that way encourages greater self-awareness and opens up the possibilities for a wider variety of strategic choices.

Knowing what our biases really are permits a more objective evaluation of the choices available to us. We are not bound in our thinking by a value system of which we are not aware. But being more aware also permits us to be more accepting of the strategies of others and puts them less in conflict with our own. Finally, and most important, awareness of the influence of our values on our strategic choices permits us to evaluate the importance of a *value* before we deal with the strategic issue directly. Once we put a value in its proper perspective, strategic choices fall more readily into place.

In writing about the formulation of corporate strategy, Kenneth Andrews comments on the role of the executive's personal values. What he says is equally applicable to personal career strategies: "Strategy is a human construction; it must be responsive to human needs. It must ultimately inspire commitment. . . . Somebody has to have his heart in it."*

Relating Career Strategy Alternatives to Social Values: What I Should Do

Whether we like it or not, all of us are part of some social environments. We are members of a family, a working organization, a committee, a club, a group at a theater, or a group traveling the same highway to a common destination.

In each situation we play a role—parent, child, chairman, boss, subordinate, or just a member. And for each role, we have certain ideas of how we should behave. What *we* think may be different from what the social organization expects of us; and what *they* expect of us may be different from what we *think* they expect of us.

Nevertheless, there is no denying the Pygmalion effect—that people try to live up to what they perceive as the expectations of others in the groups to which they think they belong. It is a potent force in human behavior and, therefore, an important ingredient in the formulation of career strategy.

But it obviously does not stand by itself any more than the en-

* *The Concept of Corporate Strategy* (Homewood, Ill.: Dow Jones-Irwin, 1971), p. 117.

vironmental and personal forces can stand alone. There is a dynamic interaction among all of these forces that complicates the understanding and analysis of career alternatives. What society expects of someone is not necessarily correct, either for society or for the individual. And what the individual thinks society expects of him may, in fact, be in error; even if accurate, it may be in conflict with what the individual feels important for himself.

Nevertheless, it is essential that career strategy be based on reality. Therefore, even with all the possible imperfections of the environment in which the individual functions, he must be aware of and respond strategically to those environmental expectations. His strategies must work within those expectations either to change the environment so that his immediate and/or longer-range objectives are achievable or to use the environment to help accomplish those objectives. To do otherwise will lead to continuing frustration and anxiety.

One's own values inevitably lead to the conclusion that in a free society people have a responsibility to more than just themselves. They are not independent creatures, able to optimize their resources solely by utilizing their own strengths in a vacuum. The mature person is dependent on others for satisfying at least some needs and for developing his own sense of identity and self-worth. These come only when he can relate to others and have them provide the feedback necessary for self-evaluation.

The broadening of interests to include more than just oneself permits the growth of the individual and of others; and as others in the immediate environment grow, interaction with them in turn permits personal growth. To learn to rely solely on oneself will create a society of competitive souls who, because of the energies spent competing, cannot optimally use the resources around them for their personal growth.

To be mature, it may be added, implies to be sensitive to the social consequences of one's behavior. As the individual grows, he needs to care and to feel the extent of his caring—to feel sorrow when those he cares for suffer, to feel joy when they rejoice. As Gordon Allport has stated: "Everyone has self-love, but only self-extension is the earmark of maturity." *

Knowing, then, what others think you should do and caring about what others feel and how your actions affect them are vital ingre-

* *Pattern and Growth in Personality* (New York: Holt, Rinehart and Winston, 1961), p. 285.

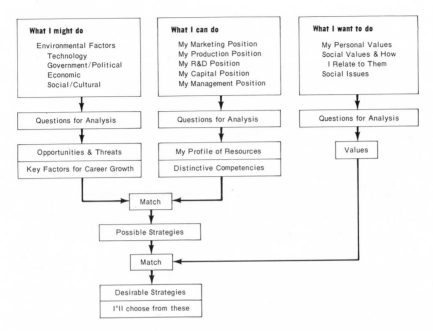

Figure 2. Selection of career strategies.

dients to the formulation of a career strategy. To ignore them means the stunting of personal career growth.

Summary

The descriptive model for the formulation of a career strategy is now complete. Its essential features are summarized in Figure 2.

As highlighted in the figure, the nature of the career strategies desired by the individual hinges on his own set of attitudes and value systems, his aspirations, and his awareness and understanding of these attitudes and values as they influence his evaluations of himself and the world around him. What he might do, can do, and should do are all tempered by what he wants to do.

5

Career Environments and Roles

Analysis before Commitment

THERE are many different ways to analyze the necessary input data for a career strategy. The preceding chapter indicates one way. This chapter will present two other models that may be of value.

The Wheel Model

Visualize, for a moment, the elements of your career as being put together to form a giant wheel that moves you along some path to a series of goals. What characteristics of a wheel can help us get a better understanding of the dynamic nature of our careers?

Symmetry

The real value of a wheel over other geometric forms becomes apparent when it is put into motion. How smoothly the wheel will progress is to some extent a function of its symmetry. If, in fact, the

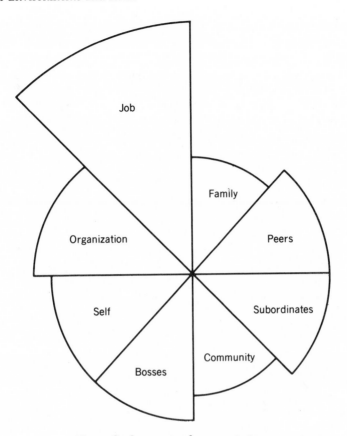

Figure 3. Segments of career strategy.

wheel is not a perfect circle, then the ride will tend to be bumpy even if the road is smooth.

The same is true of career strategy. If one portion of your total career is emphasized to the detriment of other portions, then the career strategy will lose its symmetry, and over time you will experience rough spots in your total lifestyle.

Consider Figure 3. As indicated there, the wheel has several sections to it. These represent important aspects of your total immediate career environment—the job, the family, peers, subordinates, bosses, the organization, and the community, as well as those aspects of the career related directly to your self.

Generally, as individuals think about their careers, they tend to emphasize some of these critical segments more than others. It is not unusual to find a person, particularly early in his career, attending religiously to his job and some of its related aspects, such as the organization, bosses, or subordinates, while ignoring family and/or community concerns. This situation is depicted in Figure 3. Because of the resulting loss of symmetry the individual will experience disequilibrium as he progresses toward his career goals.

This lack of balance may well be part of a planned strategy and be justifiable over a short period of time as a conscious means to shape career objectives. Because career development must in many cases be taken in stages, it is possible and indeed often realistic to plan a strategy that concentrates on one segment at a time.

The key word here is "plan." For example, a young couple may decide that "for the time being," both should concentrate on their careers, sacrificing time they could spend together, with their children, or on some other projects of interest to them. When such decisions are made without considering possible conflicts in roles to be played after working hours (who prepares the meals and keeps house, which social activities are acceptable and which are not, what time is "sacred" and saved for being together or for being alone, no matter what), one or both partners may experience frustration and anxiety.

Conflicts between family and job are not easily resolved; but when a person knows that a particular strategy is likely to create conflict in himself or in his relationship with others, he can plan for it—and it is this planning that helps reduce the negative impacts. The disequilibrium is no longer a surprise and can be dealt with on a more conscious level.

Surprise or not, however, conflicts must be resolved, and the resolution occurs most easily when all segments of career strategy are ultimately brought into proper balance. It is not enough to resolve frustrations solely on the basis of one's private concerns; family, peers, and bosses must also be considered. In short, a strategy is not isolated; it is an interactive process.

Spokes

Another way in which symmetry can be violated is by placing too much emphasis on portions of a given segment of the strategy rather than on the entire segment. In our career wheel we have identified eight segments that determine the strength and balance of the overall strategy. Within any of those segments we can identify many different issues (like spokes on the wheel) which, if properly

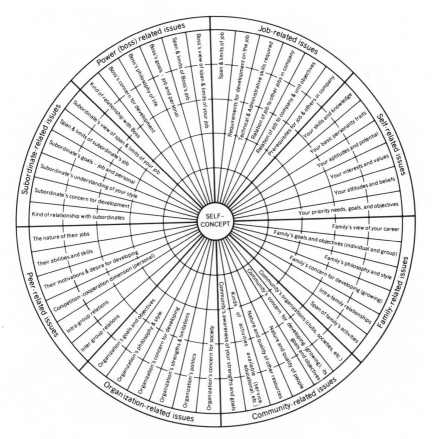

Figure 4. Career planning wheel.

understood and attended to, will give that segment added strength. Figure 4 shows the internal structure of each of these major segments. An individual should have an understanding and an awareness of each of the "spokes" of the different segments if he is to optimize his strategy. Frequently, people concentrate too much on some of the spokes and lose sight of the value of the others. For a while, such failure to develop all areas in a segment will go unnoticed; after all, the weakness of one or two spokes of a wheel will affect the strength of the entire wheel only after a period of time. Eventually, however, such weaknesses will show their impact on the segment and minimize its potential value for the wheel as a whole. The result is a general deterioration of the entire wheel and a loss of effectiveness. In short, failure to develop all of the spokes of one segment of strategy will ultimately lead to a weakening of that segment and eventually of the career strategy as a whole.

In the following we discuss some specific issues for certain of the career strategy segments.

Job-related issues. It is not unusual to have individuals attend to the span and limits of their jobs. They more or less know what the demands of their jobs are. They know something about the training programs available within and outside the company to help them develop the skills required for the job. They will even know, at least partially, what technical and administrative skills are needed for the job. But the other spokes are less likely to be as well understood. People rarely know how their jobs are related to other positions in the unit or organization, and even more rarely how they are tied to unit or organizational goals or to general company policies and procedures.

Although an in-depth understanding of these latter issues may not be absolutely essential for immediate satisfactory performance, they become increasingly important in planning future moves and career mobility. Knowing how a job is related to others at the same or a higher level allows us to develop strategies for movement within the organization. Similarly, knowledge of the requirements for other jobs in the organization permits us to structure a self-development program for possible entry into those jobs.

Furthermore, lack of strategy development at the job-related level affects peer-related issues (How do I compare with peers in other jobs?), organization-related issues (What are the demands of the organization for people in other areas? Should I even try to move into other positions?), and even family-related issues (If I don't know about the opportunities that exist in the organization, I may look outside—and that raises the prospects of moving and financial insecurity).

Boss-related issues. When discussing job-related issues, we stated that a person will frequently know only *partially* what the span and limits of his job are. Many studies have indicated that there is usually a discrepancy—as much as 30 percent—between what the boss thinks a subordinate's job is and what the subordinate thinks his job is. That is why this spoke becomes so important; individuals can be as much as 30 percent ineffective in their strategies if they don't understand what the boss expects of them.

Being aware of what your boss's job and goals are not only enables you to respond better to his needs but also gives you a perspective for your own aspirations (Do I want to be doing what he is doing?) and an idea of the organization's policies and philosophies (What do the requirements of his job tell me about the kind of company in which I am employed?).

Finally, an awareness of the boss's lifestyle and philosophy provides you with clues as to his value systems, which in turn can give you valuable information about how to relate to him on the job. How important are the human aspects of life to him? What does his lifestyle—his leisure-time activities and hobbies and his family life—tell you about his own priorities?

Subordinate-related issues. If you are dependent on other people to get the work done, this segment has a strong bearing on your own job effectiveness. This is true whether you have subordinates or are in a staff position, where you must try to get something done through others.

To what extent have you, as the boss, provided your subordinates with a clear statement of what you expect from them? To what extent do they have a clear understanding of your job and what you're trying to accomplish? Do you know what they think of your style of management, or is your perception of how you manage different from theirs? Do you know what their career and life plans are and how interested they are in developing themselves?

What, in effect, is your relationship with your subordinates? Do you really know and understand it, or is it the sort of thing you have been taking for granted and therefore have not given too much thought?

Peer-related issues. Because of the nature of early careers, people typically develop their relations in an organization with only a few of their peers. The larger the organization, the more limited the peer group will tend to be. We go to training programs with a certain few, have work contacts with those few, and limit our social contacts at work to only those few. If we're not careful, these few will become the frame of reference for our judgments about the organization and the quality of its employees.

Your view of upward mobility is at least in part influenced by your evaluation of your peer group. Are you better or worse than they? Are there many or few who are aspiring to higher positions? Are some of them in jobs that are more in keeping with your abilities than the job you now have? Do you see the group as highly competitive or as willing to cooperate? What are your relations with your peers within your own department or division? Are those relations any different from those you have with people outside your immediate work group?

The extent to which you can provide answers to these questions will give you some indication of how well that segment of your strategy is developed. If you don't know, you may have discovered a soft spot in the formulation of your career strategy.

We need not go further with our analysis of the "spokes" of the strategy wheel. Now that you have an idea of the issues involved, I suggest that you take a closer look at Figure 4 and determine the extent to which you have a knowledge and understanding of each segment and subsegment of your career strategy.

As will have become apparent, there are interactions not only within each segment but also across different segments of the wheel. Vibrations of a spoke in one area will cause other areas to vibrate; and if the vibrations become too violent, they can affect the overall strength and performance of the wheel.

The Size of the Wheel

The progress made by the strategy wheel depends to some extent on its size. A smaller wheel must make many revolutions in order to cover the same distance traveled by a larger wheel. And in the traveling, the smaller wheel has the potential of wearing out sooner.

Again, the analogy holds for careers. Suppose two individuals both have attended to the process of balancing out all aspects of their career strategies so that one segment is not developed at the expense of the others; however, whereas one has utilized his and others' resources effectively so as to develop all segments fully, the other has developed them only to a limited extent. In each case the strategy will provide for "smooth sailing"; that is, neither person will experience a "bumpy" progress toward his or her goals. The difference, of course, is in the amount of energy needed to get to the same place. The person who adopted a strategy that strives for optimum development of all segments of the career will progress more quickly and easily than the one who settled for a strategy that does not encourage such development.

One way to ascertain the size and shape of your own career wheel is to study each of the spokes in Figure 4 and rate yourself on the extent to which you know and understand each of the dimensions shown. This may be done using a five-point scale:

1. I don't know anything of what I need to know.
2. I know a little.
3. I know a modest amount.
4. I know most of what I need to know.
5. I know all I need to know.

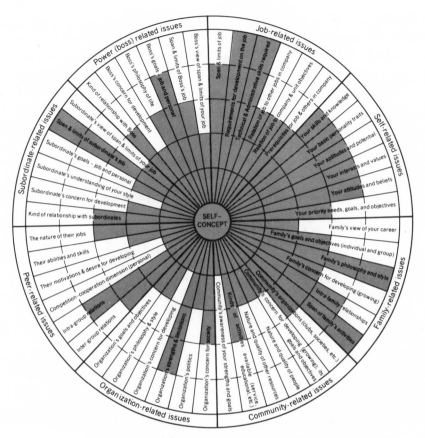

Figure 5. How the career planning wheel is used.

Judgments at the number 1 level would be placed near the center of the wheel, judgments at the number 5 level, at the periphery (see Figure 5). Note that they are not intended to measure how much you know of all that is objectively to be known but rather how much you know relative to what you *think* you personally need to know in order to have an effective strategy. Of course, your judgments may be incorrect, but that will become clear as your specific strategic activities fail or succeed.

To take an example, one young man who participated in our program scoffed at the section of the wheel having to do with family-related issues. He just could not understand why that dimension was even important.

"I really don't know what my wife's view of my career is," he said. "Nor do I know what her goals are and what's important for her. And frankly, I don't care. She's going to have to go along with any decisions I make about my job and our lifestyle. And if she doesn't like it, I can't get excited about that and worry over it. She takes me as I am, and if she doesn't like it—well, then maybe she should leave me."

Accordingly, he rated himself as "5" on each of the family dimensions, even though he had very little knowledge and understanding of them. His rating of himself was accurate in the sense that he knew all he needed to know on the basis of his value systems. However, one may suspect that in terms of his total career, there will ultimately be a void that will make for a bumpy ride.

The importance of making judgments about each of the spokes is that it helps in formulating a strategy and coming to grips with your own value orientations. A judgment of less than "5" in any of the dimensions gives you clues as to activities in which you need to engage in order to move your understanding and knowledge toward your perceived goals; the more of such scores you have, the more energy will be required to achieve the progress you envisage. Furthermore, a look at the total wheel gives you some idea of the symmetry—or the lack of it—and therefore of the prospects of smooth progress.

Figure 5 shows a planning wheel completed by one young woman. The shaded area indicates the size and shape of her wheel and her own judgments of the areas where she needs more understanding and knowledge. This woman wants to grow into broader management responsibilities but at the same time feels that she has a contribution to make to social issues in her community.

Let's take a closer look at the subordinate-related segment of her career strategy and at her plan of action for developing this aspect of her career. Analysis of the various dimensions brought to light her judgment that she really didn't know much about how her subordinates felt about their jobs and their personal careers or about her style as a manager. Because of her interest and desire to grow into broader management responsibilities, she felt the need to upgrade her own effectiveness as a supervisor. As a priority issue, she therefore planned a series of activities aimed at learning more about how her subordinates felt about her and about their own careers.

Contact with the Environment

Wheels move objects to which they are attached in certain directions because those wheels are in contact with some environment along which they can travel. Take the wheel out of contact with that environment, and the object to which the wheel is attached makes no further movement forward or backward.

It's the same with your career strategy. Keep it out of contact with the environments in which you want to function, and there'll be no progress. No matter how large the strategy wheel is, its free-spinning will never move you toward your goals. But put that wheel in touch with the proper environment, and the impact will be different. Now it matters what the size of the wheel is. The greater the contact that the wheel has with its environment, the better able it is to respond to changes and varying environmental conditions. What we are saying here is that as the individual develops, gains more experiences, and acquires a richer repertoire of skills, abilities, attitudes, and beliefs—and he does this by enlarging the environments in which he functions and his experiences within those environments—his ideas for possible strategies will also expand. In short, his broadened horizon provides him with additional resources for reaching his goals more quickly and efficiently.

The Center

Our career strategy wheel has a hub—a center around which the entire wheel rotates. The hub of career strategy is the self-concept. This, as we have seen at the end of Chapter 2, is at the heart of a sound career strategy, for without self-awareness, without a knowledge of what's important to us and what our strengths are, our actions will lack direction.

The self-concept is that series of characteristics, attitudes, values, and beliefs that, in the view of the individual, describes what he is and how he differs from everybody else. This may be quite different from what *other* people think he is, and it may be different from what he *thinks* other people think of him.

It is this self-concept which impacts on one's environment, and *vice versa*. The individual is influenced by the events in his environment, not directly, but rather as a function of how he interprets those events and how he thinks they are meaningful to him.

For example, in the job sector of career strategy, what the company says its policy is and how it actually treats the individual are not the important issues; what determines the individual's behavior is his perception of those company policies and actions. Hence punishment (for example, threat of losing a job) is only punishment when the individual understands that, indeed, his behavior may lead to loss of job and—here's the most important element—he cares about losing his job. If he does not care, then the act of punishment threatened by the company is not perceived as punishment by him.

The individual also acts on his environment, and his actions are at least partially determined by his self-concept. For example, whether or not a person volunteers his services to his boss is influenced by what he thinks he is and whether he feels he can accomplish what he wants through volunteering. To take another example, it is difficult for an individual to "act enthusiastically" toward others simply because a boss, a parent, or society says that's what he should do, if, in fact, the individual doesn't want to act enthusiastically or sees himself as a less than enthusiastic person and fears that he would fail by trying to do something he feels he can't do.

There is, then, a continuous interaction between an individual's many environments in which he functions (those eight segments of the wheel) and his self-concept. The self-concept influences how the person perceives those environments; it helps shape reality for the individual and influences the way in which he will behave in those environments.

When an individual has a good idea of what his self-concept is and when that self-concept is close to reality and to other people's perception of him, the individual can interpret more accurately the environments in which he functions. If, on the other hand, his concept of himself is distorted, then his interpretations of the environment will be proportionately distorted and he will respond in ways that will be interpreted by others as unrealistic. This, in brief, is why a realistic view of oneself is the hub of any career strategy.

The "Tire"

We have stated previously that if a wheel is to move forward or backward, it must be in contact with an environment. How well the wheel absorbs the bumps of the environment, how well it responds to the friction created, depends on the quality of the materials that make up or cover the rim of the wheel. The old-fashioned wheelbarrow used to have a steel-rimmed wheel; today we use tires on that wheel—it makes it easier to push as the tire responds to the rough surface of the earth.

Our career strategy wheel, too, must have a "tire" that absorbs the impact of the "ups and downs" of the environments in which it functions and permits easy maneuvering. Our tire on the career strategy wheel is an individual's personal lifestyle—how he orients himself and the nature of the adjustments he feels he has to make. This lifestyle, as you might predict, is influenced by one's self-concept. How we see ourselves in great measure affects the kind of adjustment mechanisms we employ to protect ourselves from the frictions of our environments. The tire with good absorption qualities can stand a lot of punishment and prevent the immediate collapse of the wheel.

What, then, is this philosophy of life? People learn, over their lifetime, to behave in certain ways that are supportive of their self-concept and responsive to their needs. They learn that certain ways of behaving toward their environments are "better" for them than other ways. Hence two individuals can have similar traits and yet respond differently to an environment because of the learning experiences they have had. We all know that two equally intelligent people reared in different families with different values can behave in different ways in a social situation; one may be socially responsive, the other unresponsive and withdrawn. This difference in adjustment makes a considerable difference in how people, in turn, respond to the individual and how that individual "sees" the world around him. These adjustment mechanisms influence dramatically how we absorb the frustrations and conflicts we perceive in the environments in which we function.

Perhaps some examples will clarify the matter. Let's consider a person—we'll call him Henry—who has a strong trait of aggressiveness. If Henry has one set of experiences, he can capitalize on that trait to act in a dynamic, decisive, forceful, confident manner. Another set of experiences, however, can turn that aggressiveness into lack of tact, insensitivity, intolerance, and maybe even ruthlessness.

Another example: consider Mary, who has a strong artistic trait. If she learns how to use this positively, she will be perceived as creative, intelligent, and socially sensitive, with a good cultural background. However, it is entirely possible for her to use this trait in ways that lead to her being perceived as impractical, oversensitive, and moody.

And then there's Tom, who is more introverted. When used effectively, this trait is expressed by Tom in his being analytical, reflective, careful, methodical, orderly, and patient. In its extremes, however, Tom can act in shy and self-conscious ways, indicating a lack of confidence and social poise and an oversensitivity in his relations with others.

In short, how we look at life, how we learn to adjust, how we learn to use whatever characteristics we possess, makes a considerable difference in how we resolve the frustrations and conflicts that occur in our lifetime. We can have a good "fix" on our self-concept and environments and still do a less effective job of adjusting than others.

The point is, just as we can change tires on a car, we can change tires on our career strategy wheel. We can learn how to make the best use of our skills, attitudes, and personalities as we interact with our many environments.

Direction

A wheel that is not given any direction may still be able to roll; however, its path and how far it progresses will be a function of the contours of the land it traverses. A person's career behaves in the same way. Without guidance, it will progress only if the environment happens to keep it moving. And the quality of that ride will depend on the lack of obstacles in its path.

What happens when the career wheel is given direction? Now the path of one's career can be determined by the driver, and its ultimate destination can be planned. The effects of potential frustrations and conflicts can be avoided or at least minimized by careful driving. It can be given more energy when the going gets tough or slowed down so as not to get out of control when things appear too easy.

Summary of the Wheel Model

In this section we have likened the characteristics of a career strategy to those of a wheel and developed the following analogies:

1. The hub of the career wheel is the self-concept. Without it the wheel collapses. As it is strengthened, so is one's career.

2. The major spokes of the career wheel have to do with issues related to work, the organization, peers, subordinates, superiors, family, community, and the self. As these spokes are strengthened— that is, as these issues are more clearly understood—so is one's career.

3. The length of the spokes determines the size of the career wheel. As the length increases, the amount of energy needed to reach career goals decreases. The length of the spokes of the career wheel is determined by the developmental efforts made by the individual in relation to career objectives.

4. The symmetry of the career wheel determines the smoothness of the ride to a career destination. If the career wheel is out of symmetry because some segments of the wheel are not developed as fully as others, then the career strategy cannot be implemented smoothly.

5. If the career wheel is to make progress, it must be in contact with an environment. This contact permits the individual to learn from his experiences. Without contact there will be no progress, and the career will be "free-spinning."

6. The cover of the rim of the career wheel is the individual's philosophy of life and his ability to adjust to his environment. This "tire" helps the career wheel to absorb the frustrations and conflicts that the individual experiences.

7. The career wheel can roll by itself, aimlessly and with no direction except that determined by the bumps and contours of the ground. Alternatively, it can be given direction to reach a predetermined end, in which case the "driver" of the wheel can pick his own route to avoid or minimize frustrations and conflicts in his career.

A Role-Demands Model

A career may be defined as a *series of roles* that you play. The nature of each role, how you play it, and the context in which you play it will have an influence on the next role you play in the series.

This approach provides yet another useful model for developing a career strategy. In this section we present such a model, along with suggested worksheets that may be of help in determining the action steps necessary to implement the career plan.

Figure 6 gives a schematic overview of the model. In the following, the various steps indicated in that figure are briefly discussed.

Step 1: Defining Your Self-Image

As in the case of the wheel model, the process must begin with a clear assessment of yourself—your needs, skills, values, attitudes, and personality traits. This should be developed using feedback from as many sources as possible.

The worksheet in Figure 7 suggests some of the items that will need to be reviewed at this stage; in particular, such questions as what you can do, can't do, and would like to do in the future must be answered.

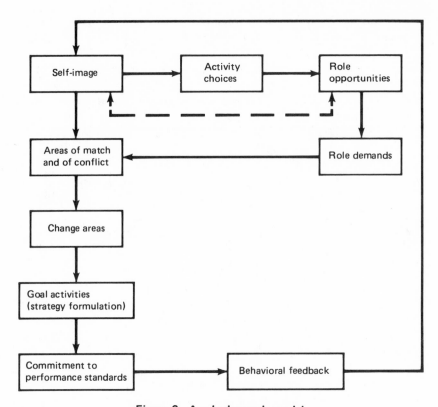

Figure 6. A role demands model.

Step 2: Defining Your Preferred Activities

Next you should compile a list of activities that you'd like to be engaged in now and in the future (see the worksheet in Figure 8). This should be based on an analysis of your environments and the self-image defined in the first step, and it should be couched in behavioral terms. As we have stressed in Chapter 3, a sound career strategy must be oriented toward specific actions (for instance, "develop a new market for product X within two years") rather than vague and general goals ("grow into broader management responsibilities").

Step 3: Defining Your Role Opportunities

The target activities from step 2 must now be matched to professional roles that are open to you (see the worksheet in Figure 9).

My needs—at work, at home, at leisure, in the community, spiritually _____

_____

_____

My values _____

_____

_____

My interests _____

_____

_____

What I do well _____

_____

_____

What I don't do well _____

_____

_____

What I can't do but would like to do _____

_____

_____

What I get satisfaction out of doing _____

_____

_____

What I dislike doing _____

_____

_____

What I avoid or try to avoid _____

_____

_____

My attitudes about people and things _____

_____

_____

What I'd like to do but never tried _____

_____

_____

Figure 7. Self-image (Worksheet 1).

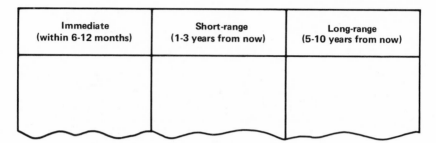

Immediate (within 6-12 months)	Short-range (1-3 years from now)	Long-range (5-10 years from now)

Figure 8. Activity choices (Worksheet 2).

This step will require some research and analysis, drawing on your own and others' experience and on the relevant professional literature. Your analysis may well bring to light certain general conflicts between your self-image and some of the role choices open to you. However, it is best to keep an open mind and refrain from rejecting role opportunities at this early stage; if there is indeed a serious mismatch, this will be brought out later in the process. Furthermore, it should be kept in mind that not all of your desired roles need be played on the job; some can be exercised in satisfying ways at home or in society—a point we observed earlier when remarking on the growing trend toward fulfilling a variety of roles that satisfy personal objectives. The accompanying table lists three major activity areas and some examples of professional roles related to them.

Step 4: Defining Role Demands

At this point you need to conduct a detailed analysis of the specific requirements (aptitudes, interests, personal characteristics,

Now	Short-range	Long-range

Figure 9. Role opportunities (Worksheet 3).

Activities	Roles
PLANNING	
Scheduling work Budgeting Setting up procedures Determining goals Preparing agendas	Production manager, regional sales manager, corporate planner, claims supervisor, controller, methods engineer, spouse, parent, committee chairman
EVALUATING	
Appraising employees Evaluating financial statements Inspecting products Judging suggestions Approving requests Grading papers	Chief inspector, chief designing engineer, university professor, suggestion plan director, medical director, chief underwriter, president, mortgage loan officer, parent, consumer
COORDINATING	
Coordinating plans Arranging meetings Coordinating training Maintaining corporate communications Developing liaisons with other departments Seeking out cooperation	Personnel director, training coordinator, corporate planner, traffic manager, city manager, stenographic pool supervisor, conference director, parent, political party chairman

and so on) for fulfilling the roles considered in the previous step. Figure 10 shows the suggested worksheet for this phase.

These role demands take on several dimensions: (1) demands of the role as *you* see it—what you think is important in order to play that role; (2) demands of the role as seen by the organization or society in which it will be played; (3) the role demands as seen by the people who actually play it. The three views may differ substantially, and any differences must ultimately be reconciled for you to arrive at a realistic assessment of what the role will demand of you.

As a relatively simple example of these differences, consider the concerns that the medical profession is experiencing today because

Role demands	Immediate roles	Short-range roles	Long-range roles
Required skills and aptitudes			
Interests and values			
Personality and temperament			
Educational requirements			
Time requirements			
People orientations			
Thing orientations			
Other			

Figure 10. Role demands (Worksheet 4).

of society's expectations regarding the profession's role in society. The medical doctor has one perspective of the kind of person he needs to be, the training required, the typical work day, and the lifestyle he can lead. The patient, however, may have very different expectations for the doctor's role; he may expect different personality characteristics and a different work day and take a different view of the doctor's training. And the medical profession itself may have a third set of expectations for that role, expectations that focus more carefully on the selection process and the training requirements and not as readily, perhaps, on the patient's expectations.

These variations in role expectations will give you a more balanced perspective of the role and help you determine how you fit into that role, now or at some future date.

Step 5: Matching Role Demands and Self-Image

Next it will be necessary to make a realistic comparison between your self-image and the role demands determined in step 4. The

	Immediate roles	Short-range roles	Long-range roles
Areas of match			
Areas of conflict			

Figure 11. Areas of match and conflict (Worksheet 5).

result of this comparison will be a list of *areas of match and of conflict*. The appropriate worksheet for this step is shown in Figure 11.

If the match is a poor one, this will suggest the need for much work and effort on your part to grow into that particular role, and you might therefore abandon it in favor of a role whose demands are more compatible with the image you have of yourself. On the other hand, you might not want to abandon it if you feel that you have the necessary resources to develop in the required direction.

Step 6: Determining Areas of Change

If you have identified an area of conflict, there will be a need for change: either your goals regarding the professional roles you would like to play must be adjusted or your self-image must be changed by reconsidering your values and priorities or, more concretely, by upgrading your skills in certain areas (see the worksheet in Figure 12).

You may also find that in order for you to achieve your role objectives, *external* conditions must change: for example, the attitude of your family or friends may be responsible for conflicts, or policies of your organizations may stand in the way of your goals. Some of these conflict areas may be resolvable if you are willing to work on them. Others may not, and they become a fixed reality for

Areas of conflict	Required changes		
	Self	Others	Environment

Indicate with ✔ those changes on which you are willing to work. Indicate with * those changes that you feel cannot be accomplished. Underline those areas of conflict that are unlikely to be resolved and therefore must be dealt with as reality.

Figure 12. Change areas (Worksheet 6).

you—that is, you may have to work around them, accepting their existence and reducing tension as much as possible.

Step 7: Formulating Your Career Strategy

You are now in a position to reevaluate your list of target activities compiled in step 2. Some of the activities initially selected as desirable may turn out to be unrealistic given the role opportunities available to you; others may have been added as prerequisites for meeting the demands of those roles that appear attractive to you (see the worksheet in Figure 13). In fact, then, this is the point at which you formulate your concrete career strategy, after having reconciled your personal goals with specific job requirements.

Goal activities for immediate roles	Short-range roles		Long-range roles		
	Immediate goals	Later goals	Immediate goals	Short-range goals	Longer-range goals

Figure 13. Goal activities related to target roles (Worksheet 7).

Immediate goals*	Standard of performance	Date of completion	Commitment made to:

*Related to immediate, short-range, and long-range roles and listed in priority order.

Figure 14. Commitment to performance standards (Worksheet 8).

Step 8: Commitment to Performance Standards

Your strategy is not complete without a binding commitment to achievement. This should take the form of a schedule (Figure 14) giving realistic dates of completion for the specific subtasks implied by your career strategy.

It is important to establish concrete criteria (such as "salary increase of X percent" or "50 percent reduction in customer complaints") that you will use to measure your progress on each of your goals. Furthermore, commitment should be made not only to you but also to those who will be affected by your achievement of a specific goal.

Establishing such measurable performance standards will provide you with the necessary feedback on how well you're doing. The information thus gained will become part of your total experience and have an impact not only on the environments in which you function but also on your self-concept.

A Case Study

Scott Konrad is working for an insurance company; he has been with the firm for ten years. One of the longer-range roles he considered was the presidency of his company.

In planning his career, he completed worksheets for the various phases indicated in our earlier Figure 6 and discussed in the preceding section. Let us take a brief look at some of the results of that process.

Self-image. In filling out Worksheet 1, Scott Konrad noted his strong need for power and recognition, and hence for upward mobility. At the same time he was aware of his strong family values: he believes that spending an adequate amount of time with his wife and children is important for his and their growth. Under the next item he noted his broad interest in corporate issues, which was a factor in his selection of the presidency as a long-range role.

With respect to skills, he admitted to his lack of knowledge of financial analysis and information systems. Also, he realized that his listening skills were weak and that he was never much of a reader.

Role demands. Based on his preliminary awareness of what his company's president and presidents of other medium-sized corporations do, he compiled the following list on Worksheet 4.

1. Required aptitudes and skills: high general mental ability; ability to plan and organize over long periods of time; conceptual and analytical skills; high reading rate; ability to listen; ability to speak well; time management; knowledge of how to read financial statements; budgeting practices; awareness of computer hardware and software capabilities; high energy level; ability to run meetings; ability to make decisions under stress and without all information; risk-taking ability; ability to make self visible; knowledge of people and how to motivate and manage them.

2. Interests and values: orientation to company as a whole; personal interests compatible with those of company; willingness to use personal strengths and influence for the good of the company; pragmatic orientation; interest in analytical work; broad perspective well beyond present job demands; social orientation; concerns for social responsibility; belief in free enterprise as a viable system.

3. Personality and temperament: leadership characteristics; high energy level; firmness; tolerance of ambiguity; planful; independent; mobile; conflict resolver; innovative; faith in others; Machiavellian (?); respect for others' opinions; self-sacrifice; loyal; patience in decision making in the face of pressure; impatience to achieve; responsible; managerial orientation (as contrasted with technical orientation); concern for development of others; learner; high self-esteem; self-awareness; objective.

4. Educational requirements: college degree, preferably in liberal arts (broad perspective); experience in company in major functional areas (marketing, production, finance, administration) and preferably in personnel; attendance at major industry seminars; advanced management development in company and university; at least two weeks of self-study each year; planned reading program throughout the year.

5. Time requirements: 15 to 20 years of effective performance internally (company's policy of promotion from within).

6. People orientations: desire to serve upwardly mobile superiors; top-management oriented; concern for development of people who will do the delegated jobs; concern for family's role.

7. Thing orientations: minimal—awareness of value of systems of information and control.

Armed with this kind of information, Scott Konrad can now (1) check his observations against the perceptions of people already in top management positions, the literature about people at the top, and so on; and (2) check his observations against his self-image to determine where areas of match and conflict might arise.

Areas of match and conflict. In comparing the role demands with his self-image, Scott Konrad noted certain areas of conflict, particularly with regard to his knowledge of financial analysis and information systems and his listening and reading skills. Also, the company's promotion policy posed a problem for him because he felt that he could not afford to wait another ten years to reach the presidency. Finally, his family values appeared to conflict with the time demands of the career he envisaged.

Change areas. In order to resolve the conflicts he perceived, Scott Konrad identified a number of areas in which changes would have to occur. Some of these were personal changes. For instance, he decided that he would have to take courses to improve his listening skills and his reading rate and then constantly practice at these skills. Similarly, he realized that he needed to upgrade his understanding of financial analysis and information systems.

Other changes were of a more external nature. For example, the conflict between his family values and the demands on his time by his career would have to be put into perspective. Although a complete resolution seemed improbable, he believed that careful planning of his time might be the answer to this dilemma.

Finally, he had to consider the conflict caused by the company's policy requiring about twenty years internal experience for the presidency. Could he possibly be the first younger president? And are the present social conditions conducive to this attempt—is society serving youth more than it did in the past?

6

Getting Started

Problems, Concepts, and Action

JUST getting started presents some problems. You have your usual work to do and your personal life to satisfy. Not surprisingly, these day-to-day activities keep getting in the way.

There are many reasons for this. For one thing, routine activities tend to expand until they fill our days so that it's difficult to ignore them, even for a little while. How often have you heard someone say, "If I don't take care of these little things now, they will keep piling up and really cause me trouble later on." Or: "I'm so used to doing these things every day; I'd feel funny if I had a day when I didn't do them."

Now's the time to check up on all those little things. Will it really make any difference if you don't do some of them, or maybe even all of them? Or can they be delayed just for an hour or two so you can fill that time with something new? Which are vital? Which are trivial?

The so-called Pareto Time Principle, named after Vilfredo Pareto, a 19th-century economist and sociologist, suggests that 80 percent of the time expended on our many trivial activities produce only about 20 percent of the desired results. The other 20 percent of our time spent on the few vital activities produce about 80 percent of the results.

Take the case of George Owen, who was frustrated daily by not being able to get some writing done. He felt he had some good ideas to put down on paper but could never find the necessary time. Once he decided that developing his writing was vital to his career objectives, he took one hour away from office duties every day, first thing in the morning, and wrote. Sometimes it was only a few pages; sometimes, only one. But he wrote every day. Today, George is the author of over one dozen books and 100 articles.

It's a matter of self-discipline. It's a matter of deciding what's really important and of taking some calculated risks to find out whether some of those trivial activities can be put aside or even ignored.

Another reason why routine activities tend to get in the way is that they are familiar to you. They don't require much thinking or effort on your part. They don't have the ambiguity that goes with new tasks—and you avoid ambiguity in your environment and extra effort whenever you can.

The typical reaction is exemplified by statements like: "I can do these things without really thinking about them much. I'll get them out of the way first, then attend to the bigger problems." Or: "I'm not quite sure I know what to do. Are you sure this isn't going to be an exercise in futility?"

These day-to-day tasks, furthermore, provide you with an immediate sense of accomplishment. They are there to get done; you do them and get immediate feedback. Not so with career strategy tasks: they are for the longer pull, so the results are not immediately apparent. This lack of reinforcement tends to make such future-oriented activities less appealing.

As one young man complained: "I've been stewing over these items about me and the future now for about two full weeks. I have something down on paper, but I'm not sure if it's any good." And in the words of another: "I like to see things move from this side of my desk to that side. I'm a doer, not a planner. This business of contemplating who I am and how I fit into the future doesn't get me anywhere. Today's job today; tomorrow's, tomorrow!"

We naturally resist the new, the strange, because it will require us to put extra effort toward unknown results. This is particularly true about activities centered on self-analysis. We've taken ourselves for granted for a long time. To ponder issues related to self and self-development opens up the possibility of having to face up to dimensions of our being that we'd prefer to keep hidden from us and from others. No wonder we delay and resist such activity except when circumstances force us into it.

Prescription: take little steps first, steps that won't produce a big hurt if you fall and—if you don't fall—move you obviously toward a goal, even if you can't see the very end of the stairs. This will reduce the ambiguity and give more immediate reward to whatever efforts you expend.

Often it isn't our involvement with day-to-day activities that prevents us from getting started but our failure to see the *need* for drastic action. You may be aware that changes are going on around you, but because you believe them to be temporary, you think it unnecessary to respond to them. "You know how the old pendulum swings—first in one direction, then in the opposite," you might say. "There's really no need to respond to each swing."

Although it may be dangerous to react to every little change in one's environment, to ignore trends and significant shifts means simply not to face up to reality. Even if some of the trends are fads and won't last long, it is still important to determine their impact on the short- or long-range goals of one's career.

Unfortunately, even pressure from our superiors doesn't always lead us to see the need for some far-reaching planning. "Things around here must change," the boss might state in a meeting with his subordinates. "We're not getting the most out of our day-to-day activities. I'd like you to think about what we can do to be a more effective unit." Chances are that everybody present thinks, "He's talking to the rest of the group, not to me. My performance is great, and things have been going along well. No need for me to change."

Some Conditions That Will Get People Started

Our experience in working with people on the job suggests a variety of conditions that seem to spur people on to doing more strategic planning about their careers.

Consistently Poor Performance

Dissatisfaction with one's own performance on the job is an obvious and often powerful motivator. The problem may reside either in the *quantity* or the *quality* of the work produced.

"I've been putting in mighty long hours for over a year now, and

I'm still on a treadmill," we heard in one case. "What I do is O.K., but I'm not keeping up with my job. I'm not getting it all done."

This person finds no fault with the quality of what he gets done. His fault is with quantity. As the frustration increases, he'll either opt to get out of it, or he'll be forced to rethink his activities. That's when some strategic planning will start.

In another case we were told: "Nothing seems to work anymore. Ideas aren't coming the way they used to. Sure, I have enough time to really do a good job, but what I'm producing isn't up to my usual standards."

Here quality of performance is lacking. Under these conditions, we can predict that the individual will start doing some serious thinking about upgrading his performance. That, too, can be the start of strategic planning.

Forecasted Changes in the Environment

You may be doing well right now, but indications are that there may be different times ahead because of changes in your environment. The environmental factors responsible for your worries can include any of the major areas covered in our wheel model in Chapter 5: peer competition, organizational changes, economic or social issues, family concerns, and the like. To alleviate the impact of that storm, you turn to more strategic planning for the future.

As one young woman reflected: "My boss is going to retire in two years. That will leave an opening that I think I'd like a crack at. I'm not sure how to go about putting my name on the list of possible candidates for his job."

But the problem is not restricted to people at the beginning or middle of their career.

"I'll be retiring in another three years," we heard in another case. "Funny, but I never gave it much thought. I thought it would be just another natural flow of events. But I'm beginning to realize that it will not be as easy as all that. I hope it's not too late, but my wife and I are giving real thought to those retirement years."

Forecasted Problems in Performance

You are more likely to spend more time on strategic issues when you know that you will not be able to do what you will be called upon to do sometime in the future. The individual who knows he'll be promoted a year from now to a job whose demands go beyond his present abilities is likely to make some strategic plans to prepare himself for that promotion. The bachelor who will be married shortly starts concerning himself more with what he must do and know in order to be a "good husband."

"This entire operation will be automated in another couple of years," one person noted. "Then what? Certainly my job is going to be a lot different. I don't know if I can hack it. All these younger people who are coming along right out of school seem to know a lot more about these things than I do."

An Environment Concerned with Strategic Planning

When a person must function in an organization where key people express an interest in career planning and development, then he or she will also be more involved with career issues. In fact, this issue is probably the single most important factor in producing concern for career strategy. Organizations report that individuals left to their own devices will readily delay or cancel their career strategy planning. However, when the organization provides the time, the setting, and the signal to do it, then people feel encouraged and indeed obliged to engage in career planning pursuits.

Previous Positive Experience with Strategy Activities

Obviously, those who "try it and like it" are more apt to continue thinking in career strategy terms. If you've had a history of concern for such matters and that concern was reinforced positively, then it is quite likely that you will be a supporter of these matters. Or, if you've not had the experience yourself, you may know someone close to you who has had good results through strategy planning. In either case, such experience enhances the probability of developing a strategy and continuing the process.

It is not surprising that people with a sense of self-esteem and of inner control are more likely to engage in these pursuits than those who are still trying to find themselves. For the latter, our previous advice to proceed in small innocuous steps is to the point.

In general, an individual just starting to concern himself with issues of career strategy will do well to ally himself with someone responsible who has had success with such strategy ventures. As we noted earlier, "reality testing" of a career strategy involves, among other things, associating oneself with individuals who themselves are reality testers.

Some False Starts

Even when we're at the point where we know we've got to do something, our tendency is to think in *operational* rather than strategic terms. That is, instead of sitting back and doing some real thinking about our objectives and the longer-range issues, we still think primarily for the moment, about how to handle the immediate issue. Typical operational approaches follow.

We Work Harder

We somehow feel that things will get better if we put in more time and generate more activity on the job, with the family, or for a community project. You will recognize this as the "virtue of hard work"—a myth we discussed in Chapter 2. But if we keep working harder at the same things without having any clear-cut ideas about our objectives (an issue with which strategy can readily deal), then we will not experience growth.

We Get Organized

This usually takes the form of doing some immediate on-the-scene structuring of our day-to-day activities. We make out time charts; we put down on paper what we want to accomplish that day or that week; we set up schedules—and usually overschedule our time. If we're not careful, we'll spend more time on developing a system to keep us organized than we'll spend on working toward the appropriate goals.

For a while, this manner of attack can appear to be rewarding. Things seem to get done, although at a greater expense of time and effort. In the long run, though, the same problems still exist. If we don't have a sense of direction, we can organize the routine, repetitive day-to-day activities, but this still won't lead us anywhere. We can keep taking aspirin to get rid of a headache and never really get at the cause of the headache itself.

We Seek Help

When the schedule gets tight and hard work and more organization will not resolve our problems, we get others involved in doing our things. The family has to help with our chores; the subordinates are required to spend longer hours; we seek out the extra hands of friends; we hire other people to "take the load off our shoulders."

If enlisting help releases you to respond to broader strategic issues, then you've accomplished a lot. However, if you're still bogged down and unable to get beyond the day-to-day chores, look again to see just how well you're using all that extra help. The load gradually returns unless we look at our problem from a longer-range point of view and sift out the priority issues.

We See Training as a Panacea

In some cases we may reach the conclusion that the best way to solve our problem is through self-development. After all, personal growth is the road to career growth.

For instance, the engineer who knows that he's reached a plateau in his career may try to resolve his problem by taking graduate courses in management—only to wonder, after completing his courses, what he can do with the knowledge he gained! Similarly, a manager may send his subordinates to a training school to upgrade their skills, not realizing that the real problem at hand is lack of motivation rather than of technical knowledge.

Training for the sake of training usually has only limited value. By contrast, when self-development is tied to strategic goals—that is, when it becomes part of a total *system* of strategic activities— then its impact is more immediate and beneficial.

Some Good Starts

We have dwelt on some of the wrong ways to launch your career planning. They make sense, on the surface, and that's why they're all the more dangerous. But what is the right way to get started?

Naturally, what strategy is appropriate for you will depend on your personal characteristics and circumstances. Nevertheless, the approach that is best suited for you will probably fall into one of the categories discussed in the following.

Strategies That Broaden Your Market Base

Once you determine what your strengths really are and how and where to use them best, then make every effort to find other situations in which you can use those strengths even more. Don't concern yourself with your weaknesses; play to your strengths.

Beyond doing nothing, this is probably the easiest strategy to follow, and it has the highest probability of immediate payoff. For this reason, it's the best place to start in order to give yourself some confidence and experience in strategy implementation. Start where probabilities for success are highest.

Take the case of Glenda Davis, who was just promoted to manager of the corporate systems unit. She knew there were some aspects of the job that she could do well: handling the coordination with other departments, setting up long-range studies, and dealing with the broad technical issues that arise in the development of systems. But she didn't like the detail work, the digging into all the little things, the record keeping that was a necessary part of that job.

In view of this situation, she decided that her best plan was to build on those things she did well and to make sure that they would be built up to her best advantage. In other words, she decided to make her mark as a manager by using her best talents.

Strategies That Complement Your Market Base

Attending solely to your strengths will set potential limits to your personal growth. Often, the job requires attending to some matters that we can't handle as readily as other people, and in such cases, the best strategy is to find some other individuals with strengths that complement our own so that more can be accomplished.

The obvious example that comes to mind is the manager who surrounds himself with assistants who do well what he can't. But it works in the opposite direction too: a subordinate who understands his boss's strengths well may often be able to use them in support of his own weak spots.

Glenda Davis—to stay with our previous example—used not only a broadening strategy but a complementary one as well. She reorganized her unit so that one of her subordinates, who was especially good at keeping books, handling budgets, and proofreading reports, handled much of the detail work connected with Glenda's job.

The value of such a strategy rests of course on your awareness of the many resources around you—whether it be peer, boss, or subordinate—and a willingness to get help from others involved in your objectives. All of that may require more effort, but it also provides greater flexibility in your career objectives.

Strategies of Diversification

Perhaps you are aware of some weaknesses that you'd like to work on and possibly turn into strengths. This would provide you with an independence of action that is not readily available when you rely on others to complement your skills.

A general rule of thumb in this strategy is to choose first some situation that involves low risk for testing out your weaknesses. After confidence and competence are established, you can move on to the medium-risk situations.

For example, if you are trying to overcome what you consider a weakness in your interpersonal relationships, test your techniques first in situations where there is strength of relationship—say, at home or with friends—so that any failure won't be catastrophic. As you become proficient, moving to higher-risk environments makes more sense. Similarly, don't try to correct a weakness in speech making by accepting a speaking engagement before a convention of your professional peers. That comes later, after you've developed a certain degree of competence and confidence.

Compromise Strategies

It's difficult to change completely, but you may be able to compromise your style to mesh better with the styles of others. This strategy is different from the "complementary" strategy discussed earlier in that it requires actual change in your approach to matters. The complementary strategy requires no change but simply support from someone else's strengths.

An additional difficulty of the compromise strategy is that it requires you to figure out ways to change not only yourself but also the other person, because both parties' objectives must be accommodated. This certainly requires a considerable amount of self-control on your part to keep your own style in a check-and-balance position and avoid major conflicts with other people's styles.

Glenda Davis found herself in this accommodating mode with her boss. He felt he needed more frequent reports from her so he'd know what was going on. She really wanted to scrap the reports altogether and rely more on face-to-face discussions. The conflict was resolved by a compromise: he got his regular reports, but some of them were given in oral form.

A Balanced View

Chances are that, within any total career strategy, all of the approaches we have discussed will be used. As you evaluate yourself and decide what to do in view of the opportunities and risks, you will become aware that in certain areas you can use your strengths in new ways. In other areas, you may feel that you should use the strengths of others to complement your own. In still others, you may find that you must branch out and work on your weaknesses or perhaps steer a compromise course. Finally, there may be areas where you feel that for the moment, you should do nothing beyond perhaps some "doorknob polishing."

These strategies require different levels of effort on your part, and they are associated with different degrees of risk. Both factors increase as we move from a "do nothing strategy" to the compromise strategy.

Some Specific Steps

As will have become clear by now, in real life the formulation and the implementation of career strategy are intertwined: feedback from your experiences as you put your plan to work makes you aware of changes required in your original strategy. Hence, formulating a career strategy is a never-ending process, and it keeps on going even while you attempt to implement the strategy. Nevertheless, this section will focus on specific steps to get the process started.

Identifying Key Tasks

Just as you were asked to analyze your environments and yourself in order to formulate your career strategy, you are now asked to analyze your strategy. The purpose of this analysis is to identify the key tasks that must be accomplished if you are to achieve your strategic goals.

Essentially, this step involves answering questions such as: How does someone who wants to accomplish the things I'd like to accomplish fail? What are the issues which, if unattended, carry a high probability of failure? The converse questions are equally useful: How can a person ensure that he will achieve his goals? What are the activities to which he must absolutely attend?

For example, career strategies will almost always include an objective of self-development. What is the key task to be performed here to achieve that purpose? Many people believe that self-development is best achieved through the pursuit of a university degree. But is obtaining a degree important for success in my business career? Will I fail without it? Will it enhance the probabilities of reaching my job goals?

The answers depend on one's unique strategy. *If* analysis of the environment reveals fierce competition for desired positions among highly qualified applications, *if* the organization that employs or will employ you values a degree, *if* time is not an immediate concern in goal achievement, *if* seeking the education does not create conflict in other spheres of your career, then seeking a degree as a means of self-development may be a reasonable approach.

On the other hand, it is not necessarily true that a formal education leading to a designated degree is the best way to implement your strategic objective of self-development. If the strategic objective is for growth in a specialty business area (finance, marketing, personnel), if the organization does not emphasize the need for a formal degree, and if your resources and commitments create potential conflicts, then self-development through other means—on the job or through noncredit seminars and specialized university courses—may more readily serve the strategic purpose.

Note that some of the questions relating to key tasks are already answered by your initial analysis of your environments. Do the various environmental factors provide opportunities or pose threats? If you do not respond to them now, what implications does that have for the present and the future? Are your present resources so thinly spread over essential activities that to add another pursuit would threaten your current effectiveness? If so, can you risk current ineffective performance to achieve a longer-range success? Or are you presently spending time on activities that really have little or no bearing on present or future total career effectiveness.

Organizing Available Resources

There is no reason to think that all the key tasks must be done by only one person. Your analysis may suggest that a number of other people be involved in the process. In fact, one of the real values of the initial analysis of environments and resources in the formulation of strategy is to find out specifically what resources will be available if needed—and *then to use them effectively* when that is necessary.

It is not a matter of asking who is *available* to help? Rather, the key questions are: Who has the strengths that are essential to accomplish the key tasks I've identified? Are these people committed to my career objectives? Are they even aware of them? Should they be aware? Does their helping me create conflict with their own strategies? Can I possibly reduce that conflict for them so that their resources can be more readily used to achieve my and their purpose?

These are not selfish questions. They should not imply that the name of the game is to exploit others' strengths for personal gain. The fact is that high achievers are those who are not afraid to utilize the services of others in the achievement of personal purpose. And if everybody who is determined to achieve took this attitude, a system of cooperative spirit would be more likely to develop.

We have stated earlier that individuals have conceptions (whether correct or incorrect) of their role and of the activities demanded of them in that role. These role conceptions frequently influence our willingness to use the resources of others. If, for example, a man believes that one of his role demands is to handle the financial affairs of the house, then he will naturally ignore the possibility of letting his wife deal with these things; therefore, he will have less time for other matters that are equally important for both of them. Or, to take an example from the sphere of work, it is not unusual for a manager to keep the decision making to himself because he views it as solely his responsibility, even though the subordinate might be able to take some of this load off his shoulders.

Utilizing the resources of others, then, requires not only that you recognize those resources in your environment but also that you are willing and able to use them effectively. Recognizing available resources may not be too difficult. And when we are in trouble, we are usually willing to seek out the services of others who appear to be in a position to help. It is when we're not in trouble that we really test our willingness to use these resources.

Your outside resources may include the whole array of professionals—doctors, lawyers, educators, brokers, counselors, librarians, computer experts—as well as those people—bosses, subordinates, peers, the family—who are directly or indirectly involved with your strategic activities. Finally, there are the myriad of physical resources—equipment (for example, typewriters or computers), money, facilities—that are needed. All should be organized around your key tasks.

Developing a Control System

After you have identified key activities and organized your own resources and those of others to achieve your purpose, your next step should be to devise a system that will help you know when that purpose is reached.

Just like your strategy, your control devices must be *future-oriented* and *dynamic*. You must be concerned with what your present behavior tells you about your future behavior. Should you continue on with your strategy, or do the signs indicate that change is necessary? Are your standards out of date in view of changes, present or forthcoming, in your environment? For example, has the organization in which you work established tougher guidelines for performance so that your present standards are no longer valid? Has society changed its ideas of what is "acceptable" behavior for the role you are playing?

Furthermore, control systems should be *all-pervasive*, in the sense that they should concern themselves with all aspects of behavior and all objectives. For some objectives, controls are easily developed; for example, it requires no great ingenuity to establish the date when a specific task must be completed, the number of items to be sold, or the number of books to be read in a month. It is more difficult to control the qualitative aspects of life—for instance, giving more love to one's family or being more attentive to one's superior or subordinate. Nonetheless, they must all be measured if you are to check your progress.

Within that context, it is possible to identify several different types of effective controls for career strategy implementation. Three of them are discussed in the following: the "go no-go" control, the "wait and see" control, and the "early warning" control.

THE "GO NO-GO" CONTROL

In this kind of control, the individual sets up a series of tasks in some logical order that is to be strictly followed; that is, in implementing the plan, no task will be begun until the preceding step is accomplished to the individual's level of satisfaction.

This approach may be valuable for those aspects of career strategy that require building on successive steps. In general, however, excessive reliance on this control device in career planning will lead to a slowdown of the process. The reason for this lies in the dynamic nature of environments and of strategy. Since events may change the usefulness of a certain strategic decision, it may be essential to scrap a particular step in the process or to accomplish it at something less than the desired standard, or even to go on to another step that appears to be out of sequence.

A typical plan of this kind might go somewhat like this: "The first thing I've got to do is talk to my boss and get his ideas, then contact the salesmen in the territory and get their reactions. Then I'll get to work on developing the materials for the campaign." If the boss is out of town or otherwise not available for a period of time, the process will come to a halt, and valuable time and opportunities may be lost.

Or you might say to yourself, "I'm going to master this if it's the last thing I do! I'm not going to pursue my technical studies any further if I don't get an outstanding evaluation in this program." In this case, the standard may be too high, and you may find yourself in a "no-go," standstill situation in your career implementation.

In short, although breaking your plan down into subactivities is a useful way of ensuring feedback, the go no-go control may retard progress when the sequencing is artificial.

THE "WAIT AND SEE" CONTROL

In this kind of system, the individual goes ahead and completes whatever he sets out to do, then checks his results against some kind of standard. If they are satisfactory (up to standard), there will be no need for corrective action; if they are not, then change is called for.

The report card system is typical of this approach. It may include wait-and-see items like: "I'll wait and see what they do for me at salary time." "I'll just have to wait and hope my wife understands." "I haven't been sick yet, so why exercise?"

There are of course advantages to this kind of control. If you know the past results of a specific activity or series of activities and you can forecast similar conditions for the future, this feedback information may be valuable for future planning. This kind of control may also provide a good incentive if the system is set up to promise some reward—a salary increase, a degree, or increased self-esteem—at the completion of the cycle.

The obvious disadvantage of the wait-and-see control is that it is applied too late to be effective for this time around. The event has already occurred before it is measured. Your spouse is already upset; your salary wasn't increased; you are now ill. The only thing you can do now is to take corrective action so that it won't happen again and spend some time alleviating the damage done by the wait-and-see approach.

It is this latter factor that can be debilitating to a career strategy: you may spend more time putting out the fires and correcting negative results than getting on with the progress of your career. That is why we recommend using an "early warning" control whenever possible.

THE "EARLY WARNING" CONTROL

In this kind of control, an individual monitors the results of his career strategy along the way. If the signs predict potential failure, corrective actions can be taken.

Such controls are constructive. Measurement and feedback devices are designed to bring actual results as close as possible to desired strategic objectives and make remedial action possible. In short, this type of control is future-oriented and dynamic.

To predict with some degree of accuracy the outcome of your plan before it actually occurs is generally difficult, but it becomes easier if you remain sensitive to clues of how you're doing. Here are two of the signs that bear watching.

Initial successes or failures. Frequently, you can get clues about potential success or failure from results early in the process of career implementation. In your school years you got clues about possible final results in a course from the first paper or test; when the early signals were negative, you could, if you wished, take corrective action. Similarly, how a young couple gets along before marriage may well predict the course of action after marriage.

On a broader scheme, the activities of your earlier life will give you clues about what will happen in the future if you continue in the same pattern of behavior. High achievers, for example, tend to have a life history of accomplishments, and their past behavior is therefore often predictive of their future behavior, provided that conditions remain similar.

Shifts in environments. Shifts that are occurring in the environments in which you work may very well give you clues as to the potential success of a given strategic step. For example, introduction of new competitive talent in the organization or dramatic changes in the economy may indicate what you have to do in order to continue meeting your primary goals.

Master strategists, it appears, are individuals who have an intuitive awareness of the subtleties, the "little things" going on around them that may affect their career strategy. It's as though they have their antennas up and are able to pick up trends that, even if they don't relate directly to their career objectives, may be symptomatic of things to come.

There is of course the danger of becoming oversensitive to the environment and responding to the slightest of clues. To take this attitude is to flirt with the danger of never achieving a desired end. It is the *consistency* of these signs over a period of time that has meaningful predictive value.

Developing Standards

It is not enough merely to collect information about your progress in implementing your career plan; to be of any real value, your control devices must be based on specific performance standards. How good is "good," or how bad is "bad"?

That kind of question cannot be answered in any general way. What outcome is desirable for one person may not be desirable for another. Hence, the ideal standard is one that is acceptable to you and to others who are crucially involved in your career strategy. If the standard you select is unacceptable to others—say, your superiors—it may create conflict and endanger your ultimate career progress; and if it is compatible with the ideas of others but unacceptable to you, it will quickly lead to feelings of frustration on your part.

We see this when an individual reaches a level of status in an organization that is acceptable to him but perceived by his boss as not high enough in view of the person's abilities. The subordinate is happy; the boss, frustrated. Depending on the situation, the boss's frustration can be a roadblock to progress.

Conversely, a wife may be perfectly delighted when her husband is promoted to assistant vice president. But if the husband's standard for "success" is to be a vice president, then he may feel that he has failed or that he needs to do more in order to achieve his career goal. As a result, the wife may complain: "You're never satisfied," and the husband may see his wife as a roadblock to his career.

It is for this reason that any control system for career objectives must provide continuous information not only to you but to all others involved in the ultimate outcome. Since your career is so closely interwoven with the strategies of others, others must be kept informed not only of your goals but also of your results. They must be in a position to take action when such action has a bearing on your or their career direction. If they don't know, they can't act.

Taking Corrective Action

It's only after you can measure your own behavior against some standard that you can decide whether further action on your part is necessary. If you performed below standard, should you abandon that goal or make a determined effort to bring your behavior up to standard? Should you perhaps change the standard?

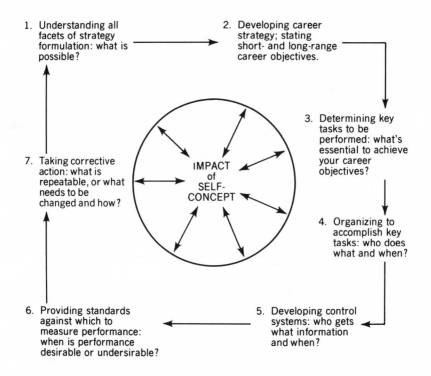

1. Understanding all facets of strategy formulation: what is possible?

2. Developing career strategy; stating short- and long-range career objectives.

3. Determining key tasks to be performed: what's essential to achieve your career objectives?

4. Organizing to accomplish key tasks: who does what and when?

5. Developing control systems: who gets what information and when?

6. Providing standards against which to measure performance: when is performance desirable or undersirable?

7. Taking corrective action: what is repeatable, or what needs to be changed and how?

IMPACT of SELF-CONCEPT

The focal point of your career strategy formulation is your self-concept. The same is true for the implementation of your strategy. How you perceive yourself affects your understanding of each phase in the sequence, and it influences the manner in which you proceed to implement that phase. This is brought out by the flowchart, which summarizes the process of career strategy implementation.

Figure 15. Flowchart of career strategy implementation.

If you performed at or above standard, should you now raise standards or go on to another objective? What does a specific result tell you about your overall career strategy? To what extent should the total plan be changed?

Personal Style

As we have seen in the preceding chapter, the focal point of your career strategy formulation is your self-concept. The same is true for the implementation of your strategy. How you perceive yourself affects your understanding of each phase in the sequence, and it influences the manner in which you proceed to implement that phase. This is brought out by the flowchart in Figure 15, which summarizes the process of career strategy implementation.

Whether you approach career planning activities aggressively or with reservation, whether you approach them with concern for others or with disregard for others' career objectives, whether your risk level in setting standards and controls is high or low—these are symptoms of your personal lifestyle and reflect directly on your perception of who and what you are.

But this personal style not only influences what goals you set and how you go about achieving them, it also interacts directly with your environments and therefore must be consistent with the expectations of those environments. Clearly, the way you behave and the mechanisms you use to adjust influence others' perceptions of you. If you are to minimize conflicts and frustrations, it is essential, then, that you develop an objective view of your environments and strive to find the best fit between their expectations and your needs.

The intimate relationship between your personal style and the system leads to a lack of stability of any career strategy. As you implement your strategy, your resources change. The very process of putting a system into action provides you with more information about you—your strengths and limitations, your interests, values, and needs. This new information in turn creates a different set of inputs for career strategy formulation—and the process starts all over again!

A winner takes big risks when he has much to gain; a loser takes big risks when he has little to gain and much to lose. *Sydney Harris*

7

Motivation and Career Strategy

The Need for Direction

SOMETIMES the incentive for change is obvious and the need for it is great, but we just don't think we can do what's required to reach our goal. At other times the incentives are not so apparent, and that makes the going more difficult. And then there are times when the incentive is there, obvious as can be, and we know we can do what is required, but somehow we just can't seem to get motivated to do anything about it. That's the complexity of motivation.

Take the case of June Sanders. She's married, career-oriented, productive, and effective in her job. The company has invited her on several occasions to enroll in a year-long management studies program that would prepare her for a management slot—something she says she wants very much. But she just can't seem to say "yes" to it.

"There are so many other things that get in the way," she observes. "My job demands so much of my time that I couldn't afford the extra time for studying and reading. And goodness, I've got to spend time with my family as well. Sure, I'd love to be a manager, and maybe my schedule will get better so I can take advantage of that course next year."

Dangling the carrot in front of someone does not necessarily move them in that direction. Incentive alone is not the answer.

Understanding what our needs are and what incentives will satisfy those needs becomes important in both the formulation and implementation of a career strategy. If we base our strategies on the wrong kinds of needs (needs that are not important to us) or if we seek, through our careers, certain incentives that are really not going to satisfy us, then our strategies will indeed fail. We start, therefore, with some basic concepts of motivation.

Need as a Motivator

Much of our behavior can be explained in terms of our needs. A need, whether or not it be one of which we are aware, creates a "tension state" in us that serves as an initiator of some activity on our part to reduce the feeling of tension.

Sometimes, when a need becomes especially strong, we are aware of the tension. If we go without food for an extended period of time, for instance, we will experience hunger pangs. In such simple cases we usually know what behavior will reduce the tension and satisfy our need.

In other cases we are aware of the generalized tension, but, since the need is not readily apparent, our activity may be trial and error until the right behavior is found. Perhaps the following dialog rings familiar.

Husband:	"Let's do something today; I feel restless and want to get out of the house."
Wife:	"Okay. What do you want to do?"
Husband:	"Oh, I don't know. But let's do something."

So off they go to the flea market. As husband and wife are looking at some "junque" on one of the tables:

Husband:	"What are we doing here?"
Wife:	"I thought you said you wanted to do something today."
Husband:	"Yeah, but not this. Let's *do* something."

And the husband might spend the rest of the day feeling this generalized tension "to do something" but never really releasing the tension because the activity in which he is engaged is not related to the need causing the tension state.

Without need, of course, we would experience no tension and consequently take no action to relieve our dissatisfaction. In reality, however, this state of perfect equilibrium never occurs; instead, we have a multitude of needs that keep vying, as it were, for satisfaction. As one need is satisfied, its strength is reduced and another need moves in. Hence, our behavior is continuous, and we are always in what is called a state of quasi-equilibrium: first off-balance (tension state high), then back into balance (tension state reduced), then back off-balance again as another need arises.

Self-Confidence and Motivation

Need alone is not enough. A person may have a high need for something and yet feel that he does not have the skill or ability to perform or that some other factors will prevent him from reaching his goals. In fact, then, he develops an estimate of the probability that he will be able to perform in an intended way. If that probability is high, he is more likely to pursue his goals actively; if it is low, the probability of his taking action is reduced, no matter how great a need he feels to change his situation.

Joseph Schmidt, for example, has a strong need to gain recognition from his boss. He knows that such recognition will occur if he does certain things, such as building good relationships with the clerical force and developing a better liaison with other departments. But Joe sees himself as rather inept in his interpersonal relations; he does not consider himself outgoing, and his experience has been that when he tries to overcome his natural shyness, he usually feels uncomfortable and performs poorly.

Evidently, the probability that Joe will perform as required to satisfy his need for recognition is judged as low by himself. We can predict that his probability estimate will influence Joe's motivation to perform.

What the example points out is the *importance of one's own experiences*. We learn much from our past performance. Joe Schmidt has tried to be outgoing on several occasions and feels that he doesn't do well under these circumstances. That, of course, reduces, in his mind, the probability that his efforts will result in effective performance.

But clearly, we must go beyond merely recognizing our past experience as the source of a motivational barrier; we must take active steps to increase the probability of our performing effectively. If motivation is influenced by our degree of self-confidence and self-confidence is built on our past experiences relating to our skills and abilities, then what's required is to increase our skills in the relevant areas. Here our earlier advice is to the point: start by developing new skills in situations that minimize failure and encourage you to persist in your efforts.

That is just what Joe Schmidt did. He realized that he had to develop a basic desire to talk to people, and he decided that the best way to start was to talk about his problems to his wife, of whose understanding he could be sure.

"Frankly, it wasn't too easy at first," he recalls. "Yet, now our evening meals seem a source of conversation. My wife is now used to my talking, and if I appear headed for a relapse, she now asks me questions. Saying 'hi' to people was actually difficult for me not too long ago. I am now in demand to (1) play golf, (2) play bridge, (3) cut firewood, and (4) sit and talk. It is a pleasant experience."

Another factor that influences our perception of the probabilities that we can do something is the judgment of others—particularly of people whom we consider mature, reality-oriented, and experienced in the situation. Our discussion of career myths in Chapter 2 strongly suggested that people sometimes have difficulty coming to grips with reality: their own concerns seem to get in the way of seeing a situation objectively. Communication with others, then, becomes a vital link to a more accurate estimate of the probabilities of our performing in the desired way. When we see others as mature, objective, reasonable, and experienced, we tend to accept their observations of us and our situation.

This is where good interpersonal skills become important for the accomplishment of career strategy. Effective communication brings us in closer touch with reality and gives us a more valid picture of our abilities and, therefore, of our chances to reach our goals.

As one young man who had been sent by his company to a career planning conference put it: "I was convinced that I just didn't have what it takes to move ahead in management at the company. In fact, I was thinking seriously of leaving when the company sent me to the career planning conference. At the conference I did a lot of soul searching and self-evaluation. But more than anything else I had an opportunity to do two things. One was to talk to other people from other departments and learn more about the kinds of people they were. The other was to talk with the professional staff about me.

"It gave me a different insight into where I should be and where I was going. When I returned from the conference, I sat down with my boss and for the first time really discussed my abilities and what I thought I could do in the future. Ironically enough, after the conference, I received a very lucrative offer to join a competitor, and after reviewing the materials from the conference and my talk with my boss, I elected to stay where I was and to work my best for advancement right there."

The example once again points out the importance of self-esteem in the individual change process. When we have a belief in our own performance capabilities, then we tend to have a higher regard for ourselves. And the higher that self-esteem, the greater the probability that we will be a better judge of our future performance. People with low self-esteem tend to underestimate the probability that they'll be able to perform in certain ways.

External Factors

How motivated a person is to work actively on his career depends not only on his perceived needs and his estimate of his abilities but also on his expectation that effective performance will lead to the desired result. If people feel that external factors are likely to prevent them from reaching a goal even if they perform well, they will lack the motivation to take action.

Dale Preston, for example, has the need to do well. He perceives that the probability is high that he'll be able to perform well. But he also thinks that the probabilities are low that his performance will lead to an appropriate outcome for him. Hence his desire to perform is reduced. "I'm no farther along in status in this company than any of those people who are just putting in a mediocre performance," he notes. "Why should I knock myself out for nothing?"

Just as a person's confidence in his ability to perform is influenced by his past experience, so it is with his estimate that effective performance will lead to the desired result. Dale Preston, for example, has learned that good performance doesn't lead to desirable outcomes. But is that conclusion inevitable? There is a real danger here of basing far-reaching decisions on hasty generalizations.

Even worse, when we lack the relevant experience, we sometimes let our behavior be influenced by the "experiences" of others without checking that their perceptions are realistic. Thus we frequently establish ideas about the "reality" of the work place that are far from the true practices or intentions of the company. We may believe, for example, that redesign of jobs will lead to greater performance demands without concomitant rewards. We believe it not because we understand what the situation is all about but because our peers told us.

Here's a typical case involving a young man who had been with his company for about five years.

He:	"Well, I guess I have no choice but to leave the company."
Counselor:	"Why's that?"
He:	"I was just offered a promotion right here in Hartford. I really don't want it. My wife and I want to transfer back to Dallas."
Counselor:	"Have you mentioned that to your boss?"
He:	"Are you crazy? Of course not!"
Counselor:	"Why not?"
He:	"You know how it is in this company. Just refuse one promotion, one transfer, and they push you aside, forget all about you."
Counselor:	"Do you know that for a fact? Anybody you know have that happen to him?"
He:	"Not really. But all the guys say it's so. They say they've heard it from a lot of people that you just don't say 'no' to this company."

This young man was about to consider a career change based on what he "knew" to be fact from his coworkers about the probabilities of his ever receiving favorable treatment again if he refused a promotion. When he was encouraged to explore the "fact" more closely, he found it to be a myth—and, incidentally, was transferred to Dallas with a promotion.

If an individual feels that he has some control over reaching a goal, he is likely to be more motivated than if he feels the attainment of that goal is dependent on the behavior of others. Hence individuals who have learned the value of *internal control* are likely to have high expectations of achieving a certain outcome. On the other hand, *externally motivated* people—individuals who believe that their success depends on external forces, such as luck, other people, or timing—are likely to have low expectations of achieving their goals.

Again, our own experiences are a vital factor here and can help us develop greater reliance on internal control mechanisms. If we have a lot of faith in our own capabilities to make a certain outcome occur, then we are much more motivated to behave in ways to make it happen. If we must depend on others, then we are much less likely to act, unless we think we can influence their behavior.

Incentives and Motivation

Finally, the nature of our goal itself is also important in determining the strength of the overall motivation to expend energy. It must of course be a goal that we want, and the more desirable it is, the more likely we are to try to reach it. A carrot is a goal only when we have a need for carrots. Dangling a carrot in front of us does nothing for us if we have a desire for peaches.

Desirability of a goal is an elusive variable; it's so personal, so much a function of one's own experiences and value systems. Although we tend to think more in terms of tangible goal objects (pay, a new car, something for the house), it is apparently the intangible results (feelings of competency, adequacy, and self-esteem) that are more desirable and sought-after for most mature adults in our society.

This is an important observation because it can explain why achieving a goal—such as a new job title or recognition from the boss—does not always bring us a sense of accomplishment. If the outcome comes too easily, if we believe it is not based on our own efforts, then we don't experience personal achievement. In other words, the satisfaction we derive from attaining a certain goal seems to be linked to the perceived challenge of the situation.

However, reaching a goal can be associated with a lack of satisfaction not only when we believe that there was no challenge but also when we feel that our success was so improbable as to be due mostly to luck. In the first situation, we have a sense of being no more than average; in the second, a sense of relief that luck was on our side. By contrast, if the probabilities are about 50-50 that we can succeed through our own efforts, then actual achievement leads to a feeling of competence and self-esteem.

Needs and Goals

Psychologists differ in their classification of needs. For our purposes those differences are really not important. We are more interested in taking a closer look at need states from the point of view of the behavior that may be elicited by them and the goals that are commonly associated with them. Based on a classification proposed by Abraham Maslow,* we will therefore categorize need states in terms of individual goals.

Our first gross classification will be in terms of lower-level and higher-level needs. This classification depends on factors such as learning required, level of maturity, and the complexity of the behavior needed to satisfy the need. Lower-level needs, since they are more primitive, require less complex behavior and less maturity on the part of the individual to satisfy them. By contrast, satisfying higher-level needs generally requires more complex activities, higher levels of maturity, and more experience.

Within this dichotomy we can identify five major need systems.

Physiological: The need to survive by securing food, drink, shelter, and other basic necessities of life.

Safety: The need to ensure continued maintenance of basic existence needs and to provide an environment that is predictable and void of harm.

Social: The need to associate with others and to accept and appreciate their existence; the need to belong.

Ego (self-esteem): The need to gain a reputation, to be recognized for one's accomplishments, to be needed, and to be responsible and independent in one's actions.

Self-actualization: The need for a sense of competence and for self-expression; the need to grow as a person.

The first two of these categories are clearly low-level; the last two, higher-level. The third—the need to associate with others—may be considered to occupy an intermediate position.

These various needs can be satisfied by a variety of goals, depending on one's experiences. The list on the next page provides some examples.

* *Motivation and Personality*, second edition, New York: Harper & Row, 1970.

GOALS RELATED TO PHYSIOLOGICAL NEEDS

On the Job

Money for purchase of basic goods; acceptable physical surroundings at work; vacations and personal time off from job; subsidized cafeterias; etc.

Off the Job

Availability of adequate stores for the basic necessities; adequate living space; availability of physicians; time to relax and sleep; recreational facilities; etc.

GOALS RELATED TO SAFETY NEEDS

On the Job

Health and medical care packages; social security; safe work place; job security; automatic cost-of-living salary increases; etc.

Off the Job

Protection against crime and fire; a savings account; an orderly family life; a freezer stocked with food; etc.

GOALS RELATED TO SOCIAL NEEDS

On the Job

Association with peers; involvement with committees; group travel; staff meetings; team incentives; contacts with other departments; etc.

Off the Job

An adequate social and family life; involvement in community and social clubs; intellectual stimulation; recreational facilities; etc.

GOALS RELATED TO EGO NEEDS

On the Job

Promotions based on performance; special assignments; responsibility and independence to schedule one's day; respect from one's co-workers and superiors; pay; contacts with other departments; developing a unique expertise; doing better than last year; etc.

Off the Job

Gaining the respect of people whom one admires; being elected to the board of education; repairing the kitchen faucet; helping with homework; learning how to paint; people laughing at one's sense of humor; etc.

GOALS RELATED TO THE NEED FOR SELF-ACTUALIZATION

On the Job

Setting one's own goals and standards; attending training programs; satisfying work; devising feedback systems to determine one's effectiveness on the job; a feeling of freedom to be open with one's peers and superiors; etc.

Off the Job

Achieving self-set standards of performance in leisure-time activities; being accepted by the family for what you are; taking night courses "just for fun"; doing volunteer work; starting one's own business; trying something new; good time management; upgrading existing skills; etc.

As will have been noticed, some of the goals listed appear on more than one level. This reflects the fact that one and the same goal may serve to satisfy a number of different needs. For example, pay may be important to you because it is necessary to buy the things you need to exist. However, once you pass that basic maintenance level, pay becomes more of an ego satisfier: it's a means by which most companies express their evaluation of your performance.

Hence the $100,000-a-year executive wants a raise, not for the sake of the money, but because the amount of the raise tells him something about the regard his company has for him. Finally, pay may become a means to satisfy our need for security—to store up and buy more than we need at present in order to have enough for a rainy day.

But the reverse of this is equally possible; that is, one need may be satisfied through many different goals or activities. For example, if you have a strong need for recognition, you may try to satisfy that need by striving for superior performance on the job; alternatively, you may seek recognition by becoming active in your community.

Determining Our Needs

The arousal of a need state demands behavior on our part to try to satisfy that need. That is why we stated earlier that behavior is motivated. It should be possible, then, to determine our true needs by examining our behavior. However, we are remarkably flexible and versatile and can find a variety of behaviors that, even though they may not be satisfying to others, provide us with a feeling of need satisfaction. Hence looking solely at our behavior does not necessarily tell us what our needs are. The real clue to understanding our needs is *consistency* of our behavior over a period of time and in different situations.

In our earlier example, for instance, the decision to become active in the community rather than to strive for superior performance on the job is not an expression of a need to do social work or to alienate the boss. Rather, it reflects a need that says: "I am a person who wants to be recognized. If my boss won't pay attention to me, somebody else—the community—will."

The relationship between needs and behavior, therefore, is something that requires our close attention if we are to do effective career planning. All too often, we find out—sometimes too late— that our behavior satisfies needs that are not related to our true priorities.

As one young man who had this experience observed: "I used

to think that if I ever made $35,000 I'd have it made. But there's still something lacking. I'm pretty well set with all the things I want. Sure, we always want more in the way of material things, but even if I'd have all the material things I want, I'm pretty sure that something would be lacking. There's no zip to my days; it's tougher getting up in the morning and going to work. The job doesn't have the excitement anymore."

This person thought that his pay was of primary importance to him—that his greatest need was to be financially secure and not to have to worry about living the "good life." But obtaining that goal left a void; higher-level needs turned out to have greater priority for him.

Achieving the goals related to higher-level needs requires behavior on our part that comes very close to what would be labeled "mature." It requires initiative, independent action, specific interests and purpose, an awareness of self, and enough inner control to make things happen. It is this commitment to mature behavior which, in the long run, brings growth and personal satisfaction.

Of course, we want the other material things associated with the lower-level needs; we need many of them to subsist. In the last analysis, however, it is the dedication to higher-level goals that brings about our personal psychological well-being. In the formulation of our career strategy, these needs cannot be denied.

There is some evidence that individuals will not attempt to satisfy higher-level needs until such time as the lower-level needs are satisfied to their level of expectancy. Hence in our recent example, once an individual reaches a level of security acceptable to him (a $35,000 salary), he may turn to greater concern for the "excitement" of the job—a higher-level need. Furthermore, it seems that people who are trying to satisfy higher-level needs will revert back to satisfaction of lower-level needs if the latter are threatened.

Whether or not individuals progress upward in precisely the five levels of needs discussed here is still a matter for research. What appears clear is that there is at least a dichotomy of need states (higher and lower level) and that this dichotomy has an importance for understanding and formulating an effective career strategy. Until we know what really motivates us and what outcomes are really important, our strategy will remain shallow.

Satisfaction versus Saturation

A major difference between higher- and lower-level needs is what happens once the need is satisfied. Satisfaction of lower-level needs tends to move a person away from the activity that brought about satisfaction. On the other hand, satisfaction of higher-level areas tends to keep the person around the source of satisfaction.

Let's take some examples. You're hungry, you go to the dinner table and eat. When you feel you've had enough to eat, you stop eating and ultimately move away from the dinner table. You may linger for a while at the table, not to eat, but, if others are present, because you want to be sociable as well.

You will recall that we categorized the social needs as both higher- and lower-level. Individuals need contact with others to develop a sense of self, to get recognition, to feel the sense of being needed, and to test out their ideas and capabilities; in short, the social need is of a higher-level order. But all of us have been in situations where we've had "enough of people," where we feel a need to be alone and just relax. In that sense, the social need is a lower-level need; it can lead to oversaturation and encourage us to move on to something else.

Not so with the higher-level needs. Once we experience satisfaction of a higher-level need, we want more of the same. When we are in a situation in which all the signs lead us to believe that we are needed and wanted, that our talents are being used well, that we are recognized for what we do well, and that we can grow and develop in these surroundings, a warm glow of satisfaction tends to envelop us. It's a good feeling, and we want *more* of that, not less.

Hence a clue to career and life satisfaction rests in our reinforcement of higher-level needs. If we can put ourselves more frequently into situations that increase the likelihood of arousing and satisfying these higher needs, we can bè guaranteed greater personal satisfaction from that situation.

It comes as no surprise, therefore, that people who set challenging goals that test their abilities and who then set out to accomplish those goals and actually reach them gain greater levels of self-esteem and have a much greater sense of satisfaction with life or work. Jobs that may be dull and boring one week can become exciting and challenging the next week if we give purpose to them and then direct our energies toward the accomplishment of that purpose.

Take the case of one young man. "I used to think that my job was not very challenging," he recalls. "My boss left me alone most of the time, and I complained to myself and to my wife that my boss wasn't giving me enough direction and that I didn't have enough to do. And then I took a closer look at my job functions, put them in a priority order, and decided what needed to be done, checked it with my boss, and I'm off and running. Once those goals were set, I had a direction to follow. So things are better all around.

"The irony is that I don't have what I thought I needed—a stable, concretely described position. It changes daily as I strive to achieve my objectives."

The unfortunate thing is that many people find this a difficult concept to accept—until they've experienced it. Our experiences seem to suggest to us that if only we could get some of those lower-level needs taken care of, life would be much better. And so we strive for "a nicer place to work," more fringe benefits, more titles, or more pay, thinking that when we get those things, somehow the work will be palatable. But more often than not, we find these pills have no lasting effect and, in the end, taste bitter. They do little to turn us on to the job, and life and work remain humdrum.

The Mature Approach: Focusing on Higher-Level Needs

To gain a better understanding of the complex relation between motivation and people's needs, let's take a closer look at the human adult. Here are some of the attributes that can be said to describe the mature person:

Dynamic and self-activating.

Controlled primarily by inner drives or needs.

Seeking responsibility.

Attempting to give order and consistency to his world in order to cope effectively with it.

Flexible and perceptive.

Able to learn and to communicate with others.

As such a person grows to adulthood, he or she is likely to continue to take the initiative, behave in independent ways, display a variety of interests and remain flexible, gain greater self-awareness, and exercise self-control.

What we are describing here, of course, are behaviors directly related to higher-level needs. As adults, we want to do those things that will keep proving to us that we are people in our own right, that we are growing, using our talents, making choices, and the like. Hence it is highly probable that in most situations, most people will attend to those needs and test out the environment to determine to what extent the environment can satisfy those needs. We dip down into the lower-level needs only occasionally when we get clues that they need attention. For the most part, our waking lives (and sometimes our dreams as well) are focused on the satisfaction of higher-order needs.

What happens when we start getting clues that perhaps these needs won't be or can't be satisfied? We don't give up very easily. We've got to survive psychologically; we can't deny our very existence, our very sense of self. We fixate on these needs. We try a variety of behaviors, all of which are an attempt to keep proving to ourselves that the situation cannot, will not destroy our sense of self.

Sometimes we attack what we think is the cause of the frustration—the boss, the company, the spouse, the children, the system. Here's an example that may sound familiar:

"I dialed that number, I bet, ten times over the period of about 30 minutes, and every time I got some taped answer. So then I shot off that letter to the telephone company, complaining about the quality of their service, the deterioration in efficiency, the increased costs. But after I cooled down, I had to admit that none of my complaints ,were justified. I can dial a number 3,000 miles away and get, almost always, an instant answer. And costs, if anything, have gone down. I guess what really got to me was the tape: it treated me like I'm a nobody, and I didn't like that. I'm somebody, and I want the telephone company to recognize that."

To find the cause of our frustration and to work on it directly is the mature approach to seeking satisfaction. If we don't know the real cause, then our behavior will not be successful. And even if we know the cause, our satisfaction will be limited if our behavior in response to it is immature.

If we can't fight the cause directly, we try to get around it some way and still get what we want—a sense of control over the situation. So, for example, if our boss is the source of our frustrations, we join him rather than fight him: we agree with him when we really don't, look busy when we aren't. Anything to avoid a hassle. Anything to avoid putting our sense of self on the line.

We emphasize this only to indicate that, as adults, we are driven by this strong need for self-esteem and for actualization of self. All of our activities to overcome frustrations of this need are aimed at an all-consuming desire to defend our sense of self.

The Way of Frustration: Returning to Lower-Level Needs

When all of our attempts to satisfy our ego and concept of self fail, we start looking for satisfaction at lower levels. After all, we must still work; we must keep on going. And if work itself does not provide us with ego satisfaction, then we'll look to social needs or safety needs to make that work worthwhile. What's more, we seek our ego satisfactions away from work—in family pursuits, hobbies, or community activities. The ego can't be denied; on or off the job it will be satisfied.

There is considerable evidence from work situations to support this observation. Workers who are in boring routine jobs that provide for little satisfaction of ego needs will become much more sociable, be more concerned with the ideas and norms of the work group, and look to the peer group for support. Lengthy conversations and coffee breaks, the "we versus them" syndrome, an over-concern for the work environment ("it's too cold in here"; "how about some planters around the place to make it look more lively"), an overconcern for fringe benefits and security—these may well be symptomatic of a heightened importance of lower-level needs because the higher-level needs are frustrated.

As Rosabeth M. Kanter wrote in her article "Why Bosses Turn Bitchy":

> [The people] in these routine jobs . . . defined their jobs as temporary and dreamed of leaving. They claimed to have little interest in climbing to a higher-status job, preferring, they said, 'easy work.' And they placed a higher value on family life than on their careers. In effect, they adopted values that rationalized the reality of their roles. . . .
>
> People in dead-end jobs cope with career limitations by getting moral support from friends and co-workers for not seeking advancement. They develop hostility to outsiders and to powerful bosses. Peer groups can make a bad job endurable or even fun, but they put pressure on a person to stay put. To leave would be disloyal.*

What does all of this have to do with your career strategy? Notice the delusions under which we can plan our careers when we regress to a concern for job goals that have no bearing on our sense of satisfaction on the job. Because the job does not satisfy higher-level needs, we tend to concern ourselves on the job with other things that, even when we get them, bring us no sense of lasting satisfaction. We believe that salary is the answer, or we settle into mediocrity because "the people are nice."

In short, we seek out goals related to security and social needs,

* *Psychology Today,* May 1976, p. 59.

only to learn that those needs don't do much for our own sense of personal growth and competence. By that time it may be too late.

Can we prevent that obsolesence, that deluding of self? Of course we can. In a general sense, it's commitment to higher-level goals that makes the difference. In a more specific sense, we can do things on the job, in the organization, off the job, and in our relations with others that will help us give direction to our activities. That requires attention to *all* our needs and values, with special emphasis on those higher-level needs that have so much to do with personal growth and competence.

"Man cannot live by bread alone"—and the effective career strategist is very much aware of that!

8

Learning and Career Strategy

Learning to Learn

AN UNDERLYING theme of this book is that the human being can
change. As new situations confront us, we bring to bear a whole
series of past experiences in an attempt to cope effectively with the
newness. But this is not an automatic process; rather, we must *learn*
how to solve new problems. And it is not enough to *want* to learn or
to identify just what it is we want to learn; we must learn *how* to
learn, how to move into new situations and solve the problems that
the newness demands of us.

In their book *Human Behavior—An Inventory of Scientific
Findings,* Bernard Berelson and Gary Steiner define learning as
"changes in behavior that result from previous behavior in similar
situations." * They go on to state that typically, "behavior also becomes demonstrably more effective and more adaptive after the

* New York: Harcourt, Brace & World, 1964, p. 63.

exercise than it was before. In the broadest terms, then, learning refers to the effects of experience on subsequent behavior." Hence our past experiences shape our behavior, and as these experiences change, so might our behavior. Change, then, is a continuous process that can be enhanced or delayed by the type and number of new experiences in which we permit ourselves to be engaged.

We will be concerned here primarily with some of the conditions that enhance or facilitate change or learning—conditions that you can create and put into practice. We will not be concerned with the myriad of explanations that prevail in the literature as to *why* certain conditions seem to be effective. Nevertheless, certain principles derived from current learning theories may be of practical significance. These we will not ignore, although no attempts will be made to link them with any specific theory. Readers who wish to dig more deeply into the subject of learning in humans are referred to the books by Ernest Hilgard, Harold Leavitt, and B. F. Skinner listed in the bibliography.

From the outset, let us keep in mind that learning may produce conflict. On the one hand, there is something intrinsically rewarding about change. It indicates that we are growing and therefore gives us a sense of achievement and influences our concept of self. It makes us realize that we can control the results of our actions and therefore increases our sense of personal power. On the other hand, it is painful and threatening. Old and comfortable ways of behaving are being challenged, and as we attempt to abandon them, we may experience failure or feel anxiety because we don't know exactly what might happen.

Above all, successes show us that we can change. In fact, change is a lifelong process—if we want it to be. That never-ending process can, in itself, produce a sense of wearisomeness, unless we learn to enjoy the rewarding aspects rather than to suffer its negative consequences.

Motivation and Learning

Personal renewal can occur only when the individual has the desire for change. Without a personal awareness of a problem to be solved, the individual has no motivation to change. Hence to get the process of change started, there must be a wish to know something new, to be able to do something you've never done before, to apply your skills to new situations, or to combine some of your old behaviors or skills into a new skill or a new understanding.

Furthermore, you must generally have a clear idea of what it is that you want to have happen. Without that clarity, you'll never know if it's happening. This point is discussed in some detail in Chapter 7, and Chapter 6 suggested some conditions that provide clues as to when a process of change should be initiated. Finally, Chapter 1 concluded with a discussion of some conditions that enhance the learning process.

Learning Requires Behavior

Learning can occur only through some behavior on your part. That behavior can be an overt, observable act, or it may be covert—an attitude, an idea, or a feeling that is not readily observable. Furthermore, it need not be something of which you are aware. Learning can be conscious or unconscious. Conscious learning is, of course, more easily dealt with than unconscious learning. What's more important, though, is that conscious learning increases the likelihood of your being able to cope with the realities of the learning situation.

This suggests, then, that learning can occur in a variety of ways. We might use *trial and error*—try something out by actually doing it to see what the results will be. We might also *observe* the behavior of others to learn how we should behave in order to achieve similar ends.

Another method, *vicarious learning,* relies on studying other people's ideas and observations rather than their actual behavior. That is the real value of reading—the vicarious learning that gives us access to a multitude of concepts and generalizations about the world in which we live.

Finally, when we organize these concepts and generalizations in a meaningful way and determine what is important to us and what isn't, we can learn by a method of *problem identification and experimentation.*

These different approaches will be discussed later in this chapter and related to learning styles. For the moment, what is important is that whatever behavior we use to learn, we will not succeed unless there is purpose. Need is what generates behavior, and behavior is essential for learning. Learning, therefore, implies living. Living is learning.

Learning Requires Reinforcement

Behavior must lead to some consequences that are directly related to the reason for initiating it in the first place. If these consequences are rewarding to the individual, then that behavior is likely to be repeated under similar conditions. If there is no reinforcement or if the behavior led to negative consequences, then chances are decreased that under similar circumstances that behavior will be repeated.

Let us take a closer look, then, at some of the findings on the nature of reinforcement. The first issue to be considered is that of timing. Generally speaking, reinforcement that immediately follows behavior is more effective in influencing learning than delayed reinforcement. That is why we repeatedly suggested setting up controls that permit more immediate feedback on behavior.

Second, the effects of rewards (positive reinforcements) are more predictable than those of punishment (negative reinforcement). When a person receives satisfaction from his behavior, he knows his behavior was right for him, and therefore he is motivated to repeat it. Not so with punishment. All the person knows from this unsatisfying experience is that what he did was not good for him. He does not know what specific behavior will lead to satisfaction.

Because of this, the impact of negative consequences may be more temporary than that of positive results. Behavior that leads to problems for the person will not be repeated as long as the feeling of disturbance remains; but once that emotion has passed, the same behavior may readily reappear, particularly if the person doesn't know what else to do or if an alternative course of action requires more effort than the individual is at that time willing to expend for the probable rewards.

There is an important lesson in this for all of us. A natural response when we experience something unpleasant is to withdraw from the situation that produced the unpleasantness. But by following that impulse, we rob ourselves of the chance to learn from the occasion. We frequently find ourselves in situations that do not allow such withdrawal but must be squarely faced. If we develop a habit of seeking satisfaction by avoiding the real issues, we may find that we lack the personal resources to deal with such situations effectively and to turn them to our advantage.

Hence, withdrawing from unpleasant or problematic situations may have unfortunate side effects. It may become a general way of life and increase the probability of wrong responses in a wider variety of similar situations. We see this when negative feelings about a boss, for example, are generalized to other people in authority ("all bosses are alike"), to the organization, or to business in general ("all business is bad").

There is another lesson. An awareness of the likely positive or negative consequences of one's behavior, a willingness to accept risks, and a basic knowledge of what climates are conducive to achieving positive results and how these climates can be created— all these are required before the change process can be initiated.

The old adage "Practice makes perfect" is just not sound. Individuals need to know what the realities of their environment are. Rewards and punishments define the limits of behavior acceptable to the person and help him know when he is learning. Without these limitations, imposed by self or society, learning cannot occur. That is why we stress the importance of setting standards and establishing feedback systems so that individuals may readily become aware of the consequences of their own behavior and thus learn more efficiently.

One other matter related to reinforcement deserves to be mentioned. Whereas immediate and consistent reinforcement is necessary in the early stages of learning something new, it is not required in such a regular fashion once the new-behavior is in place. Once learned, a new behavior can be reinforced periodically and still maintain or increase its strength. In fact, to solicit regular reinforcement after the crucial initial phase would be unrealistic and ineffective.

Creating the Conditions for Learning

It is through reinforcement that habits, or patterns of behavior, become established. We tend to avoid the unpleasant and gravitate toward situations and responses that are more likely to be satisfying to us. As a result, we become highly predictable in our behavior in situations that are similar to those we have already experienced. Unless we make conscious attempts to change our behavior (and this implies accepting the concomitant risks), chances are that we will latch on to the comfortable patterns of the past.

We can get a better understanding of these "patterns" by taking a closer look at our behavior over time. As we establish a résumé of our background experiences in education, work, and family situations, we will become more aware of our attitudes, feelings, and values, and certain patterns will emerge of how we behave in various situations. These patterns start to describe what is "typically I," and they give us clues as to how we will behave in the future in similar situations. The probabilities of that "typical" behavior emerging are high unless we make efforts to change the situation in some way so that different behaviors might emerge.

Those changes can be in the physical setting. For example, where, when, and under what conditions we have a meeting with a person can effect our behavior and, therefore, our learning. Those changes can also be in the behavior of others. Getting the other person to behave in a different way permits us to behave differently in response. Hence awareness of patterns and of the conditions that tend to evoke them is a valuable asset if we're interested in changing our own behavior or that of others.

The Career Planning Worksheet at the end of this chapter gives you a format for taking a closer look at your experiences and how they might pattern themselves. After you have completed such an analysis, you can then go back and identify the items that reappear across different experience areas (general, medical, education, work, and personal). The more consistently an item appears, the more justified you are in thinking that it is part of your personal pattern.

Important as this self-analysis is, it is only the beginning of the long process of learning how to modify your own behavior. To bring about specific change, analysis must be followed by concrete and purposeful steps. Here are some techniques that may prove useful.

1. Keep detailed records of the frequency of any behavior that you wish to change. Count the number of cigarettes you smoke, the number of put-downs you give to people (or to a certain person) in the course of a day, the number of snacks you have (or calories per meal), the number of times you could have talked with (or smiled at) people but just didn't. In this way you will become more conscious of your behavior, and attempts to change it can be charted and checked against actual results.

2. Be aware of all the conditions that accompany undesirable behavior on your part and learn to control them. They could include people, objects in the room, or your own emotions. Whatever they are, they serve as "discriminative stimuli" that cue you to behave the way you do.

For example, you may keep bringing your attaché case home every night, yet never seem to get any work done. Even if you open it up, you find yourself distracted. You just spend too much time watching TV, reading newspapers, or listening to music—and often the essential work never gets done.

Modifying the surroundings at the time you want to do your work becomes important. If you work in a chair, put the chair in a room free of distractions from TV, stereo, or pleasure reading—and control yourself sufficiently to say that you will do your work only when sitting in that chair. Whenever you're in that chair, work. If you want to read or watch TV, move to another room and to another chair. And incidentally, bring the attaché case home *only* when you know there is essential work to do (regularity of reinforcement early in the change process), and when you come home, drop it by the side of your working chair so as to develop a regular pattern.

3. Put obstacles in the way of behavior you're trying to change. Make the undesired behavior cost you something. These obstacles can be varied. For example, having to record undesirable behavior is in itself an obstacle. Another effective technique is to force yourself to give up certain pleasures associated with your behavior.

For instance, overeating typically occurs because of the number of snacks a person has during the day while reading, watching TV, or playing a game. Some other stimuli are associated with the act of eating. To bring eating under control, therefore, these other stimuli must be controlled.

Hence overeaters are told to eat to their hearts' content, but to do *only that* when they are eating. No TV, no music, no reading, no talking—just eating. When this is done, much of the joy is taken out of eating, and it quickly drops off. After that, it is possible to be concerned with *what* a person eats, because *when* he eats is under control.

Another obstacle is to create punishments for yourself when you fail to reach a goal. Contract with yourself or preferably with someone else (someone on whom you can count) to deliver the punishment if, in fact, you don't deliver on your promise. The punishment can be loss of money, loss of an activity you cherish, or a possibility of losing face.

In one situation, a married couple both decided that they would lose a certain amount of weight each week. Their contract to each other: if she did not lose the prescribed amount, she was to cancel her weekly appointment with the beautician—and explain why; if he did not lose the promised amount, he was to cancel his weekly tennis session with his buddy—and explain why.

4. Set up rewards as reinforcers for acceptable behavior. For example, the same couple who contracted to lose weight might have

set up a reward for themselves, to be reaped when they accomplish their goal—and only then. It might be that new sofa they both want or a special trip they keep talking about.

Learning Styles

Evidently, human behavior is too complex to permit a simplistic view of learning. As we have noted earlier, people differ with respect to their preferred approach to learning: they may rely on *trial and error*, on *observation*, on *vicarious learning*, or on *problem identification and experimentation*. And in the mature individual, we can expect learning to show some integration of experiences, observations, and ideas.

Based on the four approaches to learning discussed here, David A. Kolb proposed a four-stage cycle of learning.* The cycle starts with (a) some concrete experience that should lead to (b) some observations about that experience. These observations should then be analyzed to form (c) generalizations and abstractions. These latter should then be (d) tested in new situations, which provide another set of concrete experiences—and the cycle starts all over again.

We have used the word "should" in our formulation of this cycle to emphasize the fact that people differ widely in their ability to function effectively in each of these four stages. Some of us apparently prefer learning that is focused on the first stage (concrete experiences) while others emphasize the second (reflective observation), the third (abstract conceptualization), or the fourth (experimentation). The most effective learning integrates all four; however, such integration does not come automatically but is itself a learned behavior.

What is important is that we can indeed learn to learn effectively. This learning begins with a realization of what kind of learning situation we typically favor, and it progresses to an awareness of what we might do to incorporate other learning methods into our repertoire.

This is not an easy process, and it is apt to produce tension and conflict. Specifically, there will be conflict between action and in-

* "On Management and the Learning Process," *Organizational Psychology: A Book of Readings*, second edition, edited by David A. Kolb, Irwin M. Rubin, and James M. McIntyre, Englewood Cliffs, N.J.: Prentice-Hall, 1974, pp. 27–34.

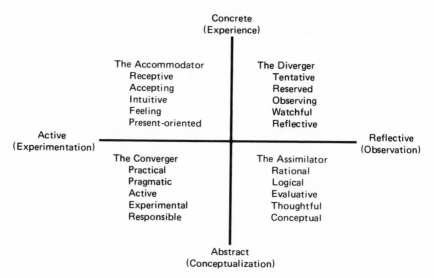

Adapted by permission from David A. Kolb, "Four Styles of Managerial Learning,"
Organizational Psychology: A Book of Readings, second edition, edited by David A. Kolb,
Irwin M. Rubin, and James M. McIntyre, Englewood Cliffs, N.J.: Prentice-Hall, © 1974, p. 32.

Figure 16. Learning style profiles.

volvement in concrete experiences on the one hand and observation
and objective, analytic detachment on the other. This conflict is
resolved through the years by us as we establish our own preferences for learning situations.

Kolb studied these preferences and related them to four different learning styles, each with its own strengths and weaknesses.
These are shown schematically in Figure 16.

The *Diverger* combines abilities of dealing with concrete
experiences and reflective observations. He can study his concrete
experiences from many different points of view and come up with
appropriate observations. He enjoys other people and has broad
cultural interests, with an understanding of the arts and the
humanities.

Opposite to the Diverger is the *Converger*. His learning abilities
combine the skills of active experimentation and abstract conceptualization. The Converger is able to deduce what the specific problem is and then practically apply his ideas. His major interest is not
in people but rather in ideas and things and in seeing how they
work. As may be expected, this type is found most frequently in the
applied sciences.

The *Assimilator* demonstrates learning abilities of abstract conceptualization and reflective observation. He is associated more frequently with the pure sciences than with the applied sciences and displays a strength for inductive reasoning and precise theory construction.

The fourth learning style is that of the *Accommodator*. In contrast to the Assimilator, the Accommodator combines abilities of concrete experience and active experimentation. He is a "doer," likes to take risks, and will rely on intuitive trial-and-error reasoning to solve immediate issues. As such, he is not very analytical and is willing to use others and their strengths.

There are two things I would like to add here. First, we can make some judgments about our own styles and the dominant abilities and skills that we possess for their implementation. (Some helpful hints on how to measure these styles can be found in David Kolb, Irwin Rubin, and James McIntyre, *Organizational Psychology: An Experiential Approach.**) This exercise also gives us clues about what skills we must develop if our learning is to be an integrated process. As we mature through life's stages, specialization must give way to the expression of those learning styles that were not previously dominant and that provide opportunities for new and innovative approaches to careers and to lifestyle in general.

Second, because we are primarily learning animals and so much a product of our experiences, learning styles affect our very adaptation to life. They influence how we see and approach life in general, what environments we select, and how we learn. In short, they affect our personal development.

As we quoted at the beginning of this chapter: "When you change what you do, you change who you are." And who we are influences our learning style. It is a circular effect. If our style does not change, our own development will be limited by the strengths required by that style. And if our development is limited, it will constrict who we are.

The Need for Proactive Learning

To break away from the stereotyping imposed by our natural learning styles and to open up new opportunities for growth requires the acquisition of new learning skills and abilities and a shift

* Englewood Cliffs, N.J.: Prentice-Hall, 1974.

in personal attitudes. As Chris Argyris points out in an unpublished manuscript,* these shifts are difficult to make, even when an individual understands what needs to be done and has the drive to do it.

The first step must be a relearning process, a reexamination of one's values and assumptions in order to envisage a lifestyle that is free from the constraints of habitual behavior. As we have indicated earlier, and as research by Argyris confirms, this first step tends in itself to be threatening to a person and frequently produces defensiveness and inhibitions that reduce the probability of change in the desired direction. That is why we suggested that such relearning and testing of new ideas and behaviors should be undertaken in an environment that minimizes the threat of failure. Without that, we tend to hang on to our old ways and seal ourselves off from doing anything but the predictable.

To a large measure, success in bringing about such basic changes depends on our ability to abandon the usual "reactive" type of learning. That is, instead of waiting for stimuli from our teachers, bosses, parents, or other power figures, we must take the initiative for our own learning. To put it differently, we must learn to take a "proactive" approach to learning.

Again, taking the step from reactive to proactive learning isn't easy. Sometimes it requires certain changes in the environments in which you function, but mostly it is a matter of adjusting your own attitudes and value systems. Not much can change if you don't want it to; commitment to change and to personal development is essential. After that come other necessary conditions:

- An inquiring mind; a curiosity about the unknown.
- A belief in your own self-direction.
- An awareness of all the resources available to you.
- A willingness to cooperate with others who can be of assistance in your efforts.
- A healthy skepticism toward authority.
- A willingness to test the validity and reliability of your assumptions and conclusions.
- An ability to become more aware of your emotional and intellectual reactions to your concrete experiences.
- An ability to collect data on these experiences through more objective self-evaluation and use of feedback from other sources.

* "Theories of Action That Inhibits Individual Learning," Harvard University, 1976.

- An ability to broaden your perspective by analyzing your experiences and the observations derived from them.
- An ability to test your perceptions and generalizations by setting goals that are in keeping with them.

The Course of Learning

Once we have the necessary prerequisites for change and know what it is we want to change, we will probably find that the course of learning will not proceed smoothly and consistently. Our rate of progress may increase or decrease with practice, and an advance made yesterday may vanish in a deteriorating performance today. An understanding of the course that learning may take will help clarify some of your own observations and feelings from previous learning experiences.

Some learning seems to go very rapidly at first and then gradually taper off to the point where further practice leads to only minor improvements in performance. This is called a negatively accelerated learning curve (see Figure 17).

This kind of performance is likely to occur when the material to be learned is relatively easy, when your previous experience provides you with a basic understanding of the material to be learned, or when you are highly motivated. Under these conditions, you will note a rapid and early improvement in performance that soon levels off.

This learning curve is a familiar one in most initial jobs in organizations. These jobs are structured so that "you learn the fundamentals of the business first before you get in over your head." Hence learning is simplistic and designed to provide you with signs of immediate progress stemming from your efforts.

This may explain the early excitement in such a job, because you see yourself in a growth or learning mode—and that is the greatest of all rewards. But if the task to be learned offers little or no challenge, a performance level satisfactory to you is soon reached, and leveling or plateauing will occur. At this point, unless new demands are made on you (by you or by others) for the learning of new skills or knowledge, plateauing may well lead to boredom and a sense of frustration.

If, on the other hand, the material to be learned is very difficult or complex, if your background is not particularly relevant to the learning task, or if your own motivation for learning is low, then you

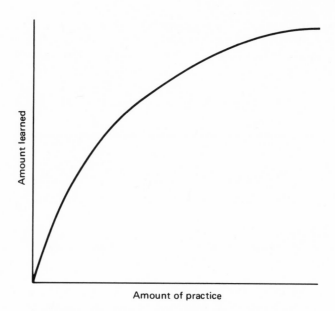

Figure 17. A negatively accelerated learning curve.

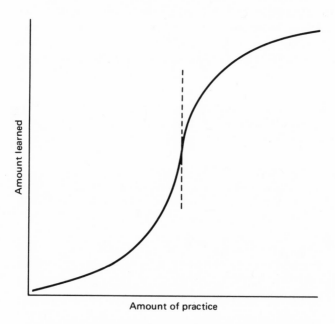

Figure 18. An S-shaped learning curve, showing positive
acceleration up to the dotted line.

can expect to find a different performance curve. Your rate of progress may be slow at first, then gradually increase, and finally reach its limit and level off. This situation is depicted in Figure 18.

Such S-shaped performance curves are typically associated with the acquisition of those complex skills so necessary for implementing a quality career strategy. That is another reason why so many people become frustrated with the entire process of trying to implement a career plan. At first, effort is high, but the returns on that effort are not apparent. Frustration is a natural consequence.

That frustration can be avoided by breaking the complex task down into distinct and simpler steps that can be implemented one at a time. In other words, the learner should set up situations where negatively accelerated performance curves can be produced. If this is done, and if, as we suggested, refined, sensitive measures of goal attainment are established, even the slightest of changes can provide a sign of learning—and such signs are important in these early attempts at changing some old and complex patterns of behavior.

Even so, however, progress should not be expected to be consistent and predictable. While the trend of learning will be either negatively or positively accelerated, actual day-to-day progress will show peaks and valleys (see Figure 19). Until the performance becomes "habitual," we can expect temporary improvements or failures. A slight change in the situation will add another dimension with which to contend, or a slight change in us (fatigue, emotion, desire) will influence the progress of learning.

Performance That Levels Off

It is a common feeling, as we move along in life, to experience periods where we seem to be leveling off, where progress seems to be at a standstill. Typically, this happens early in an individual's job—at the end of the third to the fifth year—after all the formal training has been completed and the business of settling into the job must begin.

Fear of such plateauing seems to be more frequent in young people in their late twenties or early thirties; it finds expression in such statements as: "I'm thirty already; half my life is over and I've got to get with it and make a decision on what I want to do with myself." But much has been written also about the plateauing that occurs in workers in their late forties and early fifties.

What does such leveling off really mean? One possibility is that

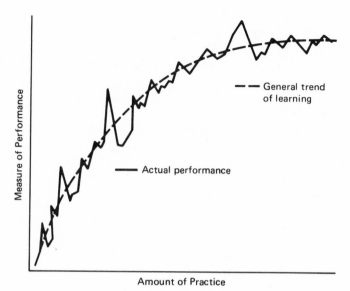

Figure 19. Actual performance compared with a general trend of negative acceleration.

the individual has literally reached the limits of performance in that area of work. Obviously, coming to grips with such a situation requires different techniques and decisions than when the individual still has much potential for doing better. However, this dead-end situation seems rarer than is sometimes supposed; in general, individuals can do much to influence the timing and level of plateauing.

Some plateauing is due to changes in the motivation of the learner. These changes can be caused by a variety of factors. For example, the novelty of the work assignment may wear off, the job design may do little to satisfy higher-level needs, or frustration may set in over the behavior of the boss or developments in the work environments.

The obvious recommendation for removing plateaus caused by such factors is to remove the cause of the lack of motivation before it leads to a situation of no return. Our chapters on the job and the organization give specific recommendations for keeping motivation at a high level and thereby minimizing the probability of leveling off.

Plateauing, according to some experts, may also occur during a period when a lot of incorrect responses are being eliminated. Effective learning includes not only the acquisition of the appropriate skills and abilities but also the elimination of incorrect responses. Performance curves only indicate the acquisition of correct behavior; hence, when plateaus occur, learning may still be going on, but its focus may be on unlearning incorrect behavior.

Such plateauing might be forestalled if the process of eliminating incorrect responses is spread out over longer periods of time rather than concentrated into the later phases of learning. This is best done by making sure that your feedback system is sufficiently precise and immediate, especially in the early stages of your learning, so that incorrect behaviors can be quickly identified and correct behaviors readily reinforced.

Finally, plateauing may occur when the task to be learned is complex and requires learning a series of habits or individual behaviors in some sequence, each building on the one learned previously. Under such circumstances, we tend to build up a series of S-shaped performance curves, one for each individual task in the entire complex.

If each of the parts is in itself not too complex, it is possible to combine some of them and try to learn them together. You may find that learning will be a bit slower at first, but it will generally pick up and surpass the level you would have reached if you had attempted to learn each part separately. In this way, the plateauing for each part will have been eliminated.

This aspect of learning is related to the controversy of the "whole method" versus the "part method" of learning. Should you practice all the material to be learned at once or in some meaningful sequence?

Generally speaking, in the early stages the difficult tasks should receive special attention. Eventually, however, they must be incorporated into the whole, because learning each part does not guarantee that the whole can be performed.

At some point, then, a switch to the whole method must take place even if initial learning followed a sequential course. Whether the whole method is appropriate from the start depends on a number of factors: generally, it will be the preferable approach if you can distribute your learning over a long period of time, if the material is not too complex and has some meaningful unity, and if you are motivated and intelligent.

It is doubtful that, even in the best of learning situations, all plateauing can be eliminated. This is particularly true as we change our behavior in the more complex aspects of our life. Apparently, the human mind needs time—time to consolidate new experiences, time to deal with old and comfortable habits, and time to appreciate the potential satisfactions of new ways of behaving. This time factor must be kept in mind whenever we see ourselves leveling off. The important thing is our commitment to change; as long as that persists, plateauing will be no more than a temporary condition.

Over Time or All at Once?

In most learning situations, particularly those usually involved in career strategy, change will be more permanent and require less effort if we implement it over a period of time rather than try to accomplish it in a mass of practice trials. Time, then, is again an important factor, especially for more complex learning tasks.

We stress this point again because too frequently people, once they have made a strategic decision, expect that something should happen right away. But change requires patience.

Here are some specifics about distributing practice that may be of help to you as you consider a learning program for yourself in areas where you feel change is desirable.

1. If what you want to learn is difficult and complex or not very meaningful to you, then spacing the learning process over time will reap greater rewards for you. If, on the other hand, what is to be learned is simple, short, and meaningful, then go at it with a vengeance and mass your learning efforts.

For example, building effective interpersonal relations is a skill that can be learned. However, it is typically not easy to master that skill; neither is it a matter of mastering only one thing. The process is complex and demands a series of communicative skills. Thus it must be built over a period of time, in situations that provide feedback and opportunities to reflect on the consequences of previous behavior. To set a goal of "mastering interpersonal skills during the next week" is simply unrealistic.

2. If you are not very experienced or capable in what you wish to learn, then chances are that spacing your learning will be better. If, on the other hand, you have some abilities or experience in the area, then some initial concentrated learning may be of greater value to you.

3. In the early stages of learning, intervals between testing a new skill should be short and regular. However, after you see signs that learning is progressing, these intervals can be increased.

4. The factor of spacing is of course related to your overall

strategic objectives. If time is of the essence, then massing your learning may be essential. But such massing requires greater investment of time and resources to gain the equivalent ends obtained by spacing one's learning. That is why we stress the *strategic* aspects of career development: to plan sufficiently into the future so that you will have the opportunity to use the most effective change processes available. With careful planning, then, you can save yourself much time and effort while getting the most out of your learning experiences.

Summary

In this chapter we have not attempted to discuss all the theories as to why learning occurs, or all the conditions that make for optimum learning. Rather, we have focused on those conditions and practices that appear to be especially relevant for one who wishes to implement a career strategy.

In the course of our discussion, we have seen that there is an important interface between learning and motivation and that learning requires consistent performance and reinforcement. We must learn to manage our own learning process and to establish the conditions and acquire the skills to do this effectively.

Four different learning styles were discussed in ways that may help the reader identify his own style and understand its impact on what he learns. Finally, the course of learning was described, with specific ideas on how to influence learning curves and optimize progress in the change process.

Throughout, the underlying message is that strategic changes take time—time to drop old habits and acquire new ones. In Anne Morrow Lindbergh's words:

The sea does not reward those who are too anxious, too greedy, or too impatient. To dig for treasures shows not only impatience and greed, but lack of faith. Patience, patience, patience, is what the sea teaches. Patience and faith.*

* *Gift from the Sea*, New York: Pantheon Books, 1955, p. 17.

CAREER PLANNING WORKSHEET

Shown here is a suggested career planning worksheet, followed by a list of the items to be considered in completing it. This form is designed to be of assistance to you in your thinking about your career planning. It is not intended to be all-inclusive in its coverage of your personal history. Rather, its purpose is to stimulate your thinking about certain key aspects of your background that may provide you with insights about yourself. These insights, coupled with information you may have from other sources, will form the basis for establishing career goals and specific strategies for achieving your objectives.

It is to your advantage to be as honest with yourself as you possibly can be. If you have not thought about some of the questions before, take some time to do just that. The form is designed to get at those things that make you a distinctive and unique personality.

Use this form as a worksheet. The main purpose is to get ideas down on paper; do not worry about correct grammar. In the notes column, do not hesitate to put down anything that comes to mind. Later you may find that some of those spur-of-the-moment thoughts will be very helpful in producing insights.

After you have completed the form, go back and try to determine how many of the same ideas crop up in all or almost all of the experience areas. The more frequently you see the same factors appearing in various areas, the more likely it is that they form part of your typical behavior patterns. Those patterns can then be checked against other available data on yourself to verify or question your subjective analysis.

Questions to ask about yourself	Things to consider in your answers	Personal notes
GENERAL		
Name and address . Length of time . . . Other addresses . . .		

Career Planning Worksheet

GENERAL

Questions to ask about yourself	Things to consider in your answers
Name and address.	Stability (or instability) of home address and reasons for it.
Length of time at present address.	
Other addresses in the last five years.	Noticeable trends in your choice of geographical locations; changes in quality of living and reasons for them.
Date and place of birth.	
	The kinds of places and neighborhoods where you lived and your home conditions; their influence on your attitudes, values, and lifestyle.
	Your age as a factor in your career plans.

MEDICAL

Questions to answer about yourself	Things to consider in your answers
Height and weight.	Are you overweight? If so, do you plan to correct this?
State of health at present and over the last five years.	Actual or potential effects of health factors on the achievement of career goals and on performance in present position.
Recurring illnesses.	The impact of illnesses or accidents on your stamina and vitality and on your attitudes, habits, and goals.
Accidents and operations.	

EDUCATION

Questions to answer about yourself	Things to consider in your answers
Schools you attended. Major courses of study. Degrees received. Overall average and rank in class.	The kinds of schools you attended and their impact on your total education or specific parts of it and on your values, attitudes, beliefs, and interpersonal skills.
Reasons for choosing specific schools beyond secondary school and for choosing major course of study.	Your motives and needs; the soundness and maturity of your decisions; factors and people influencing your decisions.

Plans for continuing education.

Which subject areas did you enjoy most, which least? Why?

In which subject areas did you do your best work? In which did you do your worst work? Why?

What extracurricular activities did you choose, and why? Which did you enjoy most, which least? Why?

Honors, awards, prizes, recognitions, and leadership roles you received.

The best and the worst teachers you ever had; the characteristics that made them good or bad.

The kinds of people with whom you associated and your reasons for associating with them.

As you look back on your accomplishments in school, do you think they reflect your true abilities?

Gaps in your education that are relevant to your career goals; ways to minimize those gaps and cost in time, effort, and money of doing so.

Things that interest and challenge you; the relationship between your interests and abilities and your actual behavior; the impact of your needs on your choice of behavior.

What sort of things do you do best? Under what circumstances? How are your accomplishments related to your perceived strengths and goals?

Do your accomplishments reflect leadership abilities?

What characteristics of people do you value most? What are the factors that determine your feelings toward people in positions of authority and toward people in general?

What do they tell you about your industriousness and energy level, the consistency and feasibility of your career goals, and your relationships with people? How well do you use your talents? If there is a discrepancy between your accomplishments and your abilities, how do you account for this? Does it give you clues on how to handle future goals? Are your goals consistent and realistic?

WORK

Questions to ask about yourself

Things to consider in your answers

Full-time jobs you held (in chronological order).

The kinds of jobs you held; their consistency and their compatibility with your career plans.

Type of work.

Salary.

Part-time jobs you held.

Your job stability.

Your advancement record.

What does your part-time record tell you about your sense of responsibility and your ability to set and achieve goals? Were they related to your longer-range career goals?

Reasons for leaving your jobs.

Were these reasons mature? Do you have a sense of direction? Do you have tendencies to give up easily, be overly critical, make excuses, or avoid reality?

What did you particularly like (dislike) about those jobs? Why?

What are the things that are important for your job satisfaction? What does this imply for your future career choices?

Behavioral and personal characteristics of the best and of the worst boss you ever had.

Your relationships with authority. What leadership styles do you prefer, and how do they relate to your career goals? Your desire for independence, · responsibility, challenging assignments, or externally imposed direction.

With what kinds of people did you work well? Why?

With what kinds of people did you work ineffectively? Why?

Your attitudes toward the ability to get along with others. What does this tell you about your management style?

The kinds of people you seek out or avoid. What does this tell you about your attitudes, values, beliefs, and goals?

The kinds of people and environments you need to be effective. What does this imply for your career goals?

On which job did you develop most, on which least?

What specific things did you accomplish or learn in these jobs?

What's important to you? How do you spend your time?

Why did a certain job develop you more than others? Can you make the most of any situation?

How does what you've learned fit into your career plans?

What are your relationships with your boss and your associates?

With whom do you have the best relationship, with whom the worst?

Are your interpersonal skills what you'd like them to be?

What kinds of things do you consider important in your relations with others?

How effective are you in these relations? What do you personally contribute to them?

PERSONAL

Questions to ask about yourself	*Things to consider in your answers*
Your spouse or prospective spouse: age, health, personality, activities, and interests.	The attitudes, interests, and activities you value in others. Your relationship with people who play an important role in your life.
Your children: age, health, interests, and accomplishments. Your evaluation of them.	Environmental factors influencing your children's personalities and behavior. Your own role in your children's personal development. What does this tell you about your values, your use of authority, your sense of responsibility, and your abilities to lead and to relate to others?
Your day-to-day behavior with your spouse. What activities do you share? Do you have common friends?	Is your relationship with your spouse and your children what you'd like it to be? If not, why?
Your behavior with your children.	What does your behavior tell you about your values and beliefs? What are its implications for your short- and long-range plans?
What people or groups have had the greatest influence on your personal development—your values, preferred roles, and relationships with others?	What kinds of people or groups are they? Why did they influence you so much?
Are these people still important to you? In what way? Why or why not?	Does this give you any clues about the things you consider important and the way they influence your decisions?
Is your financial position (earnings, savings, insurances, etc.) what you'd like it to be at this stage of your career?	The role of financial considerations in your career plans. How important is money as a motivating force?

Your financial objectives five years and ten years hence. Do your plans call for regular saving?

What factors are responsible for your financial position (own efforts, external factors)? How did you finance your major expenses (education, home, furnishings)?

Your parents, brothers, and sisters: education, occupation, and background. What do you consider their major strengths and weaknesses? Your relationships with them, past and present.

Are your financial objectives for the next years reasonable?

Your own role in achieving the financial position that you consider appropriate.

The influence of your parents and siblings on your personality, value system, beliefs, and habits. The impact of your relationships with them on your career thinking.

A winner plays the people more than the "cards"; a loser plays only the cards, and it might as well be solitaire. *Sydney Harris*

9

Interpersonal Relations

Winning Requires Others

A CAREER strategy cannot be implemented by an individual alone, no matter how well it is planned. Careers are achieved by interaction with others who are in a position to furnish information and make decisions that forward the career plan. The people integral to your career will include, but not be limited to, bosses, other management personnel, colleagues, subordinates, and members of your family. Thus an individual's personal relations, his interaction with others, are highly important in career planning and achievement.

The basis of good interpersonal relations is effective communication. When the average individual in business is asked to define communication, he will typically use such phrases as "conveying or

I am indebted to Dr. David C. Phillips, Professor Emeritus of the University of Connecticut, for the initial draft of much of this chapter and for his dedication to the principles discussed here in his working with young people in career planning settings.

	Known to self	Unknown to self
Known to others	1 Common area	2 Blind area
Unknown to others	3 Hidden area	4 Unknown area

Adapted from Joseph Luft, *Of Human Interaction*, by permission of Mayfield Publishing Company. Copyright © 1969 by The National Press.

Figure 20.   The Johari Window.

transferring information," "exchanging ideas and information," "getting others to agree with you," "listening to others," or "making communication a two-way street." But that is a limited view of the problem. In a more general sense, communication may be said to involve *perception by others of your total behavioral pattern.*

For instance, if you seem aloof, seem to listen only on certain occasions, seldom give answers or seem to tighten up physically when important questions are asked, or communicate with others only when *you* want something, you are creating an atmosphere that may get in the way of effective communication. Similarly, a smile or a compliment (or lack thereof) may be interpreted by others in unexpected ways.

Thus it is important to recognize that your *total* behavioral pattern is perceived by others. That perception is an important part of communication.

One way to think about these perceptions was first presented by Joseph Luft and Harry Ingham in their Johari Window model, shown here as Figure 20.

The first quadrant of the figure indicates that there is a part of you that is known to both you and the people with whom you are involved. This is the common area of an interrelationship.

The second quadrant suggests that there's a part of you which others are aware of but which is unknown to you. This is your blind area. (As they say in the ad: "Even his best friends won't tell him about bad breath.")

The third quadrant is just the reverse of the second one. Here you know something about yourself—your attitudes, values, motives, and feelings—that you don't reveal to others. The person who agrees with the boss when he knows he really doesn't agree is putting on a facade; so is the person who looks interested in a story when he's bored to tears.

Finally, the fourth quadrant indicates that there are parts of you that are unknown to both you and others. In good interpersonal relations, some of these areas will eventually become known, and then we may realize that they have been affecting our relationships with others all the time without our knowing.

As the common area known by both parties increases, so will the effectiveness of the interpersonal relationships. Improving relations, then, whether it be with boss, subordinate, spouse, child, or friend, rests on behaving in ways that close the gap between what you know about yourself and what others know about your ideas, values, and motivation.

The Key: Mutual Trust

The main factor that can open up the common area and create an atmosphere for good communication is mutual trust. What creates trust? There may be many contributing factors in varying situations, but at least three of them must generally be present: (1) the perception by others that you have the background and experience to make your comments worthwhile; (2) the perception by others that you are willing to tell the truth; and (3) the perception by others that you are interested in them as human beings.

1. *Background experience and trust.* We have a tendency not to trust people whose information in the past seemed faulty or incomplete. If others have the perception that you have knowledge that is valuable to them, then one step toward effective communication has been made. Past actions are often a key to such perception.

Giving people information that's helpful to them, providing an atmosphere that indicates that you want to help them achieve their goals (whether or not you actually do), indicating your willingness to be open with them—all these actions help enhance the positive perception.

2. *Truthfulness and trust.* If you are perceived as playing your cards close to the vest, the openness so essential to trust is reduced. Because others believe that you are withholding information, their natural tendency is to withhold information as well. The results are a reduced quality of communication and generally unsatisfactory interpersonal relationships.

What's required to establish the openness essential to a good trust relationship is what Luft and Ingham labeled *exposure*. It includes willingness on your part not only to provide specific facts related to the job but also to disclose your feelings, attitudes, guesses, and the like in an obvious attempt to share with the other person. If the exposure is untrue, partial, or misleading, then obviously mutual trust is not developed.

This willingness to tell the truth does *not* mean that you should spend most of your day telling others *all* you know or feel. It merely means that you must display a willingness to impart information that another individual considers of value to him. Occasionally you may have to state that you cannot discuss the matter now, but if that's the case, you should provide honest reasons why you can't.

Such openness can often reduce the amount of communication necessary, because an individual who feels you will tell him what he needs to know doesn't have to dig incessantly for information because he knows you'll let him know what's necessary. If he feels you are withholding information of value to him, he may go to any length to discover what he thinks you may be withholding, and he may find that what he got was not truly important to him. All this time and effort can be saved by providing truthful information in the beginning.

Essentially, what exposure does is to increase the size of the first quadrant and reduce the size of the third quadrant. That is, you are reducing your hidden area—that portion of yourself unknown to others.

3. *Interest in others as a trust factor.* Our chapter on motivation indicated that we are primarily interested in satisfying our own needs; but if the impression is created that this may be done at the expense of others, trust is diminished.

At times there may be no real conflict of interest, but if trust is low, a conflict may nevertheless be perceived. At other times, a conflict that appeared to be major at first may be found to be minor after the problem has been openly discussed. And even in major conflict areas, if the matter is brought into the open, people will generally feel that their interests have been considered.

What is important, then, is that you become aware of the needs and interests of other people, and this will not happen unless you encourage others to give you information and to expose their own feelings and attitudes. When such feedback is present, it will contribute to reducing the size of your blind area; that is, you may learn things about yourself and your interpersonal skills of which you were unaware.

One way to enhance this feedback is through your own openness. People are likely to be more open with you as they begin to feel that you are open with them.

Another way to establish trust is to be sure your behavior is consistent with your words. If you seem to agree to a communication but take no action on the matter, trust will be reduced. Similarly, if after separate communications, two individuals note that you seem to agree with two different points of view, they will not know where you stand. If you agree that there is a problem in a certain area but do not follow through when opportunities present themselves to reduce the problem, trust can be destroyed.

When words and actions seem to disagree, we generally take the action as an indicator of the true meaning or feeling. This, of course, supports the idea that communication involves the perception of your total behavioral pattern.

To trust a person does not mean that you have to like or even respect him. He may have personal habits that bother you, his lifestyle may be incompatible with yours, or his goals may have little interest for you. In short, there may be many reasons why you would not seek him as a friend. However, if two people share a belief that the other person is reliable, willing to tell the truth, and interested in assisting in specific situations, communications between them are more likely to be open and valuable.

How much trust is present in most communication between individuals in business? Many organizational studies show that often the trust factor is low. For example, Chris Argyris, in a study of 165 managers in six widely different companies, came to the following conclusions.

The gap that often exists between what executives say and how they behave helps create barriers to openness and trust. . . .

These barriers are more destructive in important decision-making meetings than in routine meetings, and they upset effective managers more than ineffective ones.

71 percent of the middle managers did not know where they stood with their superiors. . . .

65 percent thought that the most important unsolved problem in the organization was that the top management was unable to help them overcome intergroup rivalries, lack of cooperation, and poor communications. . . .

82 percent of the middle managers wished that the status of their

function and job could be increased but doubted if they could
communicate this openly to the top management.*

These figures are not particularly startling to anyone who has really
analyzed what is going on about him. They indicate, however, how
far we have yet to go in establishing the trust so important to good
communication and effective interpersonal relationships.

Perceptions and Misperceptions

None of us has direct contact with reality. The "real world" as
we know it is different from the real world as others may know it.
Our past experiences provide us with reference points for judgments about our sensations and hence for our perception of what
reality is—and we act on that reality.

This fact is responsible for many of the questionable "virtues"
discussed in Chapter 2. People act on those virtues, which are based
on their experiences of what reality is. If these experiences are
limited or distorted, so will be their reality.

For example, many people feel that their boss has little interest
in them as individuals, and therefore, they see little value in discussing career topics with him. However, if after encouragement by
someone else they do talk about their career with him, they frequently find that their opinion had no basis in fact. Because of lack
of previous communication between the two on the subject, the
subordinate created a "reality" that might have prevented him from
achieving his goals.

It is essential, therefore, that you analyze your perception of
others. You may be basing your actions on misconceptions, and if
that is the case, you are endangering the effectiveness of your communications and perhaps even supporting the misconceptions
others have of you. Others' misconceptions of you are formed just as
easily as your own misconceptions of other people. If, for instance,
you are shy or overly cautious in your statements, this may be perceived as an unwillingness to communicate. Failure to eat lunch or
have a beer with the "boys," talking with others only about company business, and many other actions on your part may be misin-
terpreted. It is highly important to get full feedback on how your
behavioral pattern is perceived by others. You may find that the
perceptions of others vary from your self-image.

* "Interpersonal Barriers to Decision Making," *Harvard Business Review*,
March–April 1966, pp. 84–97.

Developing an accurate picture of the impression others have of you is not too difficult if you continually look for clues and behave in ways that encourage feedback from the people around you. How do others act while you are communicating with them? Do they react to others differently? If they seem to be withholding information, do you know why? Asking others with whom you have a good trust relationship why some individuals respond unfavorably to you can often be of value. The point is that an analysis of how others perceive you is as important as a good self-analysis.

Interaction Demands Feedback

The concept of interpersonal relations implies the necessity for interaction between two or more people. Most individuals easily give lip service to the concept that communication is a two-way street with ideas, information, and feelings flowing in both directions. Much of the time it is just that, however: lip service. In the heat of a working day, when we get an idea, see a problem to be solved, seek a change or some additional information, we plunge into the communication with little thought about how others feel or are responding to the situation.

The importance of feedback has frequently been stressed, but the concept held by many people is that *any* reactive statement is feedback. That is a highly general and potentially harmful definition. Effective interactions require thoughtful and continual feedback that responds to the other person's needs and feelings. Simple unreflected reactions, however prompt, may only create additional communication barriers.

Specificity of Feedback

Another factor about feedback is that it should be highly specific. Such general comments as "Your idea won't work," "You haven't got all the facts," "You tend to dominate the discussion," or "You never say much in the meetings" are not very helpful. These statements also tend to put an individual on the defensive and therefore are likely to produce negative results.

By contrast, comments such as "It seems to me that a weakness in your idea is that the cost may be higher," "On what data do you draw that conclusion?" "It might be helpful to get all the ideas on the floor before we discuss your solution," or "Tom, we have not heard your feelings on this point" are specific and thus afford an opportunity for true interaction.

Although there is an unquestioned need for objective data, there may be times when *subjective* information about you provides an even more important kind of feedback. For instance, communicating how the other person's actions make you feel can be a valuable way to open up the relationship. Thus a comment like "When you say things like that I feel very uncomfortable" does not question the other person's motives in doing what he did but only lets him know how you feel.

This concept is important both in providing feedback and in soliciting it from others. If others are not specific in what they are communicating, you might say, "I'm sorry, but I don't understand what it is that you're saying to me. I'd appreciate your giving me a specific example." Or you might say, "I'd appreciate your describing a specific situation when that occurred" or "I have a feeling that you'd like to say more than you have just communicated."

People Factors

Ultimately, the nature and effectiveness of feedback depend on the individuals who are interacting. Communication, to put it differently, is not abstract; it is a process that involves real people.

One factor to be considered here is the attitude of the people with whom you're trying to communicate. Clearly, you would not treat a person who is open to comment in the same manner as someone who is habitually on the defense. Similarly, you would not deal in the same way with a person who has great confidence in himself or who trusts you as with somebody who lacks self-confidence or who has no trust in you. To optimize the chances for effective interaction, your communicative style and the kind of feedback you provide must be tailored to the personality of the people whom you're trying to reach.

By the same token, check your own attitude in any interpersonal relationship. If you're on the defensive, feel distrustful of the other person, or have no confidence in what you're trying to communicate, then the impact of your communication will be lessened.

Another way in which the people factor enters into the communication process is through shared background and experiences. Interaction will tend to be more meaningful when two people have common experiences and interests that can serve as a basis for the communication.

Often, finding such a common basis requires a conscious effort on our part. Of course, it's much easier to make the first comment that comes to our mind, but that feedback may have little communicative value. For example, a statement like "I don't understand what the problem is" conveys less useful information than a question that is tied to a common experience—say, "Is this problem you're telling me about similar to the XYZ situation that you and I worked on last month?"

Nonverbal Communication

The importance of nonverbal factors in communication has already been suggested by our definition of communication as involving the perception of your *total* behavior pattern. Various studies indicate that anywhere from 60 percent to 90 percent of the "meaning" gained in an oral communication situation comes from nonverbal sources rather than from the words themselves.

Nonverbal factors include the following: (1) body motion, such as facial expressions, eye movements or pupil dilation, and gestures; (2) personal physical characteristics, such as height, weight, skin color, general attractiveness, body odors, or certain artifacts, such as wigs, eyeglasses, or perfumes; (3) touching: stroking, patting, or shaking hands; (4) vocal signals, such as pitch, tempo, articulation, yawning, coughing, moaning, or sighing; and (5) physical surroundings, such as the layout of space, seating arrangements, lighting, temperature, or interior decorating.

Here are some specific examples of nonverbals and the possible messages they can convey:

■ A quiet place with no phone calls and no interruptions: "This is an important discussion; I don't want to be distracted."

■ The other person keeps squirming around in his chair: "I'm uncomfortable" or "I'm tense."

■ A quick glance at the clock: "I am concerned with time." Frequent glances at the clock: "I want this session to end."

■ If someone says, "Yes, I'll do that" very hesitantly, rubbing his hands, crossing and uncrossing his legs, and so on, there is a contradiction between the words, which say yes, and the body movement, which says no.

■ If someone says, "No, I'm not upset" quickly in a high-pitched voice, there is also a contradiction between the words, which say, "I'm calm," and the pitch and tempo of the voice, which say, "I'm upset."

■ When people lean forward, they are usually more intent than when they lean back in a chair casually. Leaning forward serves as a clue, along with direct eye contact, that the other person wants to hear what we're saying.

■ The way we place our body in relationship to another person expresses feelings of like or dislike, or of dominance or submissiveness. We usually leave more space between ourselves and someone we dislike. We may stand up and maintain distance when we want to show dominance.

■ If we say we're interested in a report and yawn, tap our fingers, look out the window, or stare blankly into space, our body movements say we really don't care about the report at all. If our behavior shows tension—if we clench our fists, move our legs back and forth, or sit up in our chair with fire in our eyes and a flush to our cheeks—this indicates interest but disagreement with the report.

The principle that nonverbal clues may be as important or even more important than verbal clues is of greatest impact in face-to-face communications. However, nonverbal clues can be misleading. If you are silent because you are doing some deep thinking on what is being said, others may feel you are aloof or withholding information. What does a frown indicate? Does sitting back in the chair indicate openness or disinterest? Is sitting apart from the main group a sign of shyness or of antagonism?

We constantly display nonverbal behavior and often attach great meaning to such behavior, based on our previous experiences in similar situations. It is essential that the correct meaning, if any, of the nonverbal aspects of communication be substantiated. This can often be done only by following up with verbal means.

We stress these nonverbal factors for two reasons: (1) to make you aware of the messages you may be sending out with your own nonverbals, and (2) to increase your awareness of the nonverbals employed by the people with whom you are interacting. Sensitivity to these clues can provide you with valuable insights and permit you to follow through with a verbal statement that can help maintain an effective relationship.

For example, to finger-tapping behavior (disinterest) by your boss, you might say, "I'll get back to you another time" or "This is taking a lot longer than I had thought it would. Shall we get back to it later?" In this way, you give your boss an "out." Or, when observing an expression of tension, you might say, "I'm sorry if I've upset you; I didn't mean to do that."

Communication Strategy

The main reason we communicate with others is to seek a reduction of our tensions and frustrations and to maintain a comfortable level of self-satisfaction. We develop a career pattern that fits comfortably with our self-image, and when we realize all is not going as planned, we become frustrated and irritated. So we decide to communicate, either to seek help or to seek changes in others or in company procedures so that we can do a better job and reduce intolerable conflicts.

From this and the foregoing discussion, we can arrive at the following definition of a communication strategy that may assist you in your interpersonal relations and help you achieve your career goals as well as other objectives:

An effective strategy must establish an atmosphere of trust through interaction of information and attitudes for the purpose of self-satisfaction.

There are at least two important practical aspects of communication strategy: (1) an understanding of the various communication approaches open to you in achieving your goals and objectives; and (2) an understanding that, while there is a risk involved in communicating, there is also a risk in *not* communicating. These two risks must be weighed against each other in determining strategy.

We are basically creatures of habit. Particularly in things that we do over and over again, we establish a certain method—be it as the result of thought or of happenstance—and we stick to it. Even when we recognize that the method is not as effective as we would wish, we keep the habit unless a real and concerted effort to change is made.

Our communication behavior grows in this fashion, and we often lock ourselves into a very limited approach in this area. It is important to recognize that in most, if not all, communication situations there are many strategies available to us. Choosing the one most appropriate to the situation may be the real key to effective communication.

Let us suppose that several people walked out on their jobs because a time-and-motion study was going to be made without proper explanation. The study cannot be done without these workers, so there is heavy pressure on the supervisor to get those people back immediately. Forgetting the message aspect of communications for the moment, what strategies are open to the supervisor?

Immediate answers usually include such suggestions as, "Call them on the phone," "Visit them," and "Send a letter." But further thought shows additional strategies: using one of the workers who stayed on the job and is trusted by those who walked out; holding a meeting, perhaps even in the home of one who walked out; holding a meeting of all the workers; using a personnel officer, a previous supervisor who was trusted, or some other member of management who is liked by those who walked out; calling or visiting one of the workers whom the others are likely to follow, persuading him to return, and using him to contact the others.

You can easily develop others. The point being stressed is that there is a whole range of strategies open to you; if you use an approach purely by habit, you may be limiting your potential for success.

To take another example: suppose you feel that your present boss is not amenable to assisting you. If after study you determine that this is a fact, you might give up and quit. But there are other strategies open to you: using a colleague who has a better relationship with the boss to get through to him; building up your relationship with someone else in management who can be of assistance to you; seeking a sidewise movement to get into a situation more conducive to communication and possible career achievement. Chapter 10 explores these matters in more detail.

You say there are risks involved in these strategies? That's true. But there are also risks if you do not consider other strategies and become frustrated, perhaps fail to reach your objectives, and maybe even seek a position in another company. You could find yourself in the same situation there! (Remember our Virtue of the Better Fertilizer?)

To assess a communication strategy, we must consider not only the risks of that strategy but also the risks of *not* communicating. If the risks of communicating outweigh the risks of not communicating, we should postpone action to a more propitious time. If, however, the risks of not communicating are higher (and this is generally the case), we must determine a strategy that maximizes the benefits relative to the risks.

Improving Interpersonal Relations

The first step in improving your communications and interpersonal relations is a thorough analysis of your willingness to give and seek information and opinions, to listen to what others have to say, and to consider other people's needs, wants, and personal characteristics. Some of the common errors in interpersonal relations are discussed in the following sections. Consider these as you make your analysis and see which apply to you.

Failure to Be Open

Your analysis may lead you to realize that you are not very open, or at least not as open as you thought before making the self-analysis. You may tend to retain information of value to others, feeling that you can control a situation better if you hold more of the cards. You may also find that you seldom seek information from others because you fear that it may have a negative impact on your self-image. Rather than hear such information or opinion, you choose to close off certain avenues of good interaction.

What are the consequences? It means you are drawing conclusions and making decisions on less than the full information potentially available to you. Your analysis of your environments is limited. It also means that others are trying to do their jobs without full information. The results are usually personal frustration, mistrust, and withholding of even more information, and hence less and less meaningful interaction.

How do people learn to withhold information? The reasons may vary from individual to individual, but there are some basic factors that are of interest here.

1. *Copied behavior.* We may be less open than we should be because of what we have consciously or unconsciously learned from others. We see that certain managers or supervisors operate primarily in a closed fashion, so we copy them without full analysis of the results. (They probably learned the same way!) We perceive that many people in the organization operate in a certain way, and we conclude, rightly or wrongly, that that is the accepted practice. Even though we may be highly frustrated ourselves by bosses who are not open, we operate in the same way.

2. *Fear of misuse of what we say.* If we view ourselves as in competition with others around us, we may try to beat them by withholding information, ideas, or opinions that would assist them. This is particularly true of individuals who have been "burned" by giving information that helped someone else without getting reciprocal information of value. We frequently jump from this one vivid experience to the general conclusion that *all* people misuse our openness, and because of this we decide to withhold information from everyone.

3. *Our upbringing.* Many of us were taught that young people should be "seen and not heard." We were told to "use tact," to "mind our own business," to "live and let live," and to "respect the other person's rights." All this tends to lead us to assume a less aggressive role in our dealing with others. If in our younger days we form habits of limited interaction, the habit remains with us unless there is a conscious and sincere effort to change.

4. *Lack of communication skills.* We may be less open than we'd like to be simply because we do not know how to go about being more open. Lack of skill makes us reluctant to try, because we don't like to fail. If we learn the required skills, then we are more apt to try.

Whatever the reason for our present approach to interpersonal relations, we will make little progress in improving our behavior until we are fully convinced that better relations will have a payoff for us. One place to start in order to gain this conviction is to analyze the logic of it. The more information we have, both about facts and about attitudes, the better our decisions will be, and the more comfortable we'll be in living with those decisions. In addition, the more information we give to others, the better their decisions will be—and those decisions often affect us.

But our discussion of motivation suggests that logic alone may not convince us to change a habit. We are governed more by emotions than by logic. Therefore, as an additional step, analyze your relationships with those around you—superiors, colleagues, and subordinates—*on an individual basis.* You may find that your relationship with some people is more open than with others. Are you more comfortable with the open relationships? Do they assist you more in your job than more closed relationships? An analysis of this kind may assist you in improving your interpersonal relationships with more people.

Also, ask yourself *why* you have shied away from more involved interpersonal relationships. If you find, for instance, that you are copying previous bosses who used a more closed approach, you may find that other highly successful individuals employ an open approach. If you determine that a major cause of your present behavior is fear of misuse of what you say, you may discover significant instances when being open paid off for both you and others. If you are afraid of negative feedback, you may find instances in the past in which this type of feedback influenced your thinking and behavior for the better. We tend to generalize a great deal, and a more specific analysis may show some of our generalizations to be invalid.

If you find that you're less open than you should be because you just don't have the necessary interpersonal skills, *then learn more about those skills* and start to practice them. They don't come naturally. Books and courses may help to give you clues to areas for improvement.

If after your analysis you decide that you should take steps to improve your interpersonal relations, proceed cautiously. First of all, heed our earlier advice and make your moves in areas of small risk, with people where some trust relationship is already established. This may be a spouse, trusted colleague, or even someone outside your job area. If the risk is small, you may have more confidence in making the move; and if for any reason the results are not what you expected, little is lost. After some successes in such situations, you will be ready to move into areas of greater risk.

Secondly, make your moves gradually and in a limited area. Taking on a great number of big tasks makes the analysis of your results more complex and less meaningful. Determine a limited area where you are either withholding information or not seeking feedback. Move into this area a little at a time and be sure to measure the results. If the results are positive (and experience has shown they generally will be), you will gain the confidence necessary to make more and bigger changes.

If your analysis shows that your approach is working with some people and not with others, find out why. Without a good understanding of the specific results, you may make hasty generalizations and abandon the idea of improving relationships.

You should be aware beforehand that any change in your behavior may at first be looked upon by others with some fear and frustration. They had you all pegged, let us say, as a close-mouthed individual, and all of a sudden you are imparting or seeking information. This change in behavior may be worrisome to them, and they may look for all the wrong reasons why the change took place.

It is only consistent behavior on your part over a period of time that can overcome this attitude. At that point they will often begin to move cautiously toward being more open with you, and a better relationship will grow.

Failure to Listen

It is natural for us to be intensely interested in what we are saying. Too often, however, this focus on our own contribution leads to failure to listen to others. Obviously, if each individual follows this same pattern, his path is unlikely to cross anybody else's.

The secret of effective interpersonal relationships is the flexibility to adapt to others' words and actions. While this might mean that we must sometimes compromise on our own objectives, the information gained in exchange helps us meet situations in a more realistic way and therefore increases our chances of success. If we continually fail to understand the feelings, desires, and objectives of others, interpersonal relationships will deteriorate.

Too often we think of listening as a passive thing—the pause between our statements. But listening is an active process demanding continuous interpretation and review, both within the mind of the listener and verbally so that all parties know at all times what they are dealing with. Furthermore, listening involves looking for nonverbal as well as verbal clues. A good listener will pay attention to the nonverbals and watch out for discrepancies with the verbal signals. In short, listening requires no less—and sometimes more—thought and effort than speaking.

There are some blocks that frequently hamper reception. One of these is *preconceived notions*. The minute anyone starts to talk about careers, communication, motivation, or any subject we have some ideas about, we often immediately assume we know what is going to be said. We then begin to prepare our next statement on the subject and fail to listen. What is being said may be different from what we anticipated, but we do not hear it.

This is often the result of habit. We have worked out a series of "meanings"—and certain responses to them—with which we can comfortably live. If we listen, we may well find new meanings that correct and enrich our habitual reaction in that area. And even if what we hear does conform to our preconceptions, we can use the statements of the other individual as a specific base to disagree, amplify, or get agreement.

A second major listening barrier to effective listening, often closely related to preconceived notions, is *semantics*. The meaning of a word may vary depending on who uses it; but typically we make the mistake of applying our own definitions to the words we hear rather than securing the meaning of the word intended by the speaker. "A good supervisor" means different things to different people. "Success" has many meanings, as do "leader" and "effective."

The point is not that you should argue over the definition—unless that is essential to the communication—but that you must understand what others mean by the key words they use in their communication. You may well be able to adopt their meaning, at least temporarily, and get on with the process of communication.

A third obstacle to good listening is *prejudice*. This means not only the common prejudices we hear about—race, sex, religion, and so on—but prejudices we have about any specific individual. We may not appreciate his values, his seeming lack of experience, his aggressiveness, his style of dress, his educational background, his role in the organization, or whatever.

As a result of such prejudices, we may deprecate what a person is saying, not because the information is incomplete or wrong, but merely because of our personal feelings. It would be nice if we could eliminate prejudice from our minds, but we are human and not perfect. Thus the answer is to be conscious of these feelings and, while listening, to concentrate on the speaker's ideas, not on his personal attributes.

To be a good listener, we must not only approach listening as an active process but also fit what is being said into some kind of organizational pattern. Thoughts in isolation tend to make for poor understanding.

One way to establish such a pattern is to mentally ask three questions: (1) What is the main point? (2) What reasons are presented? (3) What is the supporting material? As we listen, we should tie what we hear to one of these three questions. There is nothing magical in this suggested method, however; any pattern you develop that keeps some organization in what you are hearing may be effective for you.

What is important is that, as we listen and organize what is being said, we should listen not just for words and sounds but also for what lies behind them. We should be sensitive to feelings, emotions, and attitudes. We should be sensitive to the differences between an actual event or fact and the person's interpretation of that event. And, of course, as has been stressed previously, we should be sensitive to our own personal attitudes and opinions and how they filter out what we are hearing and seeing.

Depending on your purpose, then, one or a variety of listening skills might be used.

One method is simply to *restate* what the person has said. Such a restatement does several things. It shows the other person that you are listening and that you understand what he is saying. It also encourages him to talk more about the parts you have restated. Finally, it gives you a way to check your meaning against the other's. Hence you might say: "As I understand it, then, you have decided to do this . . ." or "Your reasons for this change, as I hear you, are as follows . . ."

Another method is to respond in *neutral or nonjudgmental* ways to what is being said. This is particularly applicable to situations that have some emotional connotations and therefore hold some temptation for you to make judgments based on your own value systems. By keeping your response neutral you encourage the other to keep on talking and to think through the problem himself. Responses such as "Uh-huh" or "I see" are examples.

For example, a colleague might say to you, "There are days when I'd like to strangle my boss for the way he treats me." You may well think that that's a terrible way to feel about anyone. But if you express your feeling at this point, communication may come to an untimely end. A noncommittal response like "I see" may therefore be preferable in this case.

A third approach is *reflective interpretation*. This is useful particularly when you want to get behind what the individual actually says and make him think more about the feelings or attitudes conveyed by his statement. In this way you help him clarify his assessment of the issue at stake.

For instance, to a statement like: "In front of everyone, the boss chewed out the poor subordinate!" you might reply, "It disturbs you to see someone ridiculed in public." Or if you're told: "And then they went ahead and promoted that guy!" you might amplify: "You feel you didn't get a fair shake."

A fourth method involves *clarification or summarizing*. Here, your purpose is to bring together what has been said to clarify the main issues so that you can get the other person to focus on one or more of these items or extend his thinking to new areas.

Examples of such responses are: "Up to this point, then, these are the points that you've mentioned . . ." "Is your main point that . . . ?" or "Would you elaborate on that last point?"

Failure to Be Specific

Another common error in communication is failure to develop specific ideas about a problem before beginning to communicate. We seldom do this when talking about money or equipment. For instance, you would not go to your boss and say, "I need some money to do something about something." Rather, you would go to him and say, "I need the authorization to spend $500 to buy a new electric typewriter that will be used to type letters that go out to the public. This will help create a better public image." Your comments are specific.

But often we make this mistake of being too general when we are seeking a behavioral change in someone. Examples are: "I think my job should include more responsibility," "If you want to get ahead, you must be more productive," "I've been with the company three years, and I've not gotten enough training," "I have been told the boss can be of value in helping a subordinate's career, and I want your help," or "I've been with the company five years, and I'm not making enough progress to suit me."

In these examples, your statements should identify some specific areas of new responsibility, indicate specifically what will make the other individual more productive, name areas of training needed, describe an area where the boss can help your career, or mention specific areas where you feel you are qualified for additional progress.

Being specific will allow you to develop good reasons for your request and to show how complying with it will assist the other person or the company. It will also permit the other person to respond in more specific terms, because he now knows what you mean, and his own interpretations are less likely to get in the way. This latter point is often essential for effective communication.

The issue of specificity applies to a wide range of career goals—a change in your job function, the next step in your career, getting the boss to think more along your lines, modifying a company rule or procedure, introducing a new product, and on and on. And opportunities to communicate on various matters may present themselves at unforeseen times: at lunch when a colleague unexpectedly sits beside you, before a meeting when you are chatting with others, during a meeting when an unforeseen topic comes up, in an office bull session, at a coffee break or a party, while driving with someone to a meeting, and so on. These informal sessions can be highly effective communication situations because they are less restrictive than more formal situations and because they provide valuable contacts with people who might not be easily accessible to you in any other way. If you do not have specific objectives in mind, these fine opportunities may go to waste.

Failure to Understand the Other Person

Often the best interaction results when you have taken the time to consider other people with whom you interact to see "where they are coming from." This understanding may open up approaches to build trust more quickly and enable you to strike themes that are of interest to the other and at the same time lead toward your desired goal. It may also prevent you from "putting your foot in your mouth" and thus losing credibility at an early stage and it will set the stage for more effective feedback, because it helps you adapt to the other person's situation.

The answers to several questions will assist your understanding of those with whom you interact: What is their motivation? Do they consider the matters you want to talk about real problems for them? If so, how have they formulated each of these problems, and what are their attitudes toward them? What information do they *want* and what information do they *need*?

We've already discussed the concept of motivation and emphasized the individuality of people's motives. Some people like to know the specific actions desired of them with regular feedback that all is going well; others want more freedom in their actions and need little continual support. Many people like to move slowly and take risks with great caution; others desire to move more rapidly and assume risks as a part of their job. Some individuals need a lot of outward appreciation; others get more satisfaction from within themselves and resent continuous "strokes" of appreciation as childish. Some individuals live by rules, regulations, and manuals; others look upon these as general directions to be bent or modified as the situation demands.

You should not be surprised, then, to find that many people's motivation differs from your own, and your interpersonal relations with them must take these differences into account. For instance, you may feel that rapid progress on your career goals is essential to you; but your boss, because he waited and let the company control his career, may view your lack of progress as normal. Little will be achieved until he views your lack of progress as a problem to him too. Interactive behavior shows real results only when all parties recognize that a mutual problem exists and must be handled. Until that point it reached, communication is likely to be one-sided.

Even when you agree on a problem, however, you must ask yourself whether the other person formulates the problem in the same way as you. Suppose your boss, while recognizing your lack of progress as a problem, feels that it is caused by your lack of experience, whereas you feel that the cause is his lack of assistance to you. The recognition of this difference must come early if effective communication is to result. Many times we see people contending over a solution when the real issue is the formulation of the problem.

How a person formulates a given problem is a function of his attitudes, motivations, and experiences. If, for example, your analysis determines that your boss has many reservations about trusting you, little effective communication is likely until that trust is established. This knowledge can play a major role in how you approach your personal relations with him.

Also, the other person's attitude toward himself should be analyzed. If his self-image is not very strong and he lacks confidence in himself, your approach to him will certainly be different on many matters from that which you would follow with a self-confident person. In addition, your analysis should determine his attitude toward the specific purpose you seek to achieve.

Thus, in attempting to understand your listener, three of his attitudes—toward himself, toward you, and toward your specific purpose—should be identified and used as a basis for determining your approach to him.

Finally, you must determine the kind and amount of information that the other person needs and wants. He may *need* only limited information to make the change you are suggesting, but many individuals *want* more information. He may want to learn the detailed reasons for a suggested change or its effect on a total procedure. He may want to know whether this is the first of many changes or what steps led you to make your suggestion.

Do not waste your time telling all these things to everyone. However, be sure to find out just what information the other person wants and give him that, or he may react in a negative fashion. Individuals vary a great deal in their informational wants, and they should not be treated all alike.

Effective use of feedback can assist you in making this type of analysis. However, if the initial approach is wrong because you failed to consider the listener before you started to communicate, unnecessary barriers might be erected that are often difficult to overcome.

Failure to Confront

A problem in interpersonal relations may arise when we fail to show the other person our own feelings. We may do a good job of listening, we may know clearly what our purpose is, we may be successful at understanding the person with whom we are communicating, and yet we might fail because we didn't let the other person know where *we* "are coming from"—not in terms of goals and objectives or facts and figures but in terms of our own emotions.

We have already explored possible reasons for our not being as open with others as we might be. Here we will examine the questions of when we should be more open and how to go about doing it.

How do you know when you should be a good listener and when you should express some of your own feelings rather than listen? To answer this question, determine which of you "owns" the problem under discussion. When the other person "owns" the problem, you can best help by using your listening skills. When *you* "own" the problem, on the other hand, it is best to take an active approach and reveal your feelings.*

Some examples will help clarify the issue of ownership of a problem.

Case 1: A subordinate tells you that on the way to work this morning his car broke down and he needs some time to get it to a garage to get it fixed.

Analysis: He owns the problem, at least initially, so listen to find out what happened. If he takes time at lunch or after work to get the car fixed, then listening may be all that is needed: you show understanding toward his problem and help him resolve it. However, if he wants time off from work and if that creates a problem for you (say, you have a project that he's working on that has a strict deadline), then you own the problem as well. Now you've got to "confront" him with your feelings regarding his taking time off from work.

Hence, in this situation you may have to use both listening and confronting skills.

Case 2: Your spouse tells you that it has been a terrible day at work and that she's as frustrated as she can be. You also had a tough day at work.

Analysis: Her tough day is her problem, so listen. If you counter with: "Well, I had a tough day, too!" then you are not listening or trying to understand where she is coming from. Listening skills are important here to reduce frustrations instead of creating additional ones.

Case 3: Your boss gives you an assignment that you think is unreasonable in terms of time limitations and expectations of your skills. You feel that you are bound to fail unless some compromise is reached.

* This insightful dichotomy was first discussed by Thomas Gordon in *Parent Effectiveness Training: The Tested New Way to Raise Responsible Children*, New York: Peter H. Wyden, 1970.

Analysis: The problem is yours, not your boss's. Here's a situation that calls for "confronting" skills—if you are certain of what your boss communicated to you. If you are not certain, clarification is needed first.

In confronting a person, you should give him an "I" message— one that indicates how you feel and what impact the situation has on you, without direct reference to the other person.

Thus to the subordinate who wants time off to get his car fixed you might say, "I feel uncomfortable about the possibility of not getting the project done on time, because I'd have to go to my boss and try to explain its being late, and that I wouldn't like to do."

Similarly, to your boss who has given you an assignment in which you think you'll fail you might say, "I have an uncomfortable feeling about this assignment. I'm not sure I have the skills or the necessary time, and I'm afraid I might not be able to do it, so I'd like to talk to you about my concerns."

The "I" message here has certain advantages. In the first place, you show honesty and openness, and that encourages a trust relationship. You also do it in a way that does not threaten the other person. Notice that there is no mention of "you" (as in "when you take time off . . ." or "when you give assignments like this . . ."). Your message gives the other person a clear notion of the effects of his behavior on you and throws the responsibility to the other to deal with your feelings. And finally, by expressing your feelings, you get a clearer idea of them and begin to understand your different rational and emotional reactions to various situations.

It is not unusual for us to blame the other person, that is, to put the main burden on him in our relationship. This puts him on the defensive and will lead to ineffective communications. On the other hand, when you ask the other person to deal with *your* feelings, this gives him an opportunity to respond to you, to share—and that leads to more effective interpersonal relations.

Written Communications

Because written communications may reach many individuals who aren't easily contacted in other ways, they can give you very positive exposure. A well-written progress report, memo, suggestion for a new procedure or a new product, or letter to a customer are all visible examples of the quality of your ideas and your ability to organize a problem and adapt to a situation. You should be prepared to use the potential of this type of exposure.

After studying more than one thousand pieces of communication written by individuals in business and industry and interviewing a number of people who are critical of present-day communication, David C. Phillips found that the major areas of failure were not in poor grammar, syntax, word choice, and the like. The most common mistake in written communications was failure to consider the reader—specifically failure to adapt the organization and the content of the communication to the reader and failure to lead him by visual means.

A thorough reader analysis is even more important than an analysis of your listeners because of the limitations of written communication. Written communication does not provide for immediate feedback, and therefore you cannot adapt your communication as it progresses. All the adaptation to the reader's motivation, attitudes, formulation of a problem, and informational desires must come *before* you start to write.

What are the reader's expectations? What possible objections does he have? What is his level of information? How might this communication affect his position, values, and interests? These and other questions must be answered in your mind before you begin to write. The procedure for making this reader analysis is the same as the method of listener analysis discussed previously in this chapter.

The organization of a written communication should fit the desires of the reader, not those of the writer. We may think there is one "accepted" method of organizing written material—say, background, statement of problem, solution—but that is a myth. There are many satisfactory ways of organizing written material. The important point is that it be organized in a fashion with which the reader is comfortable.

He may like recommendations first. Put them there, or he will become frustrated looking for them. He may like background first; if so, give it to him. If he likes a statement of the problem at the beginning, place it there. If you do not know what he likes, find out. Observe. He may write his communication in a certain way that indicates his preferences, or he may have commented on a report he liked from someone else. If necessary, talk to him about what he likes.

The organization of the rest of the communication will probably be determined by what is placed first. If not, go back to the desires of the reader. He may want a section entitled "Advantages and

Disadvantages," "Methods of Implementation," or "Possible Objections by Others Involved." The important point is to cover what the reader wishes in an organizational style with which he is comfortable.

Another failure that often crops up in writing is the failure to lead the reader by visual means. In oral communication we know what is important by a change in the voice or some body gesture that stresses certain statements. We recognize a movement to another point by a vocal or bodily change. We should offer the reader similar guidance.

Methods of leading include underlining, use of section heads, numbered paragraphs, indentation, subheadings, and different type styles such as italics, or even a change in the color of the type if that is available. The chosen is of no great importance, but making it easy for the reader to follow the thoughts, recognize the important statements, and keep the whole writing in mind as he concentrates on one section is very essential.

We often hear the admonition about written communication: "Make it brief!" Good point, but it often brings more problems than it solves. The admonition should be: "Make it as brief as possible but cover all the points!"

In making the writing brief, we often assume too much interest or knowledge on the part of the reader. For instance, we may assume that he will recognize something as a problem when in fact it has a very low priority in his hierarchy of problems. Failure to make it a real problem *to the reader* will make the best writing in the rest of the report useless.

In the study by Phillips cited earlier, not one of the more than one thousand written communications considered the reader's possible objections. That coverage would have lengthened some reports but made them more effective. No reader will consider a written report too long when all that is being read is of interest and value to him. However, if he has to spend time reading material that he feels is not vital to him, any length is too long. A good reader analysis should assist in determining what to include and what to omit.

Do not forget the possibility of using an appendix or attachments. This method takes some material out of the mainstream of the reading but makes it available if the reader wants it.

Two further suggestions about writing: *watch paragraph length and sentence length*. There should be no more than one idea to a paragraph. There is no such thing as a best length for a paragraph, but we often tend to bunch ideas together and thus get long paragraphs that do not make for easy reading.

Similarly, many writers try to include too much in one sentence, and thus their sentences get long and involved. Other writers make nearly all sentences short and pithy. To some readers, this seems like a children's reading book. A careful analysis of your past writing can often show you any possible errors in paragraphing and sentencing.

Meetings

Another type of personal interaction that makes for high exposure of a person's communication skills is participation in small group activities. Both formal and informal meetings would be included in this category.

Small group activity is a discipline in itself, and if we were to cover it all, it would take a book. Therefore, let us limit our discussion to the interaction between individuals that takes place during small group activity. In doing so, let us look at six common errors.

1. *Failure to agree on the objective of the group.* Each individual may come to the meeting with the objective as he sees it in his mind. Do the others have the same objective? Failure to agree on the objective early in the activity may lead to wasted time and considerable frustration.

2. *Failure to agree on the approach that the discussion should follow.* There are usually several good ways to proceed in order to reach the agreed-upon objective. If each individual follows his predetermined approach, the discussion will wander and confusion could result. Some approaches may be better than others, but if the approach being followed is clear to everyone, there will be a better thrust to the whole discussion. If a chosen approach proves a poor one, it can easily be changed.

3. *Failure to listen well.* We discussed this concept earlier. If each individual is concentrating only on his own ideas and statements, he will fail to hear what is being said. This can lead to a mixture of ideas being on the floor at once, with important ideas being lost in the confusion.

4. *Failure to build on what has been said previously.* This point is closely related to good listening but extends the point. If you know what idea is under discussion and what previous material has been presented, your contribution can be built on that. You may

quickly agree, amplify the point, modify the idea, or disagree, but what you say will consider what has gone on before. Contributions that move from what has been said toward the stated objective are the key to successful small group activity.

5. *Failure to make sure that everybody has an opportunity to participate.* Most small groups are a heterogeneous mixture of people. Some are aggressive, some shy. Some are quick thinkers, others are not. Some jump in at every opportunity, others take more time in making contributions. Some are good at reviewing and questioning, others are not.

Why is one participant silent most of the time? Is it because he has little to contribute or because he thinks slowly and others beat him to the punch? If handled properly, this quiet soul may have real contributions to make. Until you know why he is not participating, you cannot determine the value of his contributions.

This is the duty of the leader, you might say. But what if he does not assume this responsibility? If each individual in the group feels responsible for involving all members of the group, the results will usually be better.

6. *Failure to lead the group.* If all the individuals who bear the title "chairman" were effective leaders of meetings, the rest of the group could cease to worry about group leadership. Unfortunately, that situation is generally not true. The leader may be too aggressive, fail to direct the discussion, allow certain people to dominate, or fail to involve all individuals in the discussion. When this happens, another member of the group must at least temporarily exert some leadership, or the result will not be satisfactory. This is all the more important because such situations may produce negative feelings that carry into other activities.

You can exert leadership without being too obvious by using the method of review and question. Examples of appropriate statements are: "I'm sorry, but I'm mixed up. What point are we discussing now?" "It seems we have two opposing points of view here. Let's review what has been presented in support of each point of view." "John, you have obviously been listening well to what has been said; what do you think about this idea?"

The success of small groups can be measured by the quality of the final results, both in the ideas produced and in the interpersonal relationships maintained or developed. Each individual must recognize his responsibilities for making his contributions meet the criteria discussed here and for temporarily assuming the leadership role if that is necessary.

10

The Boss

Committing Power to Help You Win

EARL Bowers, at age 40 just promoted to the presidency of a large corporation, had accepted an invitation to talk with a group of young people in the company about their own career plans.

> Question: Mr. Bowers, you have just been promoted to the presidency of a very powerful organization at a relatively young age. I'm sure there are some of us in this room who aspire to similar successes in our own careers. What advice would you give to us so that our bosses might recognize our talents and put us on a fast promotion track, such as the one you experienced?

> Answer (without hesitation): I can best answer that by telling you about the kinds of subordinates who always got the outstanding marks from me—the ones I was most likely to put on that so-called fast track. They were the people who constantly kept control of my time. By that I mean, they kept dropping information to me—either directly, in brief conversations, or by informal notes—about what they were doing and the progress they were making. "Here's the latest news on the XYZ case"; "I just want you to know that I'm about to contact the ABC department about such and such"; or "The proposal to our new line of clients is just about ready to be delivered."

> They were things that the subordinates knew were important to me so that I had to attend to them. I knew what was going on. The people I worried about—and felt uncomfortable about—were those whom I had to seek out, who kept me in the dark. I felt I had to spend a lot more time with them in the long run. The people who initiated contacts with me on items that really mattered, they were the fast-track people.

We've already mentioned in Chapter 2 some of the misguided virtues about the role of bosses in our own careers. We have the feeling that a good boss would be an answer to our effectiveness. And that we can't deny. Good bosses can be most supportive of our job activities and can provide the kind of counsel and experience that can help us be more effective. But that kind of relationship does not occur automatically. As we also indicated in our discussion of some questionable virtues, we should not wait for the "they" of the organization (the people above us) to concern themselves with our problems. We might have a long wait, depending on organization climate and the motivations of the boss. Relations with bosses—just as with all individuals—must be fostered. Initiation for that relationship rests with you.

It is unfortunate that most of us spend more time concerning ourselves with how we can work effectively with subordinates and peers and less time thinking about how we can be more effective with those who are in power positions. And yet it is this relationship that is critically important to the achievement of individual purpose. It is for this reason that we say that next to managing yourself (understanding yourself better and then organizing your competencies to optimize your potential), the most important thing to learn is how to manage your boss—training him to understand your needs and style so that he can help you achieve your goals.

Unfortunately, this is not an easy task. Our relations to power may be rooted in our past, when we developed habit patterns for coping effectively with people in power positions—our parents, teachers, and the like. These relationships created a variety of feelings in us and, in fact, initiated a variety of frustrations and conflicts to which we were forced to adjust.

As adolescents we strove for independence at a time when we knew we were still quite dependent on our parents, and our parents may have behaved in conscious or unconscious ways to encourage that dependency relationship. We got caught up in a love-hate ambivalence, and that led to feelings of guilt. We feared the consequences of violating the guidelines of those who tried to control us;

but at the same time we wanted, for the sake of self-esteem, to be in control of our own destiny. Love-hate, independency-dependency, fear, guilt, desire for control—they are feelings which, like it or not, get caught up in our relations with people in power.

We bring these feelings with us into new situations and frequently create a "reality" around our boss or other power figures that has a powerful effect on our perceptions, even though it may be fictitious. If we've had negative experiences with people in authority ("They fail me, they make me feel inferior, they ridicule me in front of others, they threaten me with the loss of something I want and need"), then it's difficult for us to perceive even new figures of authority in a positive light. We are legitimately wary as we begin our relationships with these power figures.

When we believe that bosses behave in ways to frustrate our desires and maximize their and the organization's benefit, then we ordinarily "see" things that will eventually "prove" to us that we are right. We will withdraw, fail to communicate ("After all, what's the use?"), and then use the subsequent voids as evidence for our boss's lack of concern. It will take persistent and consistent behavior on the part of the boss to change such perceptions.

That is why, once again, we return to a focal point of career strategy: an understanding of how we relate to others. Are our perceptions accurate, or have they been distorted to protect our self-image? If we have consistently negative feelings about people in power ("All my teachers are inconsiderate"; "Bosses just love to exercise their power over you"; "Politicians don't care about anyone but themselves"), then it's time to check them out against the perceptions of others.

Checking Your Attitudes

Before considering various strategies that might be used in working with your superiors, you should take a closer look at your own feelings and beliefs and your expectations about outcomes in your relationships with power figures. Awareness of such attitudes and values is essential to an effective strategy. Unless those attitudes are generally positive, strategies will not be very effective or will altogether fail.

Here are some of the questions you should explore first.*

* These ideas are based on material from Alan C. Filley, *Interpersonal Conflict Resolution*, Glenview, Ill.: Scott, Foresman and Company, 1975. See especially Chapter 5, "Attitudes and Problem Solving."

YOUR EXPECTATIONS ABOUT OUTCOMES

- To what extent do you believe that, if there are differences of opinion between you and your boss, a solution is *available* that will be mutually acceptable?
- To what extent do you believe that, if there are differences of opinion between you and your boss, both of you *desire* to find a mutually acceptable solution?

These questions all have to do with your feelings of either competition or cooperation with your boss. A belief that, in relations with power, someone always wins (usually the power person) and someone always loses (usually the subordinate) makes it difficult to go into a relationship optimistic about a positive outcome for you. Negative responses to these questions tend to move you away from working with your boss on your career strategies.

YOUR ATTITUDES ABOUT THE BOSS

- To what extent do you believe your boss can be trusted?
- Do you believe he has some strengths that are valuable to you for your personal growth?
- To what extent do you believe he is willing to cooperate with his subordinates?

If you answer these questions in the negative, it suggests, of course, that you will have difficulty in initiating any strategy that gets your boss directly involved. And that means that you will ignore an important resource for reaching your career goals.

YOUR ATTITUDES ABOUT PERSONAL DIRECTION

- To what extent do you believe that you can control, in large measure, the major factors which impact on your career?
- To what extent do you believe that conflict is natural and a healthy source for giving direction and perspective to your behavior?
- To what extent do you understand your major career objectives and the priorities they create for both short- and long-range activities?

Again, negative reactions to these questions would indicate that you are less likely to initiate strategies for getting power figures involved in your career plans, because you tend to feel that these matters are largely outside your control and/or that it is impractical to set career objectives, let alone establish priorities for them.

Observations about Power

The typical pyramidal organization chart is drawn in such a way as to indicate that the people at the top of the pyramid have more power than those at the bottom. The organization, by title and other signs of status, "bestows" more power on some than on others. At least, that's what the message is supposed to be.

But you will recall that in Chapter 1 we made some observations about changing social values that have impact on career strategies. One of these shifts has to do with the concept of where power resides. The era of self-expression, rising entitlements, and self-actualization is making people see that power resides in each of them. Who controls whom? The pyramid should perhaps be inverted, for subordinates are at least raising the question whether power resides with the boss.

That concept comes as no surprise to the behavioral scientists. In the first chapter we also made some observations about conditions for effective individual change. In that regard, we emphasized the need for *internalized* motivation as the basis for change. External controls do little to change people's behavior if the need for that change is not internalized.

Power is the ability to influence the behavior and thinking of others. When a subordinate influences the thinking or actions of his boss, he is exercising his power.

The power of a subordinate can be exercised in a variety of ways. Whatever process is used, it is a means to keep proving to oneself that his self-esteem is still intact. As Abraham Zaleznik has stressed in his studies of power, a person's sense of self-esteem develops in parallel with his sense of possessing power.* Hence, if I can prove to myself that I do indeed have power, my sense of self-esteem is heightened.

Whether those in authority will be able to exercise their power over the governed is a decision that rests ultimately on the consent of the governed. This means, of course, that the power the boss exercises over you rests largely with your own set of needs and value systems. His use of threat and punishment as a means of control will be effective only if what he takes away from you is what you need or value. As your alternatives increase for satisfying various needs, the strength of his power decreases. Therefore, aware-

* "Power and Politics in Organizational Life," *Harvard Business Review*, May–June 1970, pp. 47–60.

ness of what things are important to you and what alternatives you have to obtain them is a powerful tool for exercising control over your own environment.

If *you* know what is important, and if you are in an organization that makes it possible for you to commit yourself to its goals as well as yours, then your boss no longer needs to exercise his authority over you. The mere commitment to joint goals, the identification with the boss and his objectives, means that there is no conflict and that both you and the boss will be satisfied. You and he have joint power in this situation.

But we know that power does not always work in our behalf—or at least appears not to. Power can be used for the aggrandizement of one's own position. This is what David C. McClelland and David H. Burnham have referred to as uninhibited power; there are no personal controls on it.* Power can also be used to help others grow along with the power figure and the organization. In this case, the power figure puts enough control on his own use of power so that other people benefit. This is socialized or inhibited power.

At the "uninhibited" end of the power continuum is a more "closed" boss. He is inclined toward precise definitions of duties and responsibilities. Rules and procedures are clearly defined and enforced; instructions and decisions flow downward. Subordinates are the people who accomplish what needs to be done; bosses are the planners and decision makers. Some authors have labeled this system task-oriented or authoritarian.

At the "inhibited" or socialized end of the power continuum is a more "open" boss. He is inclined to be more adaptable and share his power with those who need it and can use it effectively in order to get something done. Communications take on a consultative tone, and independence of action rests equally with the boss and the subordinates. Organizational design and jobs will change to meet the needs of both organization and individual. This system has been called people-oriented or democratic.

How people react to these two extremes is of course an individual matter. I have seen situations where a fairly closed system has been beneficial to an individual in forcing behavior that the boss felt would lead to a sense of competency and growth. The subordinate appreciated this structure for early development, even though he might initially have fought against the boss's high-handed ap-

* "Power Is the Great Motivator," *Harvard Business Review*, March–April 1976, pp. 100–110.

proach. In these cases, the power person utilizing a more closed system really had the developmental interests of the subordinate in mind.

On the other hand, I have witnessed situations where a democratic approach was perceived by subordinates as ambivalent, abdication of authority and responsibility, or lack of direction and concern for personal growth. Subordinates with these perceptions found it difficult to get a sense of competency; they wanted more direction than they were receiving.

These differences are stressed here to emphasize that people frequently misjudge the motives of the person in power. One must look not only at the behavior of the power person but also at the values and needs behind that behavior. This requires a willingness on the subordinate's part to be sensitive to the organization and the boss *over time* so that he can learn as much as possible about their underlying needs.

What appears to be authoritarian may be just that; but it may also be a genuine attempt to assist the other person in his own growth. What appears to be democratic may be just that; but it may also be a lack of interest or ability to commit oneself. The only way we can determine which hypothesis is accurate is to remain sensitive to what's going on around us.

Changing the Boss

When is your boss most likely to go along with an idea of yours? When is change in him most likely to occur? How does one go about developing a cooperative stance in a situation that may on the surface appear to be competitive or risky? If you are willing to take a risk in order to achieve your goals, then evidence from the study of conflict gives us some excellent clues.

The main concept is this: *Apply unrelenting but moderate pressure on your boss and at the same time reduce his defensiveness so that, as it is reduced, you can apply additional pressure.* That does *not* mean applying pressure that keeps him off guard, raising problems without indicating possible solutions, or threatening his power position.

Often, people get nowhere because they interpret "applying pressure" to mean: "I'll just go in there and tell my boss exactly how I feel." They say, "Boss, you're not doing right by me. What are you going to do in my behalf today?" And they may be unrelenting—

day after day, week after week: "Boss, remember me; you're not doing right by me. I'm unhappy. Do something for me." And finally, after several months of nothing happening, they state: "My boss knows I'm not happy but doesn't really care about me. He's done nothing to help me get out of this situation." Well, that's unrelenting, certainly, and it's open. But it's not helpful, and it's threatening.

It has been my experience that people are frequently reluctant to "put pressure" on their bosses. They see the power game as something manipulative and negative, as dominance/submission or as a zero sum game ("If I win, the boss loses; if the boss wins, I lose"). But to be aggressive does not mean to destroy or to make other people hostile. We can use our influence for the good of both. In fact, the effective use of influence over others can lead them to feel more powerful and confident if it allows them to accomplish their goals as well.

One of your main tasks, then, is to reduce your boss's defensiveness. But just how do you do that? Let us look at some of the conditions that must be met if you are to succeed.

1. *The need for change must be internalized by the boss.* How many times have you written a memo to your boss or talked to him about something that ought to be done—and he just doesn't do anything about it? The need for action may be more apparent to you than it is to him. As we have seen in our chapter on motivation, need gives rise to tension, to a sense of discomfort that we want to reduce or avoid. What this means is that the boss will act when *he* feels uncomfortable, not when *you* do—unless he has a sense of discomfort about your being uncomfortable, in which case he'll act out of concern for you. At any rate, he won't change until there is a need for him to change.

What follows from this is that you must create a situation (say by collecting appropriate data or pointing to a pertinent incident) that heightens the need for action on the boss's part. Mere plaintive cries for action will not move anyone. A sense of heightened discomfort will.

2. *The boss must be aware of alternatives.* Once the boss recognizes that "something oughta be done," he's more likely to move when he has some choices of action available to him. When he feels he has only one alternative—and that alternative may not be all good—he's likely to delay in order to resolve in his mind the negative aspects of your proposal or, even better, to seek out a different solution that will produce less conflict.

Take the case of Chris Holloway. He worked long and hard on a report for his boss on a very ticklish internal problem. He turned in the report, got an acknowledgment of receipt of the report, but nothing more specific than: "I'll be getting together with you as soon as I've had a chance to think it through."

Says Chris privately: "What's there to think about? I defined the problem, analyzed it, and made a recommendation. If he didn't want to buy my idea, why did he ask me for a recommendation?"

Says the boss: "Granted, I've been remiss in not sitting down with Chris and discussing the report with him. But I honestly don't know what to say. I'm the kind of guy who doesn't like to tell a subordinate to change a report unless I can also give him some ideas on how to change it. Chris's report indicates a lot of hard work, but his solution to our problem—to reorganize the entire division— is just not an acceptable one. And he gave me no choices. I wish I could give him some other ideas to play around with. Until I come up with some, I'll delay the discussion."

Both parties are of course wrong here. Chris's boss could and should sit down with him and give Chris some reasons why his reorganization solution is not acceptable, and then tell him to try again and bring in several solutions with Chris's ideas of the pros and cons for each. Chris, on the other hand, should have been aware that his boss would be more likely to act if he were offered several solutions to the same problem so that he could pick the best one. The best, incidentally, may very well be what Chris recommends, once all the other choices are known to the boss.

But what about the situation where you have a personal objective you want the boss to attend to?

The same principle applies. Communicate a rigidity about your important goals but be open-minded about means to achieve those goals. If you don't know what it is you want to accomplish, you will only invite your boss and others (consciously or unconsciously) to take advantage of your ambivalence. Self-respect dictates respect from others.

By being open-minded about the means to achieve your goals you indicate to the other person that you are aware of his needs, that you are realistic, and that you accept the fact that there may be many ways of accomplishing an accepted objective. Forcing your methods upon an individual who has different habit patterns and different ways of thinking about and evaluating issues increases the probabilities of frustration on his part and therefore encourages defensive behavior.

Hence we must think carefully about different ways to achieve what we want. Is our way the only way we will accept? Is it the way it is done that is important? Or is the fact that something is accomplished more important? Staff people in particular often learn the answers to these questions the hard way. Too frequently they try to exercise power in order to force the *way* things are done. They soon learn that their ends are rarely accomplished. When they focus on goals and permit others to behave in ways that make them feel comfortable, they find that their purpose is more readily achieved.

3. *The alternatives offered must be compatible with the boss's values.* Any proposal you make will be judged by the boss within the context of his own value systems. In our earlier example, Chris's boss will see the "best" solution as the one that forces the least compromise with his own values.

Entangled in those values are those of the boss's peers. We have repeatedly stressed the power of one's peers as motivators: we want to identify with them, gain acceptance from them; in short, we see them as another source of feedback for our own sense of self.

The influence of peers seems to get stronger the higher one goes in the organization. A boss is more likely to accept an alternative, not because he finds it congruent with his values, but because he believes that it will not conflict with the values and actions of his peers. This is especially true in organizations that stress team spirit at the top and whose executives identify strongly with the organization.

4. *The potential for failure must be minimized.* Bosses don't like to fail anymore than you and I do. That does not mean that they are not willing to take risks. And some are willing to take greater risks than others. But whatever the risk, we all like to feel that we'll succeed and that, if we fail, this will not be disastrous.

We have already mentioned some of the ways to minimize risk for yourself. Those same rules apply to helping the boss minimize his own risks. Good feedback systems, short time intervals between behavior and feedback, minimum resources commitments, pilot projects, and isolated settings that permit trying out new projects without committing larger parts of the organization or publicizing the activity—all these will encourage the boss to find an alternative more acceptable.

5. *Problems and solutions must be depersonalized.* This may appear to be in conflict with a previous criterion for change that suggests the value of support from peers and identification with personal values and needs. Indeed, no decision will be entirely

independent of one's value orientation. Nonetheless, it is important to keep the situation as *objective* as possible; in particular, your proposals should be devoid of attack on the ego of any individual.

Specific data and descriptions of experiences without personal judgment will create a picture of objectivity. Hence your statements of objectives should rely more on quantitative measurement and less on the judgments of yourself or others. In this way, personalities and emotions are not as likely to get in the way of taking action.

6. *The boss must be able to identify personally with the success of change.* This criterion is the corollary of our first one. A sense of competence comes to an individual when he feels that he has had a meaningful part in the accomplishment of a goal. If good things come his way through no involvement by him, then there is no sense of competence or of success.

The effective subordinate recognizes this and plans a course of action that, whenever possible, permits his boss not only to experience success but also to identify with it. When the boss can perceive success as a probable outcome of a change in his behavior, he is more likely to change.

7. *The boss must be able to identify with the source of proposed change.* You have undoubtedly seen situations in organizations where ideas have been rejected or accepted not because of the value of the idea but more because of its source.

One factor that facilitates people's identification with you and your ideas is the *sharing of common likes and dislikes.* When two people share common feelings, cooperation tends to increase. Such sharing cannot even begin unless there is increased interaction that encourages expression of feelings. As our chapter on interpersonal relations emphasizes, other people are more inclined to be open with their feelings when you are open with them in a nondefensive way.

People sometimes fear that, as they become more open and communicate feelings and goals to people in power, they become more vulnerable to the whims of the power person. "The more he knows about me, the better able he'll be to destroy me. Therefore, keep your head down below the trenches and never reveal yourself unless you have to. The boss has too much control over me!" Possibly, but not probably.

Too frequently, because of our concerns with power and its potential threats, we wait for the power figure to do something first. Hopefully, it has become clear that this attitude is wrong. You can do much to change your environment for your personal and professional growth, and initiating such change is preferable to waiting to respond to whatever the environment has to deliver. This requires risk taking on your part; but if you know your direction and the potential payoffs, then risk taking becomes an inevitable aspect of implementing a career.

Identification by the boss with you and your ideas can also be increased by locating areas where you have a *common problem.* This was already suggested by our discussion of the first condition—the requirement that the need for change be internalized by the boss. The key is to deemphasize differences so that conflict will be less apparent. This will permit both of you to work on the problem together—and this in itself increases the likelihood of more frequent interaction.

Charles Stewart, to take a specific case, was concerned about considerable turnover among his 3–5 year service people. It meant more training problems for him, to say nothing of the cost. He felt that this turnover issue should be of vital concern to his boss, whose feet were to the fire on expense control problems. After accumulating some facts and figures relating to turnover and translating them into dollar amounts, he presented a proposal to his boss whereby he and the boss could work together on the turnover issue. Charles solved his training problem, and his boss reduced the expense budget.

Finally, it is easier for the boss to identify with you when there is a feeling that you need and value each other.

When are you attracted most to another individual? When the other threatens your sense of self? When you perceive the other as of no real importance to the satisfaction of your needs? Hardly. You are more likely to be attracted to people who do things to enhance your sense of self-esteem, adequacy, and growth.

It's the same with your boss. He is no less human than you; he also seeks support of his own ego. The issue, then, in dealing with him is to behave in ways that will enhance his self-esteem. This means that you must be perceived by him as somebody who can complement him and help him meet his responsibilities without appearing as a competitor.

On the other hand, it's important to make the boss feel that he's needed and valued by you. How can this be achieved? An obvious way is to let him know whenever he does something that was helpful to you. "Boss, I appreciate that reference you gave me on the XYZ project. It gave me a lot of answers I was looking for." "Boss, thanks for including me in your session with the new customer. I never had that kind of experience before, and it gave me new insights into my job." As we've seen in our chapter on learning, reinforcing people's good behavior will increase the probabilities of their repeating it.

In essence, what this means is that you should seek help from your boss in his areas of strength. Bosses are not all good or all bad. They achieved their level of status because they brought some strengths to the job. Understand what those strengths are and utilize them, particularly in those areas where you are deficient.

In short, be willing to learn from people in power. Sometimes subordinates dwell too much on the mistakes their bosses make; they see these errors as signs of weakness, of stupidity, of not knowing what's going on. The critical point is not whether the boss makes mistakes but whether he learns from them—and, from your point of view, *whether you learn from them*. Often, what's required here is an attitude not of tolerance but of acceptance. The difference between the two is aptly summarized by Harry Levinson:

> Tolerance implies condescension, putting up with someone else's thoughts, feelings, and behavior out of one's generosity. . . . Acceptance means that one understands that people are different, therefore see things differently, and each, therefore, has as much right to his distorted view as you have to yours. Tolerance makes understanding, and therefore compromise, impossible. Acceptance, putting all views on an equal plane to be examined on their merits, makes for give and take.*

Many times we misinterpret the behavior of those who are sensitive to their boss's wishes and who don't want to create unnecessary conflict. We see their behavior as a sign of giving in, of mollycoddling the boss, of being a yesman. But that's not so at all, if the behavior comes from the right motive. Your main objective should be to grow, to mature, and to learn. You can't do it if you isolate yourself from the main forces in your environments.

Partial Summary:
The Power Concept and Changing the Boss's Behavior

Up to this point we have indicated that, because our relations with people—especially people in power—are so tied in with our

---

* "What an Executive Should Know about His Boss," *Think*, March–April 1968, pp. 30–33.

past experiences, we should take a closer look at our own attitudes about these relationships. We suggested three areas of problems: (1) your expectations of outcomes from your relationship with your boss, (2) attitudes and feelings toward your boss, and (3) attitudes about your own personal direction.

We then made some observations about power in general and emphasized (1) the ineffectiveness of power through authority and status only, (2) the potential ineffectiveness of external controls as power sources, (3) the effectiveness of identification with objectives and peers as a power source, and (4) the inhibited and uninhibited power concepts. These points led us to suggest that the power to influence rests primarily in your hands rather than your boss's.

It was at this point that we raised the question: When will the boss feel the need to change? Several conditions were explored: (1) when the need to change is internalized by the boss; (2) when the boss is aware of alternatives; (3) when the boss accepts one or more alternatives; (4) when the potential for failure is minimized; (5) when the problems and solutions are depersonalized; (6) when the boss can identify with the success; (7) when the boss can identify with you as the source of the proposed change.

In this latter regard, we indicated that your boss is more likely to identify with you and the proposed change when you (1) share common likes and dislikes with him; (2) are perceived by him as valued and needed; (3) reinforce his helpful behavior; (4) seek help from him in his areas of strength; and (5) are willing to learn from him.

If the Boss Doesn't Agree

There are those situations where you try all the techniques suggested here, and yet the relationship still isn't what you'd like it to be. What then? Here are some thoughts to consider.

1. *Be sensitive to the cause of the conflict.* Warren Schmidt and Robert Tannenbaum offer some insights here by pointing out that when issues remain unclear, two parties can be talking *at* rather than *to* each other about differences of opinion.* They suggest that differences may exist about facts, goals, methods, or values. Differences about facts and methods may be more readily resolved and handled than differences about goals and values. The latter come closer to the heart of the self and require more effort before change

* "The Management of Differences," *Harvard Business Review*, November–December 1960, pp. 107–116.

can occur. Awareness of where the differences actually are, then, will provide clues for future action.

2. *Don't reveal your total plan; have a plan without a plan.* People often get overly concerned about the priority of goals and the necessity to achieve goal one before goal two. While that is essential in certain strategy moves where in fact the accomplishment of the second goal is dependent on the accomplishment of the first, for the most part strategy goals can be achieved in a variety of priorities.

Sensitivity to environments becomes an important ingredient in the setting of priorities. The general rule of thumb is to work on those goals first, if possible, that are least likely to lead to defensive behavior in power figures. Then, as you and those in power both experience success, other goals can be introduced.

It is generally not wise to present a total strategy to those who are likely to resist. Instead, introduce your plan in stages as the power person is perceived to be ready. An avalanche of goals is much more difficult to cope with than goals that come rolling in one at a time. Although the total plan must be in your mind, you should share with others only those goals that involve and concern them at the time when they care to be involved and concerned. Their sense of timing and of being pressured is an important factor in their willingness, or lack of it, to respond to your demands.

3. *Concentrate on building your own power rather than competing with the other's power.* Some bosses have difficulty in relating to subordinates because they believe that they must exercise their power over them. There are some subtle ways, however, to broaden your power base and change the power relationship with your boss, if not in fact then at least in perception.

- Develop the boss's self-confidence by minimizing his weaknesses and building on your own strengths.
- Build effective relationships with other people in power by developing ways to work with them and providing services to them.
- Make yourself more visible in the organization by actively participating at social functions, conventions, and business meetings.
- Volunteer for task force assignments that build contacts with other departments and provide you with opportunities to learn about things going on in the organization that may have a bearing on your job, present or future.
- Provide strength to the organization through your own com-

petencies and therefore attract strength to you; your competence makes you a center of influence.
- Strive to increase your influence in the organization by upgrading your job functions so that you now work with other
individuals who have a power base.

4. *Never plan strategy moves that do not have support from at
least some members of the power group.* In keeping with our emphasis on reality orientation, we suggest here that defensiveness of
people in power positions will, in fact, be enhanced if tactics are
introduced that are unanimously rejected by the dominant group.
If, however, the strategy has support from some in the group, then it
may lead to a giving in or a compromise.

Take, for example, the case of George Leopard, a member of a
sales force who mentioned to his boss that he was going to register
for some night courses to upgrade his technical proficiencies in an
area central to the company's functions. The boss, with great intent,
leaned across his desk and replied: "The day you register for that
course is the day you will be fired. Your job is to sell, and if you have
any spare minutes, they should be spent selling, not studying and
going to classes."

We can argue, of course, that the boss is a very narrow-minded
individual and that any young man worth his salt wouldn't work
under conditions like that. Indeed, George could opt for leaving the
company as a strategic alternative. But he likes the company and
the work he is doing. It didn't take George long to determine that
his boss's point of view was an isolated one; many other managers at
his boss's level encouraged self-development activities, and those
above the managers, including his own boss's manager, were in
support of such activities.

Under these circumstances, the young man, while taking a risk,
calculated that the boss's comments would not be supported by
others in the dominant group. Not in defiance, not in secret, but in
careful discussion with his boss, George indicated that the course
was, in his estimation, important to his development and his career
plans and that, as he perceived the company, such activity was
encouraged generally by the company.

George enrolled in the course. He was not fired. And, in fact, his
achievements on the job led to greater responsibilities shortly after
course completion. Of course, if George's survey of the organization
had turned up major support for his boss's position, the decision to
enroll would have been more difficult to make.

5. *Be politically sensitive.* Resistance to your plans can be minimized by responding to and being sensitive to the political climate of the organization. The good strategist knows where to put his ideas so they won't die. He knows who in the organization will pick up his ideas and do something with them and who will just let them drop. He knows who might spread the word so that the ideas become "planted" in the organization.

He knows when his ideas are more likely to be distorted so that his personal attention to them is important, and when it is possible to let someone else move on his behalf. He knows that changes in the organization on his behalf rarely occur because of his own actions alone. He knows that change requires the support of many people who feel that the change might bring some good for them as well, or who at least see no threat in your ideas.

6. *Look for "corridors of indifference" in the organization* and try to achieve strategic goals by working within those corridors. This is, in one sense, the reverse of the previous concept. Introduced by H. Edward Wrapp in his article on how effective general managers get things done,* the concept has equal validity for those who wish to reduce resistance to their personal strategies. The principle is one of looking for those places in the organization that appear to be indifferent to what you want to do, and to introduce the idea there first. Since resistance will be minimal in these "indifferent" corridors, it's possible to do many things in them without having people interfere.

In my experience, there are many more corridors of indifference in organizations (and the number increases with the size of the organization) than most people want to believe. People build up feelings that bosses care more than they actually do, that bosses would somehow be shocked, angered, or threatened if subordinates went ahead and did things on their own. But if we conduct our activities with a sense of responsibility and a genuine concern for helping people in power positions as well as ourselves, then such actions are typically not met with resistance.

We often hear people complain that the only time they hear from their boss is when they do something wrong. Although lack of reinforcement for doing a job well is unfortunate, such a situation can readily work for the good of the effective career strategist, for it suggests that he has a lot of freedom to act. It implies that there are indeed corridors of indifference of which he can take advantage in

* "Good Managers Don't Make Policy Decisions," *Harvard Business Review,* September–October 1967, pp. 91–99.

working for his goals. In fact, our advice in such situations is to develop feedback systems within those corridors which give the individual information about achievement of objectives, measured by standards acceptable to the individual. The boss then becomes incidental for feedback purposes.

A case in point is Bill Bradley, who became aware of the fact that no one in his bank really knew what the affirmative action requirements were, what they should be, or what the legalities of the situation were all about. He sensed that it was an important concern for the bank and started to collect data. He called the local and national authorities and built up a wealth of information. He started looking internally at the bank's operations and determined weak spots and possible courses of action. And, then, gradually, armed with this information, he started feeding it to those who should have been caring.

He became known as the expert in the bank—and indeed in the town—for matters pertaining to affirmative action. His stature in his own eyes, and in the eyes of the bank, increased notably as a result of his initial playing in a "corridor of indifference."

7. *Don't be afraid to say no.* Bosses impose a considerable number of demands on their subordinates' time. When those demands are planned and are part of the job, then they are legitimate. But frequently bosses get so used to the idea of contacting their subordinates for every little thing that this gets in the way of doing effective work.

This is not the place to give lessons in assertiveness training; you may wish to learn more about how to say no by reading one of the many books on the topic. What's important here is that a polite but firm "no" even to power figures can have great impact on training the boss.

There is nothing wrong with saying: "Boss, I'm right in the middle of a project that's part of our major objective. Could I delay seeing you until later in the morning? Or maybe we could set up a date for later in the week." Or, when the boss gets tied up with one of those lengthy telephone calls that interrupted your session with him, why not get up and jot a note: "Your call probably will take a while. I'll check with you later about continuing this session."

Sometimes, too, the things that come across our desks from the boss with the note "Please handle" can get cursory or delayed attention—or even no attention at all, if they get in the way of mutually agreed-on objectives. The key is that saying no to some of the boss's demands is much easier if both of you know and have agreed on what your job is and what he expects from you.

8. *Don't be afraid to use threat or to display hostility.* This is a difficult concept because (1) "the science of threat" is still not very well understood and (2) the concept seems counter to our admonition to avoid defensiveness. But there are some situations in which the use of threat or hostility, either overt or covert, may bring about more cooperation between two parties initially in conflict.

It is unrealistic to believe that even the best of interpersonal relationships are devoid of what Morton Deutsch labels "escalatory spirals of force and counterforce."* As two people attempt to assert what they think are their prerogatives, occasional escalatory spirals will arise. Those spirals tend to clear the air and make the feelings, attitudes, and values of each known to the other. They tend to heighten awareness of mutual dependence and set the stage for cooperative efforts to resolve the differences.

Unfortunately, the conditions that must exist for such spiraling to be optimally effective are not clear. But our anecdotal data suggest that in the best of situations (for example, in an open trust relationship between boss and subordinate), heated confrontations play a central role in the process of change. Through this process people learn what the limits of their behavior are before they become threatening to the other person; they learn "just how far they can go." Through threats, they learn the extent of their value to the other person and what priorities the other person has.

As we mentioned, little is known about this area, but it seems reasonable to assume that the use of threat is not an appropriate procedure in the *initial* development of cooperation. Before two parties understand their common ground of values, beliefs, and needs so that they can indeed perceive situations at least partially from the other's point of view, the use of hostility and threat will limit rapport and increase resistance (overt or covert) to change. Once a healthy relationship is established, then threat may be legitimate behavior. Even then, however, it should probably be your last resort, when all other attempts to resolve conflict have failed, because it may endanger a relationship or the creative spirit in the achieving of career purpose.

Some Special Situations

In dealing with people in power positions, it is often important to adjust your strategies to their personal style. There is a major

* *The Resolution of Conflict: Constructive and Destructive Processes,* New Haven, Conn.: Yale University Press, 1973.

problem here, however: it is really not possible to classify people into neat categories. The boundaries are hazy and not at all clear-cut. One individual may have a unique characteristic that makes working with him just a little bit different from working with another person.

Nevertheless, a discussion of personality types may be a useful springboard for developing and implementing your own career strategy, unique as your situation may be. As you become aware of the boss's personal style, you obtain important clues about his values and needs, and this knowledge may help you predict how he will react in his relations with subordinates.

As noted in Chapter 5 in our discussion of the wheel model, how we express our personalities largely determines how we are perceived by others and influences their behavior toward us. Hence a dominant characteristic that would normally be considered a strength can be a weakness if expressed excessively. As we take a closer look at various types of bosses, we should keep that observation in mind. When does a given characteristic of the boss become a weakness? And do you have the necessary strengths that might complement that weakness?

The Action-Oriented Boss

In many respects, this kind of boss exemplifies the stereotype of the typical business person. He is a man of action; he gets things done—and now, not tomorrow or next week. He has to translate his resources, whether they be people or ideas, into some practical results. He is a pragmatist, concerned primarily with making sure that whatever he does, with whomever he works, whatever idea he espouses leads to something tangible. He is a decision maker. Not to act, not to decide is simply delaying. And he measures his effectiveness by his results. Those results are based on tasks and projects, not on judgments about people and their feelings.

He is energetic. Since things must get done in order for him to judge his effectiveness, he works in a tireless manner. He is a dynamo of activity, handling many different projects at the same time and not hesitating to make a quick decision when he feels it can bring a prompt and profitable return.

To many he may be the ideal boss because he gets things done. But there are those who would criticize his insensitivity to people, his lack of awareness of the longer-range implications of his quick decisions, or his cocky assuredness in moving ahead without seeking ideas from others. His subordinates may be afraid to go into his office and talk over ideas with him because "he'll take the ball right away from you and start running with it before you're sure you want him to have the ball in the first place."

With this kind of boss there's a lot of opportunity for action and for growth. But you've got to know precisely where you want to go.

He's not the kind of boss who will take kindly to an introductory comment like: "I'd like some time just to sit down and mull over an idea with you. I'm not sure where it will take us, but let's just talk." Rather, the approach with this boss must be practically oriented; it must tickle his pragmatic values. Hence statements like: "You have this problem; here's a way that it can be solved" or "We need a 5 percent increase in sales; here's an approach that will get us at least that" are more likely to elicit a favorable response from him.

In his excesses, the action-oriented boss may push people too hard. He may set tasks that carry a higher risk than people are willing to take or deadlines that are too tight. Others may feel that they are being used and that the situation is all one way: his way, with no concern for other people's feelings and thoughts.

If you are a sensitive, people-oriented person, this kind of boss may cause some frustrations. He will be more insensitive than you'd like. To make him more aware of people issues, you will have to appeal to his action-orientation: "Boss, this won't get done if we keep pushing people this hard. Here's a course of action that is more likely to lead to the results you want." Or you may have to be the buffer and handle the people aspects of the job yourself; your style will complement his. But to try to change him—to get him to think in terms of his impact on others' feelings—will only make him uncomfortable.

The same strategy is essentially applicable if you are idea-oriented. Your ideas must be presented to him in ways that respond to his interest in action and results. Thus you might say: "Here are the issues that you must resolve in order to move on that question," "Here are the people to whom we will have to respond in order to get the results we want," or "Here are the action steps I'll take in the next few months to achieve our objectives," not: "Let's sit down and talk about it" or "I'll have to think about it; it's a complex issue."

Do your thinking about the complexities *before* you approach this person, and use him as a test for the practical nature of your ideas. He's not the kind of person who will attend to your feelings very much, unless they get in the way of accomplishing his goals.

Then he'll be interested, but only in the sense of how they impact on potential performance. He'll talk career with you, but only as it relates to the job at hand. Don't expect that he'll get personally involved with you.

One thing is certain: whatever your own orientations, do not ignore this kind of boss. He will not like it when his subordinates ignore him or fail to let him know what's going on. In short, he wants his subordinates to behave in ways that keep indicating to him that indeed he is the boss. But neither does he want people around him who have no purpose. He responds best to those who have the courage of their convictions and who give indications of wanting to achieve.

The People-Oriented Boss

Some bosses place a high value on human relationships. They believe that their effectiveness relies primarily on the development of personal and close relationships with their subordinates.

Such a boss tends to emphasize social relationships and sees the work situation as a means for building and maintaining harmony and a team spirit. He is therefore likely to be more perceptive and sensitive to the feelings of others and may have a tendency to react more to feeling than to the content of messages. On the other hand, he is tuned to the ways people are likely to respond to changes and therefore may be helpful in reducing possible resistance to such changes.

He may be perceived as not very practical, as a person who is more interested in the political and personal intrigue in a situation than in a practical solution to the issue, as an individual who believes that nothing much happens if the "personal relationships" are out of tune.

He emphasizes informality, mutual acceptance, team effort, conflict reduction, and harmony and sees these primarily as ends in themselves rather than as means to achieve individual or organizational effectiveness. In his extremes, he may prevent the solution to issues by becoming too concerned with his or others' subjective feelings.

In one sense, this boss is good to work for, primarily because he listens and cares about other people's needs and feelings. He wants to help. As a result, you will not find it difficult to get your feelings across to him.

The problem with him is precisely his overconcern for your

feelings. Since he also wants to be accepted, he may not tell you how he really feels if he thinks it would hurt you. He may therefore find it difficult to disagree or to give you a clear picture of reality. That focus on your feelings may be detrimental if it does not ultimately switch to the practical issues at hand.

Hence this kind of boss must be kept "on the track" by providing him with objective data. Communicating with him solely about your feelings will encourage conversations at that level. Skillful preparation before a meeting becomes essential. Such preparation must accomplish the following:

- Provide you and your manager with relevant data.
- State the problem in a specific, objective manner.
- Recommend a course of action that de-emphasizes peoples' feelings and reactions and focuses on results.
- State how the people issues can be handled.
- Provide you and your manager with a clear understanding as to the desired end result.

Another possible approach is to go about the *task* requirements of your position without much communication with your boss. Limit your interviews with your boss to those aspects of your job to which he can most readily and enthusiastically respond—the social and interpersonal contacts—and simply give him routine reports on the accomplishment of tasks.

Whatever your approach, however, you cannot isolate yourself from him. He values social relationships and needs them to meet his own criterion of success. Accordingly, you may set challenging job goals and pursue them independently of the boss, without getting "permission" beforehand, but in so doing, you should show a genuine interest in helping him meet his own need to have friendly subordinates. This approach, of course, requires a faith on your part in your ultimate objectives, an understanding of how you can best serve organizational needs, and a self-assurance in your ability to succeed in your task.

The Idea-Oriented Boss

The idea-oriented boss is the kind of person who can "run with an idea," not in the sense of implementing it, as is the case with the action-oriented boss, but rather in the sense of projecting the idea into the future, of seeing it in a broader perspective, with greater imagination and creativity than the originator of the idea.

He is a concept man, interested in exploring all the possibilities. He is therefore willing to "dream," to consider what could possibly be. Because of his vision, he is perceived by others of less vision (and especially by action-oriented people) as being "blue sky," "idealistic," "more intellectual than realistic."

Because of his theoretical orientation, he is the kind of person who is excellent for probing, helping in planning, identifying key issues, and seeing complex interrelationships that are not immediately apparent to most people. But don't expect him to get involved with nitty-gritty detail and with the process of defining and laying out a plan of implementation. In fact, he may readily avoid these matters and need the services of others to put his visionary ideas into some practically applied program of action.

Discussions with this type of person, then, will be devoid of any emotional content, and solutions to a problem will be attacked in as objective a way as possible. Comments from you that reflect your feelings and your subjective concerns will be handled by this person in what may appear to be a cold way: "What evidences do you have for that?" "I find that difficult to believe—is it what *actually* happened?" He will press you for ways of testing your predictions. Therefore, to go to him without specific data and expect to freewheel it with him is to be blind to how he functions best.

In his extremes, the idea-oriented boss may be perceived as a mechanical, impersonal robot. He will hide his feelings, fearing that any display of emotions would lead people to think of him as too subjective. By the same token, he may ignore your feelings and stick close to facts and figures. He may also be so analytical that he becomes overcautious and won't act fast enough. And when this leads to problems, he may in fact use them as evidence that he's not been logical and analytical enough in the past.

If you are an action-oriented person, this kind of boss may be a drag. You may feel that he drives you to distraction with "study, study, study, but never any action."

The most effective strategy in working with the idea-oriented boss (as with almost any boss) is, of course, to utilize his strength in your behalf. Proposals for action or discussions about detailed operations will not readily get his attention. These are matters that you should work on by yourself or with people other than the boss. Reserve for him those discussions that have a longer-range perspective, that demand ingenuity to prove for new ideas, and that involve concepts of planning and strategy rather than of implementation.

This in no way means that you can or should ignore an action orientation. In fact, an action-oriented subordinate can be the perfect balance to this type of boss and make him look especially good. On the sidelines, such a subordinate can and should be involved with the detail, with the process of implementing, and with the collection of information necessary to put a program into action and check its validity. Your boss won't be interested and can't be bothered with that, so don't attempt to push him into action. Just do what's necessary, for his own success may very well depend on that great idea of his being put into some practical activity. If it is put into action and if you are the one who did it with a minimum of frustration to him so that he can keep on developing ideas, you will be more readily perceived by him as a valuable member of his staff.

His value to you becomes apparent when you need ideas, new vision, some blue-sky thinking. Expect that sessions with him will take time, that they may "wander all over the lot," and that you may have to separate the practical from the impractical, from your point of view. But don't try to pin him down to one small issue. Let his abilities help you bring order into what may seem to you a maze of unconnected issues. He likes it best when he is respected for his logical approach to problems.

He will not seek out people. He prefers to function independently. Therefore, if you are people-oriented yourself, you may have to pick and choose your times carefully to approach him. Nevertheless, you may be of real service to him in the accomplishment of organizational goals. It is unlikely that the idea-oriented person will achieve long-lasting success if he attends solely to the objective aspects of the issue. He needs the sensitivity of a lieutenant to make him more aware of where the resistance to his ideas might be and to develop the human relations aspects of the project so that it can be "sold" more readily. He needs, in short, the help of someone to provide the human touch to his unemotional, mechanical approach to issues.

The Security-Oriented Boss

There are many bosses who believe that most workers seek a career that will provide them with the creature comforts, with pleasant working conditions, with security, and with assurances that work will always be there. "Give the worker decent pay, good working conditions, good benefits, and you have him hooked," they say. "Most people want just that. They really don't care about having any responsibility or getting ahead. They want their eight to four-thirty job and then no more worries until the next day."

A manager who holds such views will himself typically show

great concern about security, and as a result, he may become preoccupied with matters that are peripheral to the work itself and to most workers. He is likely to spend time working out standardized approaches, procedures manuals, organization charts, and specific job descriptions and then make certain that his shop functions strictly according to the stated procedures.

A situation that does not fit neatly into that system will create a panic until the issue can be resolved either by revising the procedures manual or forcing the situation to meet the requirements of the manual. His subordinates quickly learn that flexibility in approach and risk-taking are not part of the boss's *modus operandi*.

Opportunities for personal growth are difficult to foresee in this kind of environment. Questioning a procedure, suggesting changes to presently functioning systems, or forcing the boss into ambiguous situations will be a threatening and frustrating experience for him. He will avoid it if he can or structure it or give you every reason why it can't work.

Change, therefore, must be presented within his framework: as an orderly progression of what already is. The boss must see you as a part of that system and not as someone who is fighting or ignoring it.

However, as an organization progresses and becomes more concerned with responding effectively to rapid changes, this kind of security-oriented boss is not held in high regard. Executives tend to plateau him; young mobile employees tend to be effective in spite of him. He's a solid citizen and kept in the organization to handle the routine. Changes in the organization are given to others to handle.

Frequently, therefore, ambitious young people who are frustrated by the procedural obsessions of bosses like this do the absolute minimum on the present job to get by. They may delegate much of it to the clerical function or routinize the reports just to get them out of the way. Most of their time may then be spent building relations with the people in the organization who are important to them in terms of their career strategy.

This may or may not be done with a Machiavellian philosophy; but there is generally no desire to "go around" the boss and ignore him. After all, he must be served. But, as the young achiever evaluates the situation, he sees his boss as not too important in the decisions that will affect him early in his career, so he spends his time on those matters that have a greater probability for payoff.

Young or old, the same concept applies. If you seek self-fulfillment on a job that rewards stability and routine performance, you must usually figure out ways to redesign your job activities without frustrating the security-oriented boss to the point where your freedom of movement is seriously limited.

Such redesign can take different forms. It need not rely on delegation or development of relations with others. Educational programs that prepare you for future jobs may serve your purpose indirectly. More directly, you may be able to enrich your job by a plan of action that deliberately raises legitimate questions about the procedures and shows that the task can be accomplished better, faster, and at less cost using different procedures.

Of course, if you are preoccupied with security too, then the security-oriented boss may seem appropriate. However, if you decide to live with such a situation, don't expect excitement. And more often than not, you'll find that your attitude on the job carries over to your behavior off the job. In the end, a security-orientation may show debilitating effects such as tardiness, fatigue, absenteeism, low productivity, or an escape into social activities. There's a risk to everything—including career strategies that focus on avoiding risks.

11

The Job

Commitment to Activities

AS we noted in Chapter 3, a good career strategy should be ac-
tivity-oriented. This follows from the fact that a given activity can
be a part of many different roles a person might play, either on or off
the job. Hence, a strategy that is based on activities that you can do
well and that are of interest to you will provide you with a wide
variety of options as to the roles you can play.

With that in mind, let us take a closer look at jobs from the point
of view of activities. There are many ways to categorize job activities; the one chosen here follows Thomas A. Mahoney, Thomas
H. Jerdee, and Stephen J. Carroll, who classify activities into eight
different groups.*

1. *Planning:* determining courses of action, establishing
   policies, procedures, and strategies.
2. *Investigating:* "collecting and preparing information, usually in the form of records, reports, and accounts."
3. *Coordinating:* "exchanging information with people in the

* *Development of Managerial Performance*, Monograph C-9, Cincinnati, Ohio:
South-Western Publishing Co., 1963.

organization other than subordinates in order to relate and adjust programs."
4. *Evaluating:* "assessment and appraisal of proposals or of reported or observed performance."
5. *Supervising:* leading and directing the work of your subordinates.
6. *Staffing:* those activities that help maintain the work force of the organization.
7. *Negotiating:* contracting for goods or services; purchasing and selling.
8. *Representing:* "advancing the general interests of your organization through speeches, consultation, and contacts with individuals or groups outside the organization."

These activities can be found in many specialized or technical assignments. For example, planning is an activity that can be carried out in a personnel assignment or in marketing. Supervising can be found in a manufacturing assignment or in control systems. Therefore, we can also classify activities according to the operational or technical context of the job:

1. *Research and development:* basic R&D, applied R&D, production engineering—design, test, follow-up.
2. *Production:* plant engineering, industrial engineering, purchasing, production planning and control, manufacturing, quality control.
3. *Marketing:* marketing research, advertising, sales planning, sales promotion, sales operations, physical distribution.
4. *Finance:* financial planning and relations, tax management, custody of funds, credit and collections, insurance.
5. *Control:* general accounting, cost accounting, budget planning and control, internal auditing, systems and procedures.
6. *Personnel administration:* employment, wage and salary, industrial relations, organization planning and development, employee services.
7. *External relations:* public relations, creditor and investor communications, civic affairs, association and community relations.
8. *Legal and corporate relations:* corporate legal matters, patents, employee legal questions, stockholder relations, board of directors activities, corporation secretarial affairs.
9. *General management:* top management concerns that cut

across all operations and require general knowledge rather than in-depth technical understanding.

The following list enumerates the kinds of activities that are related to each of the eight activity groups. Note that activities 1 through 7 are all considered "planning" activities, items 8 through 14, "investigating" activities, and so on. This listing makes it possible for you to take a closer look at those activities that are related to what you do now or would like to do in the future and allows you to determine how they relate to your abilities, training, and on-the-job development.

PLANNING ACTIVITIES
1. Scheduling work.
2. Developing budgets.
3. Setting up procedures.
4. Setting up objectives and standards for those objectives.
5. Preparing agendas.
6. Developing total programs or systems.
7. Establishing policies.

INVESTIGATING ACTIVITIES
8. Developing inventory records.
9. Measuring output.
10. Keeping records.
11. Doing research; conducting special studies or projects.
12. Writing job analyses.
13. Preparing reports for internal use.
14. Preparing financial statements.

COORDINATING ACTIVITIES
15. Advising people other than your subordinates or agents.
16. Expediting.
17. Developing liaison with people in other departments.
18. Arranging meetings.
19. Informing superiors.
20. Seeking cooperation of people outside your department.

EVALUATING ACTIVITIES
21. Evaluating output records for accuracy, quality, etc.
22. Evaluating financial reports.

23. Inspecting work output.
24. Approving requests.
25. Judging proposals and suggestions.
26. Appraising employee and/or agent performance.

SUPERVISING ACTIVITIES

27. Counseling subordinates and/or agents.
28. Training.
29. Explaining work rules and procedures.
30. Assigning work.
31. Handling complaints of subordinates and/or agents.
32. Disciplining subordinates and/or agents.
33. Maintaining cost control.

STAFFING ACTIVITIES

34. Recruiting employees and/or agents.
35. Selecting employees and/or agents.
36. Placing/transferring/firing employees and/or agents.
37. Promoting employees and/or agents.

NEGOTIATING ACTIVITIES

38. Contacting suppliers.
39. Dealing with sales representatives.
40. Maintaining day-to-day relations with outside business contacts.
41. Conducting negotiations to establish leases, purchases, contracts, etc.
42. Selling goods and services of the company.
43. Contracting for goods or services.
44. Negotiating with others re taxes, unions, or the like.

REPRESENTING ACTIVITIES

45. Making public speeches.
46. Getting involved in community activities.
47. Preparing and distributing news releases.
48. Attending/participating in conventions and business club meetings.
49. Answering customer or client complaints and inquiries.
50. Preparing reports for public use.

Figure 21. Categories for personal evaluation of job activities.

	Importance for Present Job					Intrinsic Satisfaction				Time Spent			Performance Judgment					Training			Importance for Ideal Job		
	NI	LI	SI	VI	E	+	O	I	N	H	M	L	O	S	A	K	D	OJC	TI	SO	E	A	N
Planning 1																							
2																							
3																							
4																							
5																							
6																							
7																							
Investigating 8																							
9																							
10																							
11																							
12																							
13																							
14																							
Coordinating 15																							
16																							
17																							
18																							
19																							
20																							

	Column A	Column B	Column C	Column D	Column E	Column F
Evaluating						
21						
22						
23						
24						
25						
26						
Supervising						
27						
28						
29						
30						
31						
32						
33						
Staffing						
34						
35						
36						
37						
Negotiating						
38						
39						
40						
41						
42						
43						
44						
Representing						
45						
46						
47						
48						
49						
50						

Figure 21 takes these same job activities and shows you a way to do some personal evaluation.* Column A of the figure provides you with a means to describe your *present* job by simply checking each of the activities in one of the categories: *NI, not important* to my job; *LI, of little importance* to my job; *SI, of some importance* to my job; *VI, very important* to my job; and *E, essential* to my job.

A careful look at this column after you've gone through the exercise will give you *clusters* of activities that fall into one of the eight broader classifications. If three or more of the items in a given classification are checked in the Essential and Very Important columns or in the Not Important or Little Importance columns, that classification is of significance and should receive more attention in later analysis.

Incidentally, it is a good idea to have your boss complete this column as well for your job. This will give you a good idea about how he looks at your job and provide a good starting point for a discussion of your initial career goals.

Column B of Figure 21 gives you an opportunity to indicate which of these activities you find intrinsically rewarding to you. In order to know this, you must have had some experience on this or some other assignment to know that the activity is personally satisfying. As you check these items, you may find it of value to keep asking yourself *why* you answer the way you do. The four subcolumns in Column B designate the following:

+ = more satisfying than unsatisfying.
0 = not particularly satisfying or unsatisfying.
− = more unsatisfying than satisfying.
N = no experience with this activity, so you
     don't know whether it would satisfy or not.

Column C of Figure 21 is a general time analysis for each of the activities and asks you to make judgments on how you spend your time. Here *H* stands for *high,* or something that you do frequently in a typical week; *M,* for *medium,* or an activity that you do occasionally in a given week; *L,* for *low,* or an activity that you pursue rarely or never in a given week.

Again, for this analysis you may want to get your boss's ideas of how much time he feels you should spend on these activities. That

* I am grateful to Seigmar Blamberg, Professor Emeritus of the University of Connecticut, for his discussions with me on the value of such an analysis for career development purposes.

information will serve as another good base for discussions with him on your job objectives.

Column D of Figure 21 asks you to make your own personal judgment of how well you perform those activities. *O* stands for *outstanding* (upper 10 percent of those who perform that same function); *S*, for *superior* (upper 30 percent); *A*, for *average*; *K*, for *satisfactory* but not average; *D*, for *need improvement* in this activity. Why not have your boss check you out on these activities as well?

Column E of Figure 21 asks you to indicate what kind of developmental experience you've had. *OJC* means that you had on-the-job coaching—that is, that someone has evaluated your on-the-job performance and given you help in developing that activity. *TI* means that you've taken actual training programs internally offered by your company. And *SO* indicates that you have taken special courses outside the company—self-study, correspondence courses, credit or noncredit courses, conferences, and the like. A given activity can have check marks in all three subcolumns depending on the extensiveness of your developmental experiences.

Finally, Column F of Figure 21 asks you to define what activities you think your ideal job would include. Checking under *E* means that you feel that the activity in question is essential in your ideal job and should fill a lot of your time; *A* means acceptable but not a steady diet; *N* means you'd prefer to do it never or only rarely.

We now have information on the following:

1. How important (IMP) you feel a given job activity is.
2. How much intrinsic satisfaction (SAT) that activity gives you.
3. How much time (TIM) you spend on that activity.
4. How well you think you perform (PERF) that activity compared with other people in the company.
5. How extensive your developmental experiences (DEV) have been with that activity.
6. How essential that activity is in your ideal (IDE) job.

These data will give you some excellent clues about potential areas of frustration with an activity and about possible career strategies to reduce those frustrations. At the same time, it will provide you with a good indication of your accommodation potential (ACC POT) for different activities—that is, your general sense of comfort with them and your potential for integrating them into your career structure.

We can expect that an individual's accommodation potential will be highest for activities that have high importance to him, that provide him with the highest satisfaction, on which he would spend most of his time, that he could perform especially well, for which he has been best developed, and that therefore will be part of his ideal job. To the extent that this relationship does not exist, we can predict some sense of conflict and therefore lower accommodation potential for the individual in that activity.

Hence if a person spends a minimum amount of time on a highly important activity because he's not been developed well in that area and therefore does not perform it well, we will expect low accommodation potential. If the activity remains high in importance, then the accommodation potential can be increased through a strategy of more developmental experiences that would improve performance, increase satisfaction, and undoubtedly lead to more time being spent on that activity.

Similarly, if a person has identified certain activities as essential for his ideal job but has had little or no developmental experiences in them, then obviously a strategy of training is called for. If his ideal job includes activities that bring him little or no satisfaction, then again we would raise serious questions about the dimensions of that ideal job. Or if a person judges his performance to be poor in areas where he has already had considerable developmental experiences, then he needs to take a closer look as to why his performance is poor.

Without trying to cover all of the possible combinations among the personal evaluations in Columns A–F of Figure 21, here are some hypotheses to consider:

High IMP and high SAT = high ACC POT
High IMP and high SAT and high TIM = high ACC POT
High PERF leads to high SAT which leads to high TIM = high ACC POT
High IMP and high DEV and high PERF leads to high SAT = high ACC POT
High SAT and high PERF and high DEV = high IDE
Low IMP and low SAT = low ACC POT
Low SAT leads to low TIM and low PERF = low ACC POT
High IMP and high PERF and low SAT = low ACC POT
High TIM and low PERF and low SAT = low ACC POT
High TIM and high PERF and low IMP = low ACC POT
High TIM and high SAT and high PERF = high ACC POT = high IDE

Let's take a different look at these concepts by studying the results of Ed Hastings, who went through these exercises. Figure 22 shows you where Ed Hastings put his check marks. Certain checks are circled to indicate clusters of consistency in the groupings. Three or more items checked in a similar subcolumn within a specific activities group are considered a reasonable clustering for further analysis.

We note first that Ed Hastings considers planning activities to be of little importance on his job (6 out of the 7 activities were so labeled). He's had no experience on the job with them, spends little or no time on them, judges his performance as low or needing improvement, and gives no indication of having had many developmental experiences. Yet he lists planning activities as being generally important in the ideal job as he describes it.

If he truly wants these activities as part of his future job, then his strategy must include some opportunities for developmental experiences and also for performance on a job so that he can determine his own performance effectiveness. One may wonder why these activities rate so high with him. The fact is that prior to his full-time employment he had a lot of positive experiences in college and in part-time positions with this type of activity and feels he'd like to pursue it in an industrial setting.

Note the clusters in the coordinating area. He reports a high sense of satisfaction with these activities, spends little time on them, believes he performs well in them, has had practically no developmental experience, but believes he'd like them in an ideal job. This suggests that he should try to develop a strategy whereby he could spend more time on these kinds of activities, obtain more developmental experiences, and keep testing his performance and satisfaction levels as he moves into his ultimate ideal.

Note also the supervising clusters. Ed sees these activities as essential in his present job, gets little satisfaction from them, spends a lot of time on them, judges his performance as average at best, and yet has had a lot of developmental experiences in this area. He does not see these activities as part of his ideal job.

This particular clustering finds its explanation in the fact that Ed works for a company that believes in developing all of its young college recruits to be "potential managers." He felt he had to go along with the company's wishes if he wanted to stay, and therefore he was forced to spend time in areas of real frustration for him. Unless he finds ways to avoid spending a lot of time on activities

Figure 22. Sample job activities analysis.

	Importance for Present Job					Intrinsic Satisfaction				Time Spent			Performance Judgment					Training			Importance for Ideal Job		
	NI	LI	SI	VI	E	+	O	I	N	H	M	L	O	S	A	K	D	OJC	TI	SO	E	A	N
Planning																							
1	✓			✓		✓					✓						✓		✓			✓	✓
2		✓							✓			✓					✓					✓	✓
3		✓							✓			✓					✓						✓
4		✓							✓			✓				✓			✓				
5	✓								✓			✓									✓	✓	
6	✓								✓			✓		✓	✓						✓		
7	✓	✓							✓			✓		✓							✓		
Investigating																							
8	✓								✓			✓									✓		✓
9				✓	✓			✓		✓								✓					✓
10								✓		✓						✓	✓	✓	✓				✓
11									✓			✓			✓	✓	✓	✓	✓			✓	
12		✓							✓			✓				✓	✓			✓			✓
13		✓	✓					✓	✓	✓		✓		✓					✓	✓			✓
14	✓								✓											✓			✓
Coordinating																							
15	✓	✓							✓			✓			✓					✓			✓
16		✓	✓	✓		✓						✓	✓	✓							✓		
17	✓					✓	✓				✓												
18						✓			✓			✓	✓	✓							✓	✓	✓
19			✓						✓			✓											✓
20			✓	✓		✓						✓	✓								✓	✓	✓

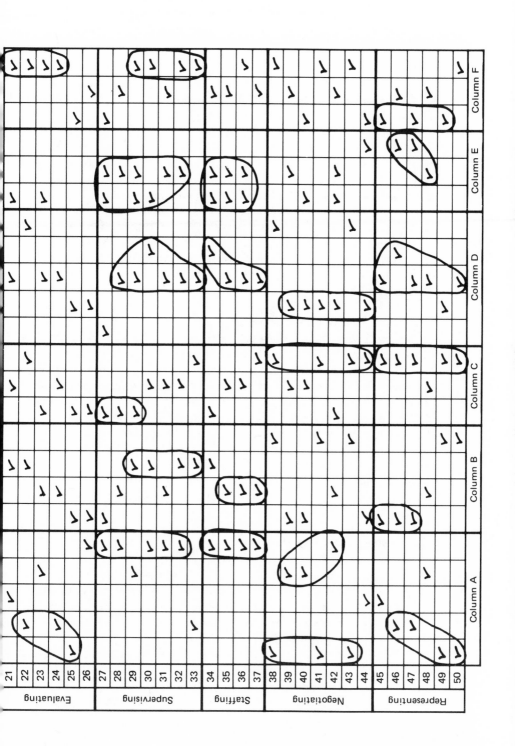

that he does not perform well and that are not satisfying to him, we predict continuing frustrations.

Finally, it can be seen that Ed Hastings includes as essential in his ideal job a broad cluster of "representing" activities. His present job assignments in this area tend to be satisfying to him. However, he spends little time with them and performs them only average. He will find it to his advantage to try to integrate these activities into his present job or to move into a job that requires these activities so that he can get some on-the-job coaching (now conspicuously absent) and thereby improve his performance. Improved performance will be important if he is to grow in his ideal job in this activity area.

This analysis of job activities gives some information to Ed Hastings about possible strategic moves. As he relates these data with other dimensions of strategy formulation, he will come much closer to developing a precise and effective course of action.

You can do the same kind of analysis. Figure 23 is provided as a means for you to list the specific clusters and the individual activities for each of the evaluation areas.

You will note that the last two columns of Figure 23 ask you to think about the different roles you could play by using various activities that are satisfying and important to you. Earlier in this chapter, we presented a classification of nine operational or technical areas in which individuals could perform their various activities. Within those operational areas you could perform strictly as a technical/professional person, or you could decide to move into management. This decision implies, of course, different roles, and your awareness of jobs in the organization, how they fit together, and what career paths lead to them or from them gives you clues as to likely roles for you to play, based on your job activities analysis.

Jobs and Individual Motives

Our chapter on motivation suggests that a good career strategy must respond to individual needs within a reality orientation. Behavior is self-motivated; personal needs must be satisfied. We may therefore ask what kinds of characteristics a job must have in order to meet the major motivations of a person.

In one sense, it is impossible to answer this question, because we might insist that each person is unique and that the needs that direct his behavior are different from those of other people. Hence we might conclude that each person must have a job specifically structured to his needs.

Figure 23. Job activities analysis: personal worksheet.

	Activities important now	Activities in which:		Activities important in my ideal job	Possible positions and roles (at work or away from work) that relate to my:	
	Activities that give me satisfaction now	I do well now	I need improvement		Present activities of satisfaction and importance	Ideal job
Activities in which I need preparation for the future roles at work and away from work						
The nature of the preparation needed and a plan of action (now and long-range) in order to reach current and future activity goals						

But this view is too extreme. First, it is possible to classify needs into categories that have some general validity for workers in our society today. Second, the career options actually pursued by people are a function of availability and accessibility and not solely of individual needs.

With this in mind we can describe some generally accepted prime motivations for individuals and relate these to appropriate job characteristics.* We should emphasize that individuals do not have just one of these needs; we usually have all of them, but in varying degrees. It is therefore a question of how strong these needs are and to what extent they give primary direction to our job searches.

1. *The person with a high need to achieve.* Affirmative answers to the following questions indicate that you have a strong need to achieve:

Do you consistently look for new ways to improve your performance?

Are you interested in doing things where doing better than others is a primary concern?

Do you consistently set high standards of performance for yourself?

Do you respond to difficult, challenging situations?

Do you try to find out how well you are performing by getting as much specific feedback as possible?

Do you stick to an assignment once you accept responsibility for it?

Are some of your activities involved in long-term career objectives?

If you have a high need to achieve you will typically like jobs with the following characteristics:

Latitude in setting your work pace and work methods.

Availability of help or direction from others.

Required skills that must be improved.

High standards of performance (as perceived by you).

*Our classification is based on George H. Litwin and Robert A. Stringer, Jr., *Motivation and Organizational Climate* (Boston: Graduate School of Business Administration, Harvard University, 1968) and *A Brief Scoring Manual for Achievement, Affiliation, and Power Motivation* (Boston: McBer and Company, 1970).

Opportunities for innovation and creativity.

Opportunities to know how well you are performing, with a sense of achievement coming from that feedback.

Opportunities to further your career.

Opportunities to learn from your mistakes and thereby improve your performance.

2. *The person with a high affiliation need.* Such individuals will typically give affirmative answers to the following questions:

Do you feel uncomfortable when you have to work alone for long periods of time?

Do you go out of your way to seek out situations where you can find out if you are liked and accepted by others?

Do you concern yourself with developing lasting friendships?

Are you concerned when there is a disruption of a positive inter-personal relationship?

Do you like to get involved in group projects?

Are you sensitive to other people, especially when you think they are angry with you?

Do you like to be invited to parties, reunions, or small relaxed bull sessions?

Do you try to get personally involved with your boss or others?

If you have a high affiliation need, you will typically like jobs in which:

There is a lot of opportunity to interact with people.

People seem to be happy.

You can get to know people.

Cooperation with others is required to get things done.

You can listen to people's problems and help them out.

3. *The person with a high power need.* Such individuals will typically give affirmative answers to the following questions:

Do you try to have influence on others?

Do you give help, assistance, advice, or support to others when they don't ask for it?

Do you try to influence other people by regulating their behavior or by obtaining important information that would affect their behavior?

Do you do things to or with others that arouse strong positive or
negative feelings—pleasure or delight, fear or worry—in them?
Are you concerned about your reputation or your position?
Do you enjoy a good argument?
Do you seek positions of authority because you'd like to give
orders rather than take them?
Do you try to take over?
Do you seek symbols of authority (such as titles or office
trappings that set you apart) in order to gain influence over
others?

If you have a high power need, you will typically like jobs in which:

You can personally direct the work of others.
Other people must come to you for decisions.
You will have some obvious status.
You have responsibility for seeing to it that things run smoothly.
You have to influence others to get things done.
You are required to deal directly with your boss and other
people in power positions.
You have control over the scheduling of your work.

Good Jobs and How to Spot Them

As we have noted repeatedly, the great majority of people seek
to satisfy their self-concept on the job. That is, they have a need for
competence, for recognition, for feeling needed, for growth, for responsibility, for a sense of adequacy. These, then, seem to be the
things that are important for a "good" or "enriched" job.

Specifically, recent studies* suggest that a good job will have
the following characteristics.

1. *Direct feedback.* There should be opportunities for frequent,
direct, and nonsupervisory feedback on how well you are doing. We
emphasize nonsupervisory feedback, not because you shouldn't
seek feedback from your supervisor, but because such feedback
should be obtained even when supervision is not available, and it
should come directly from those for whom your work was per-

---

* For instance, Nicholas J. DiMarco and Charles R. Kuehl, "Winning Moves in
Motivating Junior Staff," *SAM Advanced Management Journal,* Summer 1975, and
David A. Whitsett, "Where Are Your Enriched Jobs," *Harvard Business Review,*
January–February 1975.

formed. Hence if you are doing work for another department or another client, feedback from that source is more important than from your supervisor.

2. *A client relationship.* As suggested above, you should be responsible in your work to those who are affected by what you do. Developing relationships with those people or groups gives you an opportunity to see what your work is all about.

3. *A natural module of work.* You should know where your work begins and ends so that you know exactly what you are responsible for. If what you do is dependent on someone else or if the end product is not yours, then you will feel less responsibility for your performance.

4. *Personal accountability.* Responsibility for the end result should rest with you. This way you get a sense of identification with the job.

5. *Decision making and other control.* You should be able to make decisions and to control the resources you need in those areas that involve your immediate module of work. This will of course depend on your abilities and training and the extent to which others must necessarily be involved in a given task. This control should extend to the scheduling of work and the setting of priorities.

6. *Demand for a unique expertise.* The job should offer opportunities for you to grow, to learn specific things, and to develop unique skills and knowledge.

The evidence is fairly clear that a job that has these characteristics has some general appeal to most workers. You can still be unhappy in a job that offers all these things because, of course, job satisfaction rests on more than just job characteristics. Your boss, the organization's policies, the environment, or a better opportunity may act as factors that move you away from this kind of a job.

Nevertheless, other things being equal, these are characteristics to look for in jobs or to try to create in your present job. They can form the basis for discussions with your boss on what might be done to change the structure of your job or for some strategy decisions regarding what *you* can do to make your job more enriching. The chapters on interpersonal relations, the boss, and the organization, in addition to this chapter, may give you a number of important ideas on how to initiate action on your own.

With these characteristics of a "good job" in mind, David Whitsett suggests that the following things are indications that a job is *not* an enriching one.*

* Op. cit.

1. *Watch out for jobs that stress inspecting, checking, or reviewing.* Chances are that some other position has been deprived of responsibility for the quality of the work. Therefore, the checker's job is probably not a complete module of work, and the client relationship may be ambiguous.

2. *Watch out for jobs that have you handle someone else's errors.* Certain jobs require you to handle problems with customers or other departments. For instance, some companies have an office of consumer information—a place where customers can call to get information about products or register complaints. The job takes responsibility from the line function and places it in the hands of the people in this office. In other words, someone else's wrongdoing or responsibility to a client is transferred to this office. The office has no control over operations and therefore cannot prevent such errors. Both the office and the line function jobs are not as enriched as they could be.

3. *Watch out for jobs in departments emphasizing a high level of technical competence.* In such departments, the important jobs are given to people with a lot of technical or professional expertise, who are the fountainhead of all knowledge. When a big problem arises, it is turned over to them; they'll know how to handle it—and they do handle it. The problem is, of course, that this takes some of the decision making, growth and learning opportunities, and control functions away from the people who have to abandon the job to these experts. The job is enriching for the technician, but not for you.

4. *Watch out for jobs that take an inordinate amount of time for training.* Look somewhere else if you're told: "In this department we really can't tell whom we'll promote to an assistant management function for at least seven to ten years. The job is very complex, and only the most knowledgeable can handle it." Aside from the problem of deciding what a person needs to know before he can enter a first-level management function, it is highly unlikely that it takes that amount of time to "learn the job." Along the way there must be a lot of sameness, where learning is stifled.

5. *Watch out for jobs where you will be reporting to two people.* A person in such a job just doesn't know to whom he's responsible and what the priorities are, unless the people to whom he reports have a clear understanding of the job responsibilities and agree on the priorities.

6. *Watch out for jobs that are poorly delineated.* Some jobs are so complicated that it is unlikely that you'll ever finish an assignment. Since the work depends so much on what other people do or

don't do, control in the job is weakened, and the module of work is unclear.

7. *Watch out for jobs that overlap functions.* When this happens, no one really knows who is responsible for doing the part of the work that overlaps. In a large company that does "corporate planning," one person in a department is typically responsible for "financial planning," another person in another department, for "human resources planning," and still another person in still another department, for "strategic planning." Since these functions, out of necessity, will overlap, some of the work doesn't get done, and some of it is duplicated. Feedback and performance standards are confused.

8. *Watch out for jobs that don't change with a title change.* We mentioned earlier the tall, thin pyramidal organizational structure that organizations use to give an indication of career paths and status opportunities. But there is no sense of growth or of competence when you are promoted into a job that doesn't make new or greater demands on you.

And, of course, watch out for jobs that lack any of the characteristics of a "good job." That list of characteristics provides you with an appropriate checklist for talking to incumbents in a job, observing what people do in a job, and scrutinizing job descriptions, career paths, and the like.

A winner walks when he can, and
runs when he has to; a loser runs
when he doesn't have to, and is out of
breath when he should run.

Sydney Harris

12

The Organization

Its Impact on Commitment

THIS chapter will discuss some major differences in organizational design and the impact those designs have on jobs and individuals. We will then take a closer look at some important dimensions of organization climate and show how you can analyze an organization in that regard and, more importantly, what you can do about those dimensions in relation to your career strategy. Finally, we will examine what companies are now doing about various components of career strategy, suggest things that you can look for in order to analyze the organization from that viewpoint, and indicate what your commitment to action should be.

Open and Closed Organizations

Over the years there has been a considerable amount written about different kinds of organizational structures and their impacts on human behavior. Our classification here is a simple dichotomy between a mechanistic or closed organizational system and an organic or open system. The differences between the two systems are described here in terms of the perceptions and attitudes of the people in positions of power and control.

218

Closed System   *Open System*

CONTROL

The power person assumes that he has control and exercises his power over others to change their behavior. He keeps reminding his subordinates of his position.

The power person assumes that his subordinates know he's in the power role. He believes that he cannot exercise complete control but that subordinates control their own behavior and, therefore, the achievement of organizational objectives.

Control comes through discipline —the use of rewards and punishments, the exercise of fear and threat. "Let them know where the power is." "They won't do it on their own." "When the cat's away, the mice will play." "That's my job: to keep them in line." "I reward those who do well; those who don't do well know they're in trouble with me."

Control comes through training and development and through counseling of subordinates. If people know what needs to be done and how to do it, they will direct their own behavior. Self-control is the major determinant of direction of behavior. If an individual gets out of line, peer pressures and social sanctions will bring him back into the fold. There is a high correlation between a person's performance and the rewards he seeks.

Reporting forms, budgetary controls, rules and regulations, and procedures manuals let a worker know what is expected of him and keep the power person informed when anyone gets out of line.

While the power person has a healthy respect for necessary controls, he is skeptical about control systems as the ultimate solution to most organizational problems. His faith rests more with people than with systems.

GOALS

The power person accepts the idea that his goals are probably different from those of his subordinates, and he tries to work within that diversity. To find areas of mutual support is to deny the difference in roles and demands between the power person and the subordinate.

The power person strives to establish common goals for himself and the people under him. He accepts the idea that support for each other's goals will be necessary if the goals of each are to be reached.

Orientation is to the present. There's a job to do now. Training

Orientation is to the present *and* how it relates to the future. Train-

and development is done to develop those skills needed now. Crises are avoided by making sure that people know what and how to do what's needed now; future goals are too hazy to respond to now.

ing and development is used to provide opportunities for personal growth. Crises are avoided by preparing people for the future issues before they arise.

DECISION MAKING

The power person expects to make the decisions, especially the important ones. To ignore this is to abandon his role and to display weakness.

For developmental purposes, individuals at all levels should have an opportunity to make decisions about those aspects of their function that affect them directly. However, decision making by subordinates should be kept within boundaries that protect both the individual and the organization from severe consequences.

COMMUNICATIONS

Communications are unilateral. Relevancy of issues is decided at the power level. Whatever is communicated comes at the convenience of those in power. Feelings and social climate are unknown and/or disregarded.

Communication requires a mechanism for feedback. What's relevant is a function of the person receiving the communication. Communication is an ongoing process where feelings and social climate must be analyzed and understood.

Concerns are primarily upward: "I relate best to power, and my job is to do what my boss wants done."

Concerns are upward, downward, and horizontal, particularly where related functions may have a bearing on achievement of objectives: "I must respond to what is demanded of me, but I do this best through open communications with people at any level directly involved with my objectives."

Techniques are *directive;* control comes through carefully structured communications, job descriptions, and organization charts.

Techniques are nondirective. Jobs and organizations are structured to use people's strengths and permit achievement of personal as well as

Find out what needs to be done and then mold the person into the appropriate shape needed. Dissension and conflict must be discouraged. To show disagreement and to raise questions about management decisions is a sign of not being a good "team player." Consistency is a central value.

organizational goals. There is a reliance on "subtle signals" to provide direction and interest. Dissension is a natural human behavior. Conflicts should be confronted openly and in an atmosphere that conveys that the conflict will be resolved for the good of all. Differences in policies and procedures will be tolerated if it is for the good of the organization and others.

These descriptions might suggest that the closed system is not as supportive of career strategy concepts, as we have been discussing them, as the open system. While that is generally true, it should be kept in mind that systems and jobs are perceived by individuals— and it's the individuals' needs and values which ultimately determine the degree of comfort with a given organization. However, if your objectives include personal psychological growth, then the open system is undoubtedly the one to seek out and have work for you.

Edward Lawler has provided us with some insights into this relationship between job design, organizational design, and a person's need to grow.* Here are some of the factors that, according to Lawler, determine the sense of comfort or discomfort of an individual in a given job.

If you have a *low need for growth* and are employed in a *closed, mechanistic organization,* then:

■ In a routine job, you will probably perform at an adequate level, particularly if you are satisfactorily rewarded monetarily.

■ In an enriched job, you will probably not respond effectively to the demands of the job and will express some confusion because the demands made on you by the organization often differ from those made by your immediate job.

If you have a *low need for growth* and are employed in an *open organization,* then:

* *Motivation in Work Organizations,* Monterey, Cal.: Brooks/Cole Publishing Company, 1973.

■ In a routine job, you will probably perform adequately if the extrinsic rewards are satisfactory, but you'll feel uneasy about management and its seeming inconsistency and unpredictability.

■ In an enriched job, you will be initially confused by both organizational and job demands. Unless the organization has the patience to work with you carefully to develop your growth needs so that you'll be taught how to succeed in your job, you will be unhappy and either withdraw or grow hostile; in either case, inadequate performance will result.

If you have a *high need for growth* and are employed in a *closed organization,* then:

■ In a routine job, you will feel underemployed, overcontrolled, and dissatisfied with your job; performance will decline and frustration will increase, leading to withdrawal, absenteeism, and possibly hostility.

■ In an enriched job, you will perform well but will be concerned about the "kind of organization" you are in and will try to change it to remove the frustrations.

If you have a *high need for growth* and are employed in an *open organization,* then:

■ In a routine job, you will feel underemployed and try to change the design of your job; if you don't succeed, you'll withdraw.

■ In an enriched job, you will be highly motivated to perform well, and your enthusiasm for both the company and the job will be high.

We stress these relationships here to make you more aware of the deeper reasons for your feelings in a particular job. It's important to distinguish among personal needs, organizational and job factors, and their impact on us. If we're not careful, we'll point a blaming finger at the job and try to change that, only to find that changes there don't resolve the feeling of discomfort. Not uncommonly, we think we're different from what we are and seek out organizations or jobs that are in conflict with our basic self.

To wax philosophical for a moment, it is likely that we are going to find in the future more people who are underemployed with respect to their abilities and training. While organizations can still do much to redesign jobs in an attempt to respond to these variations in the work force, the limitations of capital resources, the rising technology, and the growing numbers in the worker market make it unlikely that companies will respond directly to the higher-level needs of employees. Workers will have to rely more on their own ingenuity to respond to these problems. They will have to do things on their own in their jobs, be agents for change in the organization, and be more aware of what's important to them and to the organization and the society to which they are responsible.

Organizational Climate

Just as the weather may affect our behavior—rain and snow retard some activities, sun and clear skies seem to buoy our spirits—so, too, the climate of the organization affects the behavior of its members. Let us take a closer look, then, at some of the dimensions of organizational climate with two questions in mind: (1) what should I look for in the organization to determine whether the organization rates high or low on that dimension? (2) what can I do to have an effect on that dimension if I want to change it?

There are many different approaches to the study of organization climate; we will follow one that is based on the work of McBer and Company.*

1. Conformity

People in organizations that emphasize conformity find that it's difficult to get their ideas accepted and that people are more interested in the rules and regulations than in getting the job done.

How to detect high conformity: Look for these factors: difficulty in getting ideas considered; procedures and policies that get in the way of doing the job; management that is highly oriented toward formal organization and lines of authority and deals severely with deviations from policy; and people who generally "toe the line" and do what the rules say.

What you personally can do about it: When you think your ideas are good, but likely to be resisted by the organization, make your appeal on the basis of facts and specific data. Depersonalize your proposals and make sure they center on *key tasks* necessary to reach organizational goals. Learn how to listen to others so you can understand their objections and respond to them. If you're convinced

---

* *Organizational Climate Survey Questionnaire: Scale Definitions and Profile,* revised edition, Boston: McBer and Company, 1975.

your idea is good, be persistent but flexible in pursuing it. Try to find some person with power who likes your idea. Take the risk and implement your ideas without approval, but only after weighing the potential damage to you and the organization if they fail.

When you think there are unnecessary rules that get in the way of your doing your job, determine whether the rules are prompted by law; if so, accept them as reality of the system. Know what it is that needs to be done, get an agreement on standards of performance, and then do it your best way—with an assurance on your part that standards will be met. Present your boss with new sets of procedures, but depersonalize them and don't put him in the position of having to question his objectives; rather, cater to his objectives and show him how he can get his job done better.

When there is an overemphasis on organizational hierarchy, understand your strengths and cater to them in job design. Volunteer for new responsibilities, but define them carefully in your own mind before you volunteer. Encourage your boss to create task forces that cut across departmental or divisional lines. Try to do those things that complement your boss's weaknesses; take on things that he doesn't want to do or has been ignoring (he'll bring you into his fold when he sees you have his interests at heart). And generally, don't wait for the other person or the organization but initiate action yourself!

2. Responsibility

People in organizations that emphasize the responsibility dimension feel that they have a lot of responsibility delegated to them and that they can do their jobs without too much checking with the boss.

How to detect low responsibility: Look for these factors: bosses who want their subordinates to check everything with them, even when the approach is agreed upon; subordinates who aren't given much opportunity to make individual judgments or to take calculated risks; a general feeling that, if you want to get ahead, you can't stick your neck out; people waiting to be told what to do. Such organizations rarely produce new ideas, and good people tend to leave them after a while.

What you personally can do about it: When there's no delegation, don't rely only on yourself to get your job done: delegate to others to show them that you have faith in them; that may encourage others to try. If you know what has to be done and you have faith in your performance, swallow hard and do it without asking the boss first. Learn how to confront the boss, particularly if you have been performing well and both you and he know it. If he fails to delegate, try to build up the trust level in order to obtain increased responsibilities. Get a clear understanding from your boss on objectives and performance standards. Volunteer for assignments elsewhere (within or outside the company) that will provide you with greater responsibility.

When risk-taking is low, push for higher standards and convince your boss that you can meet them. Know your own strengths and center your job activities around those strengths. Help the boss in his areas of weakness so he can see that more can be done; in that way he may set higher standards. Help in every way to make the boss a winner and increase his self-esteem; in that way he'll be more willing to take calculated risks. Make your appeals on the basis of fact and data, not emotion; show in specific terms what the actual risk might be. (But make sure that you'll be comfortable in a risk situation.) And again, don't wait for others; initiate action yourself!

3. Standards

People in organizations that rate high on the standards dimension feel that the company has high expectations for its employees to do a good job and encourages them to set challenging goals.

How to detect low standards: Look for lack of emphasis by management on improving performance; people not taking much pride in their work; standards of performance that are average or below; management goals that are not challenging; achievement-oriented people leaving or being highly frustrated; and plateauing or declining share of market.

What you personally can do about it: When there is a lack of emphasis on improving your performance and setting challenging goals, set your own goals, on and off the job, that have developmental potential, and keep monitoring your progress. Keep your boss informed—by reference to trade journals, news articles, and so on—about changes and innovations in the field. Make changes to improve your operations. Attend seminars and other meetings to keep up to date. Associate with innovative and creative people. Ask to be sent to company or other training programs. Volunteer for new assignments that require further development. Even if standards for performance remain the same, set your own goals on

the job to try to meet these standards more effectively and efficiently. Keep aware of your own strengths and how they relate to a
changing environment.

When there is no pride in the work, develop a feedback system
that gives you more immediate information on how well you are
doing. Seek out appraisals from your boss and others. Be aware of
your accomplishments and talents. Develop more short-term goals.
Try to perform in areas where probability of success is high. Get
involved in activities that have high importance to the power
figures and are essential to the achievement of corporate purpose.
Try to use your strengths and maximize their impact on your performance. Work with peers in a cooperative atmosphere where you
can provide feedback to each other. And once again, don't wait for
others but initiate action yourself!

4. Rewards

People in organizations that rely heavily on rewards to get
things done feel that they are being properly recognized and rewarded for good performance; threat and punishment for failure are
not nearly so apparent.

How to detect a reward-orientation: Look for emphasis on encouragement rather than on threat and criticism; a promotion system where people rise to the top not because of seniority but because of the quality of their performance; a compensation system that
is competitive with at least the average of the industry; people in
the organization who are less preoccupied with status trappings and
more with doing their jobs; few titles and differences in job demands from one level to the next; a willingness to take risk without
fear of failure and a management structure that supports this philosophy and encourages development when a worker fails to reach an
ambitious goal; signs that people are willing to commit themselves
to a course of action.

What you personally can do about it: Within some limits, set
your own reward structure (like treating yourself to something
you'd not ordinarily have) for whenever you reach a stretch goal. Be
aware of what rewards are really important and long-lasting for you.
Request frequent and *specific* information from your boss about
your performance and how you can improve it. Get into projects
outside work that provide recognition for a job well done. Collect
facts to determine if the reward structure in your organization is
really different from the industry; sometimes perceptions don't

match reality. Get other people to keep power persons informed about inequities between performance and reward. Ask your boss for "rewarding" assignments during your discussions with him about inequities between performance and reward. Ask your boss reward you another way—say, through special training programs, trips, contacts with new people on new jobs. Be persistent but not threatening in your observations about the *system;* stay with facts, not emotion. Make sure you gain the perspective of the key people who administer the policy so you can determine what their rationale is for the policy; from their broader perspective, the problem may seem different. Whenever people help you or do something nice for you, let them know that you appreciate their efforts. Try to set up feedback systems that give you information about your progress toward goals. And again, don't wait for others; initiate action yourself!

5. Clarity

People in organizations that place a high value on clarity have the feeling that things are well organized and that they know what is expected of them.

How to detect low clarity: Look for people who don't know what's expected of them in the organization; lines of authority and corporate policies that are poorly defined; indications that productivity is not what it should be because of poor planning and lack of organization; signs that people don't know what the corporate objectives are and how the objectives of their own division fit into them; lack of communication between bosses and subordinates regarding the nature of the job and objectives; subordinates who are anxious about their relationship with their bosses; signs that people don't take policy changes very seriously because they "know" it's just a passing fancy and not in keeping with any perceived objectives; people who are confused as to why their unit, division, or company is organized the way it is.

What you personally can do about it: Be willing to admit that you don't understand a particular assignment and ask for clarification. When you work with someone else, get clarification ahead of time regarding end results and measurements for them. When you give someone else an assignment, make sure he understands what he is supposed to do. Describe to your boss what you think your job is, have him do the same thing independently for your job, and then see how well you agree. Keep the boss informed on what you are doing, what you're about to do, and what you have done, and be assured that if you're doing things that are not "right," he'll let you know. Ask for regular sessions with your boss to determine objectives and standards for a given period.

Read company and divisional literature, speeches by top executives, and so on—anything that will help you understand what the company is and wants to be. Make contacts with other people in power positions and be sensitive to what they say about the corporation or the division. Be willing to accept the fact that there may be differences of understanding and difficulties in communicating objectives; don't make evaluative judgments about misunderstandings but try to get to the reasons for them and attack their cause. Be clear in your own mind about your own objectives and communicate them to those people who should know. And, as always, don't wait for others but initiate action yourself!

6. Team Spirit

People in organizations that stress team spirit have the feeling that people in the organization are warm and trusting, that there is a sense of pride and identity with the organization, and that there is a good relationship among the people in the work environment.

How to detect low team spirit: Look for a large number of people who are cool and aloof, particularly when it comes to talking about company issues and problems; a lack of personal loyalty to and pride in the company; a high degree of formality in the relationships between managers and subordinates; a lack of warmth in the working relationships; a lack of willingness to be open with people; a highly "political" working environment; a sense of competition rather than cooperation among colleagues; turnover to other companies in the same industry because "I like the people better; it's a nicer place to work"; lack of willingness to help others when the going gets tough; and a general lack of interaction among the members of a working group.

What you personally can do about it: Practice consciously and conscientiously to develop a more trusting relationship with the people with whom you interrelate (see the chapter on interpersonal relations for clues). Practice the same simple social amenities at work as you would in situations outside work. Ask people with whom you work for advice and help. Be willing to listen without making evaluations. Praise people, including your boss, when they do something good for you or for others. Let people know what their strengths are and how they can use them better. Share common experiences with people at work. Go out of your way to congratulate people who are promoted. Whenever possible, get face-to-face contact with people. Seek assignments that will require you to work with others.

When a work group's sense of identity is low, let your boss know (but depersonalize the problem) and help him figure out ways to increase team spirit. Get other people in the work group together and discuss the issues with them—find out, for example, whether you are expecting too much. Dispense with the formal communications process in memos and in personal relationships and try to develop more informal techniques; for instance, where titles get in the way of effective cooperation, it may be best to de-emphasize or altogether ignore them. Remember that power people are human, too, and need acceptance. And don't wait for others; initiate action yourself!

As we have looked at these dimensions of organizational climate, it will have become apparent that there is interaction among them; each impacts on the other, and activity at one level will have repercussions on all other levels. The organization, then, is not only the organization; it includes the jobs, the people, and the process of work itself. It is, in fact, a system.

You function within that system. You influence the system, and it influences you. When you work with your boss to improve the clarity dimension, for example, it not only changes clarity but also affects your boss, your job, the people who also work with your boss, policies and procedures, and people outside your immediate environment. The movement may be—and usually is—unnoticeable at first; but as all these changes emerge, they create a dramatic snowball effect.

What is important is not that we "move" or change the entire organization. It is the concerted effort of many people over a longer period of time that increases the probability of such changes occurring. But it is important that we try to move or change that part of the organization that affects us and our effectiveness. Bosses, jobs, and immediate climates can be changed to help serve common purpose. But ultimately it is only our own sense of effectiveness that leads us to higher self-esteem. And we have a lot to say about how effective we can be as individuals in our working environment.

The Personnel Function and Individual Commitment to Careers

Within any given organizational climate, major technical and operational functions are being carried out in support of organization goals. These include manufacturing, marketing, finance, control, and human resources. The human resources functions are directly related to the careers of individuals and therefore play a vital role within the total system. In this section we will focus on those personnel activities that have direct bearing on your career. The intention here is to discuss not so much what an organization *should* do to enhance your career as what most organizations are actually doing in their personnel functions, how this affects individual career actions, and what you can do about it.

Recruitment and Selection

The reality. We have yet to see recruiting literature that paints anything but a rosy picture of the corporation, the positions available, and the people in it. All the graphs depicting "success" go up; all the "failure" graphs go down. After all, the literature is designed to sell the potential employee on considering that company further. And what the literature doesn't supply, the recruiter will. Recruiting interviewers spend most of their time talking with the attractive applicant about the "exciting, challenging opportunities," the "variety of jobs available," the "phenomenal success of a person just like you who came from the same college just two years ago." As a result, they frequently sell expectations that deny the reality of most jobs.

Apart from the selling problem of the recruiting interview, the training of the recruiter looms high as another hurdle. Most companies have so many people involved in the selection process ("After all, we've got to get this candidate around to meet as many people in the organization as possible; that way we'll have more inputs for our selection decision") that few have had the kind of in-depth training that would enable them to gather meaningful information about the applicant and to interpret those data. The result is that typically the decision as to whether you are suitable for a job in a given organization is made by people who are guided more by "gut feeling" than by facts.

This is compounded by the fact that a recruiter is usually given information only about the company and the jobs available. How those jobs might fit together and to what kinds of *careers* they might lead is a more complicated scenario to which many recruiters are not trained to be sensitive. Yes, they can recite for you job paths ("You'll be a management trainee for 6 to 12 months, then you'll be promoted to assistant supervisor for another 1 to 3 years, from there to supervisor . . ."), but they can't talk with you about total careers. Somehow you have to find this out for yourself.

Your commitment. Because of these inadequacies, the responsibility for assessing an organization and the career opportunities it offers rests primarily on your shoulders. And you cannot make a meaningful analysis unless you know what your career goals are. Without that awareness, the data provided you cannot be properly evaluated.

Since the data you are receiving will be biased (just as those you give the recruiter will be!), you should have a carefully worked out set of questions that will provide you with the necessary information to make a good career decision. Go back to the chapters on formulating and implementing a strategy and take a closer look at some of those self-analysis questions. They will give you clues as to what you need to ask people in the organization about the potential job and how it relates to what is important to you. Further ideas for the right questions to ask may be found at the beginning of this chapter and in Chapter 12.

Initial Orientation

The reality. The early stages with a new organization are critical. It is a time when most of the attitudes about the people and the organization are developed and the first steps toward learning the required skills are made. And yet, in many organizations it is a very haphazard time for the new recruit. Challenging assignments are slow in coming because "you've got to learn the business first, and that takes a while because it's a complicated process. So be patient, work hard, and you'll be given more responsibility as soon as we see how you make out."

Orientation, then, involves getting acquainted with the company's history, acquiring a smattering of knowledge about the various departments and divisions of the company, and then attending a preplanned series of training programs to learn the necessary skills for the initial job. It is as if the company had forgotten all about that very careful selection process it went through to learn all about the unique strengths and experiences you bring to the job. All trainees are dropped into the same funnel to be carefully poured into the mold that the company, with its years of experience, considers appropriate for its new recruits.

This early orientation before you are settled into a job takes somewhere around one to three years, depending on the company. It is during that period that the company is careful to communicate to you the dimensions of each of the early jobs, what it expects you to do in order to grow into them, how you will be measured, and what standards will be expected of you in order to move in the organization. As our "virtue of a better fertilizer" suggested in Chapter 2, it is the honeymoon period. When you sense that the honeymoon is over, you start asking in more conscious ways, "What's this marriage all about, anyway?"

Your commitment. One thing to remember is that this is an orientation period for both you *and* the company. It is a time, therefore, to initiate those actions that will inform the organization of the kind of person you are, the interests you have, and the initial exposures you feel are essential for your own development. Of course, that will be impossible or tenuous if you have not gone through some initial analysis prior to taking the job.

This is the time for you to make a point of learning as much as you can not only about the job you're in but also about the kinds of development programs that the organization carries on in other functions. Some awareness of the other career possibilities in the organization will help you make the next career decision a more valid one.

This is what Sam Lewis did. Recently hired by a large financial institution and having gone through the typical orientation to each of the major functions, he planned a series of meetings with some key people in each of the functions that he thought would be especially appropriate for somebody with his strengths and interests. In the spare time he had in the training programs (and most work weeks have some slack built into them), Lewis would telephone a key person, introduce himself, and continue with: "I was very much impressed with the information I received in the orientation program about your function. It sounds like an exciting one, and as a new person in the organization, I'd like to learn more about it. As I inquired around, I'm led to understand that you're the best person to fill me in on the major activities of that function. I'm wondering if you'd have some free time soon to spend a few minutes with me and share with me what you do?"

A flattering inquiry that's difficult to refuse! In this way Sam Lewis (1) learned a lot more about the company, (2) made contacts with relatively important people, and (3) increased his visibility tremendously. Since he was an impressive young man with apparent purpose, he moved into the consciousness of a lot of people who were in positions to make career choices for new people in the organization.

With this new-found information, Sam then did the next important thing: he started doing some planning for job changes into an area that he thought would be better suited to him. To give his present training a "chance," he stuck with it, because he couldn't be sure just what it would eventually bring. But he did some contingency planning as well.

We applaud Sam for this. Companies tend to think in one-career-path syndromes, expecting people to move in only one division. Inter-department transfers are offered to a chosen few at best, and inter-department orientations are carried out, if at all, as a kind of necessary evil. The responsibility for finding out what's available is really left to the person who is committed to action, who takes charge.

Training and Development

The reality. The most effective kind of personal development occurs in an atmosphere in which an individual is given a problem (a real-life one) and is told to learn whatever tools he thinks he needs in order to solve the problem. Available to him are physical resources and the supportive hands of people who have had experience and know something about that problem but are willing to let the trainee commit himself to a course of action, even if they think it is in error, so that he can learn from his mistakes. Making mistakes in early learning in a supportive climate is a major key to effective development.

Most companies don't operate that way. The management trainee is placed in a world of competition with other trainees; he may even be in a probationary period where his performance is watched very closely and only the "fittest" survive. Acquisition of knowledge of training materials is given higher priority than the effective and innovative use of that information. "Good" present performance is stressed over good potential performance. "After all," says management, "it is a dog-eat-dog world, and we've got to put these people to the test. They're not kids anymore, and they've got to learn the bumps and bruises of the tough competitive world of business."

As we noted in Chapter 1, trends are changing—but they're not changing fast enough to catch up with most young people who are debating their early career choices right now. There is evidence that some of the larger corporations are responding to the developmental issues with more challenging initial jobs under the tutelage of capable people-oriented supervisors who have demonstrated their talents for developing people. Assessment centers or other practices that better match talents to opportunities are emerging. Still hazy are the formal and informal counseling procedures that are so much a part of the developmental process.

On the whole, companies still are not doing the job of providing their managers with the necessary training in coaching for *career* development; some are stressing the interviewing process for management by objectives sessions and for performance appraisal. But personal career counseling is wanting.

A good indication of present trends is the spending of millions of dollars every year by companies in their educational reimbursement programs. Employees are encouraged to take credit or noncredit courses related to their jobs and are reimbursed for tuition and books—in some companies, totally, in others, some preannounced percentage. The point is that little or no counseling is available to employees before, during, or after the courses are taken. While we can never doubt the value of added experiences in the developmental process, we can question whether enrolling in courses without careful counseling is the optimum use of time and resources.

We are seeing more signs of corporations training managers in the behavioral dimensions of their jobs; we are not seeing corporations rewarding managers for better people management per se. Where we do see rewards being handed out is in the general area of EEO requirements—and that strategy works! Companies like General Motors, Ford, or General Electric that set objectives—often tough ones—in this area and reward managers for doing the expected job get the desired results.

Your commitment. If the company isn't doing the necessary things, your options are (1) to try to get them to do those necessary things (a strategy that is admirable and should be pursued, but not alone); (2) to leave and find another company that has these things (probabilities are not in your favor that you'll find many companies like that, so your problem will probably still exist); or (3) to try to do some things on your own.

The last is the cat that I keep putting on your back. As you keep having these new business experiences—new jobs, new training, new acquaintances—you are changing. Periodic checks on yourself, along the lines of our recommendations in the previous chapters, become essential. New self-evaluations and awareness of opportunities and risks may lead to new career strategies, different developmental needs, and relationships with different people.

The formula for your commitment is brief and simple. I recognize that the doing of it is not so brief and not so simple. I urge you nevertheless to give it a try.

Evaluation, Rewards, and Placement

The reality. Earlier in this chapter we discussed these items at length as factors contributing to climate (see especially the sections on standards, rewards, and clarity). That discussion gave you specific ideas about what you can do to change negative conditions. The fact is that more corporations are concerned about establishing the right relation between performance and the reward structure and about finding the right ways to evaluate performance.

What is not yet clear is to what extent corporations are interested in the evaluation-reward processes as they relate to career planning. There is evidence that some corporations are showing a greater concern about career management.* Research is wanting in many areas, especially as to the impact of company practices on career planning and strategy. We know more about what companies are *not* doing and what they probably *should* do.

Companies are starting to be concerned with job redesign and job enrichment; they are less concerned with *career* enrichment. We are beginning to get glimmers of interest in *contractual arrangements,* especially for key people; in the concept of *tenure* for individuals who are evaluated at some earlier stage of their career on rather strict standards; in *skill banks* and *tracking systems* that take a closer look at what the employee may be able to offer in a wider variety of jobs within the company; in *personalized compensation packages* that link the compensation for an individual to a variety of benefits that are attractive to him; in *job posting* and other *self-nomination* systems that put more onus on the employee to initiate interest in his placement and/or development; and in *joint ap-*

* See for instance Douglas T. Hall, *Careers in Organizations* (Pacific Palisades, Cal.: Goodyear Publishing Company, 1976), especially Chapter 6, "Redesigning Organizations for More Effective Career Management."

praisals where subordinates evaluate their superiors and superiors are expected to respond to the valid concerns of their people.

The larger, more people-oriented growth companies are finding that these practices pay off in increased productivity, cost reductions, lowering of absenteeism and turnover, innovativeness in jobs, and the like. And the payoffs for the employees are more satisfying careers, better personal growth, and increased self-esteem.

The probabilities of your finding these practices in corporations are increasing but still far from high. As the concept of quality of life in our society keeps shifting and as people increasingly demand opportunities for self-actualization, corporations will be forced to pay closer attention to these matters. The day of the human resources professional as an influential member of the corporate family is fast approaching.

Your commitment. Again, the key is awareness of what's important to you. For example, a corporate policy of job posting has little value for you unless you know what you want. By the same token, joint appraisals put you in a delicate balance with your supervisor if you don't really understand the kind of climate that would be best for you or if you don't know the value of a trust relationship.

Granted, you can't do it all. But that cat's still on your back.

Leaving: Termination, Retirement, and Internal Transfer

The reality. Companies need to know more about why their people leave. The typical termination interview by the line and/or staff function makes it difficult for the employee to express the "real" reason, particularly if it is of a personal nature. "Better pay," "better opportunities," "more in keeping with personal lifestyle"—these are generalities that really don't tell corporations why the person even considered another position.

The "hidden agendas" are becoming more apparent as companies are starting to provide more attractive packages for early retirement. "Golden rainbow" retirement inducements that permit individuals to retire ten or more years before the prescribed date of 65 or 62 are showing corporations that it's the individual with the enlarging lifestyle, the person who knows what he really wants from life, who is taking advantage of these inducements. He can readily see the excitement and challenge of a different career path. The less purposeful, the shelf-sitter, the person the corporation would like to see retire hangs in there.

Again, there are glimmers of changes. Corporations are doing more to make palatable—in terms of perception by others and in terms of award to the person—a shift from a higher-status position to one of lower status, so that individuals don't feel compelled to stay in a job that is constantly aggravating to them. Preretirement clinics are starting to pop up, but few within corporate corridors. Outplacement programs in some companies help the person who is leaving find another suitable full-time or part-time position that is in keeping with his aspirations.

At the Harvard Business School there is now a popular course for students and spouses in which both are expected to work together toward understanding and developing a life/career plan—a strategy that best reflects the needs, strengths, and wants of each as individuals and of both as a unit. Such involvement of spouses at the corporate level is limited at best; it is a wave of the future.

Your commitment. We progress through stages in our careers, and at each stage a reassessment can affirm our dedication to our career strategy. If you've been practicing what has been prescribed herein, your activities today are tied in some definite or vague way to the future. The future, then, does not suddenly come upon you as a surprise, as a sudden barrier to be hurdled. Second, third, or fourth career options are more apparent to you, and the preplanning has set the stage for your entry into them.

Within that context, you owe it to yourself, of course, to know *well* in advance of retirement or transfer just what that change will mean to you and to those with whom you interact most directly. Retirement plans and benefits, preretirement seminars, skill and information seminars for those new activities in the new career, reassessment of your strengths based on these new experiences—all these must get your attention. Companies, communities, churches, schools, and friends can make opportunities available; but only you can decide the direction of your behavior. That direction demands awareness of purpose; and awareness of purpose demands self-assessment.

13

The Individual

A Case Study

IN THIS chapter we will take a closer look at the person as a product of the many environmental forces acting on him. In previous chapters we have been doing something similar, but there we took a particular slice of the total issue of career strategy—the job, the organization, the boss—or considered factors that cut across all of these. Here we will take a longitudinal view of one person, starting with his family background and proceeding to his college years and the early part of his career with his first company. We will try to analyze the events, develop some hypotheses for further scrutiny, and conclude with some indications of appropriate career action plans.

Women and Careers

Our case will center around a male, Ed Hastings. Before we get into it, however, it is appropriate to make some comments about women and their careers. Do the same rules and processes apply?

As the research data accumulate, we are becoming more aware

of the issues that may be more relevant to women in careers. Here are a few:

1. The entry of more women into the work force and the changing concept of careers for both men and women have opened up greater options for both sexes. In the past, women "have had more freedom not to be employed, or to be employed part time, as alternatives to full-time employment." * The implications for the need for formal career strategy planning are apparent.

2. The stereotype of what the female should and should not do in the world of work has created strong conflicts in both men and women when women seek careers outside the stereotyped roles. Women who seek them do so with some self-doubt and fear of discrimination and failure, and men who have to deal with the entry of women into their role domain express a concern about "how to act."

These apparent conflicts need resolution if people are to perform optimally. They also imply the potential for lack of satisfaction in a career unless the woman enters a career fitting her and society's perceptions of her "appropriate" career role. The options are fewer but gradually increasing in number.

3. Because of their background, the expectations of women are different. In an unpublished study, I found that women tend to establish lower levels of aspiration and lower expectations of what they can do than do their male counterparts. Until recently, women were not encouraged to broaden their horizons about careers. Neither were they encouraged to develop their strengths and skills beyond those needed to carry on only certain jobs in society. The result, understandably, was the setting of lower standards of achievement. This, happily, is changing.

Martina Horner found evidence in women for what she labeled "a disposition to become anxious about achieving success."† She found that many women avoided success by doing worse in competition with men. There is the case of the young adolescent girl who was competing with boys of her own age group in a physical skill. She won the contest, burst into tears, and cried, "I'm sorry! I didn't mean to!"

As society encourages women to enter more competitive situations, we would hope to see a diminishing of that feeling.

4. As women show greater upward career mobility, their con-

---

* Douglas T. Hall, op. cit., p. 34.
† "Toward Understanding of Achievement-Oriented Conflicts in Women," *Journal of Social Issues*, 28 (1972), p. 159.

flicts, in large measure, are similar to the conflicts of the male. Conflicts between job and career, between family and career, between job and personal development start gnawing at them. The concerns stem largely from the role conflicts that society subtly forces on us. And as a result, incidence of symptoms of physiological and psychological stress in women is growing.

5. A major problem that women face and that is quite different for men in business is the absence of adequate role models for women. The number and distribution of women at higher levels of organizations are relatively small; indeed, in many organizations they're still not represented. As a result, when a woman has to make the decision of placing herself or being placed on the career ladder, she has no model against whom she can make appropriate comparisons, to whom she can go for counsel, or who can be used as an effective "sounding board." The career woman is pretty much on her own, creating her own book of strategy and procedures. Because there is more risk inherent in such a pioneering effort, it requires a more supportive environment.

6. Whether such an environment exists in most organizations is still questionable. It appears that women who move into management are abandoned just as much as men, if not more so. New male managers frequently complain that they are tossed into the responsibilities of managing without being given any training on how to do it or what it is that is expected of them in the management role. At least they have other managers with whom to commiserate.

Women managers, on the other hand, tend to be a statistic, another member to help meet the federal regulations. Hence there is a danger that, once the spot is filled, they are abandoned and the organization's expectations for their performance are even lower than for male managers.

That appears to be a cruel hoax and may well be denied by many organizations. Nevertheless, there is that gnawing question in the minds of many women who succeed: Have I succeeded because of what I've done or because I'm a woman?

A Case History: Ed Hastings

Five years ago Ed Hastings joined the field staff of the Excelsior Insurance Company in Philadelphia. At the time he remarked to a friend of his that it seemed like the right thing to do.

"You know how it is. You go to college and get a liberal arts education. It prepares you for everything and yet nothing in particular. All I knew was that after I was through with college, I wanted to work in some business. Not that I particularly had in mind a sales job, mind you. But I knew that I liked to work around people: I like to talk with them; I like the idea of getting them to work with me, of meeting them and getting to know them. Working in the sales end of a business seemed to be one of the best places for that."

Ed looked forward to his interviews with company recruiters with great enthusiasm. He enjoyed the prospect of meeting people from different companies and of learning something about the various opportunities available to a person like him. He recalls that he had a difficult time making a choice among the many offers he received. After visits to six different offices, he finally chose Excelsior.

"A lot of my friends thought I was crazy. The salary wasn't as high as some of the other offers I received, but neither was it out of line. In fact, I was hard pressed to see a real difference among the various companies: they all seemed to have good training programs, good pay scales, opportunities for growth, and an excellent history of growth and profit. Company literature didn't seem to help much, either.

"In the last analysis, I guess, I was impressed with the caliber of the people at Excelsior. I enjoyed my day with them. They seemed to like their jobs. They knew what they were doing, where they were going, and were enthusiastic about it. I just felt I could fit in better there than in any of the other places and make the most of my talents."

His choice of job was based on a different set of criteria from those for his choice of college. Dickinson was close to home, and that helped a lot to reduce the travel costs. Ed knew that he was being sent to college at considerable financial sacrifice by his parents, so he wanted to minimize that as much as possible. Summer jobs and part-time work during high school and college provided the funds for most of his education, although his parents did have to go into some savings. But they all agreed that going to a highly selective school like Dickinson, even if it was more expensive, meant more than an education from the local community college. This was for the long pull, and a sacrifice now would pay greater dividends later.

Ed's father never had the opportunity for a college education, but one would never know it after talking with him. He was an avid reader and would talk with anyone who would be interested in discussing the issues of the day. His small grocery store served as a vehicle for meeting with neighbors, friends, and salesmen more than for making a profit. Ed's mother worked closely with his father and kept most of the books for the business. But she still managed to find time for a lot of church work and seemed to be the one person to whom many in the town turned for help when there was any kind of trouble.

At college, Ed managed to find time for just about everything: studies, rap sessions with the gang, extracurricular activities, volunteer work, and a part-time job. Although he would have liked to get a varsity letter in some sport, he knew that his slight build would be a handicap. His attention turned to debating and dramatics, along with his continuing interest in music through the college band. By his senior year he was an accomplished debater and a member of Phi Beta Kappa and was voted one of the outstanding young men on the Dickinson campus.

People who become acquainted with Ed Hastings through this sparse account of his college years and his choice for his first full-time job usually voice a common set of concerns. They wonder if he went about choosing the job at Excelsior in exactly the "right" way. They have questions about some of his values and about the role and influence of his parents on his life, and they wonder about the significance of his activities in college as they relate to his abilities and interests. We shall approach our discussion of this portion of Ed's history through these perceptions.

Ed's Selection of His First Job

There are those who express concern at what appears to them to be a haphazard approach to selection of Ed's first job. They feel that his choice of a sales job and of Excelsior was based on a wrong set of criteria. Choosing sales because it "seems to be one of the best places" for working and relating to people and choosing Excelsior because "I was impressed with the caliber of people at Excelsior" does not seem based on any rational analysis of the company and the job in relation to Ed's talents and abilities.

People who voice these concerns have usually been through their first job and are now in a position to recruit and select inexperienced personnel for a specific position. They believe that the new recruit should be able to relate in precise ways to specific positions and "know" whether he wants a job in sales, personnel, marketing, or whatever. They frequently ask such questions as "Tell us, Ed, would you like to be a claim adjustor?" or "Would you like to work as an underwriter?" In other words, they try to focus the individual on specific roles and see it as a lack of direction if he claims ignorance of how such positions relate to his interests and talents.

In fact, however, a person's experiences are always a limiting factor in his ability to perceive and judge a situation. Thus if Ed's experience (actual or vicarious) in a business setting has been limited, he can make judgments about career possibilities only from that limited perspective. To expect him to make the same kind of valid observations about jobs as an individual who has had experience in the insurance business (other matters being equal) is to deny the importance of experience in helping individuals to make choices that are "right" for them.

To look at the situation from a slightly different angle, we can simply note that the recruit (Ed Hastings) is in a different stage of his career than the recruiter. Although there are several approaches to the study of career stages (see the works by Donald Super; Douglas T. Hall and Khalil Nougaim; and Delbert C. Miller and William H. Form listed in the bibliography), they all suggest essentially the same process.

In the later years of high school and college education, there is an *exploratory period,* in which one tries out various activities—in education, in part-time work, or in leisure—to become more aware of one's interests, values, needs, abilities, and beliefs. This is usually followed by a *learning or testing period* in a full-time work setting, in which the person tests out some of his self-evaluations and expectancies. This leads either to further exploration (because the experiences did not match the self-evaluations and expectancies) or to an *entrenchment or establishment phase* in some specific professional role.

Once the commitment is made, the individual attempts activities that he expects will promote his own sense of *psychological growth and success* in that role. When indications of plateauing occur, there will be attempts either to maintain that role or to generate further personal growth through retooling and/or a shift in career roles.

The chances are that, while Ed Hastings is in this early exploratory stage of his career, the recruiter and those bosses with whom he comes in contact early in his career are more firmly entrenched in their careers. They have made the decision of commitment; they have resolved the major career choices and have justified that decision in their own minds. They put Ed's choice process in the perspective of what they think was their decision-making process and believe (in retrospect) that their own occupational choice was the result of a "rational, logical thought process."

Choices are typically not made that way, however, especially not the first one. In fact, our experience has been that almost 50 percent of all people make their first job decision primarily on the basis of an *organizational* rather than an occupational criterion. The organization happened to provide an employment opportunity or, as in Ed's case, a job that seemed congruent with perceived individual interests and needs.

The point is—and this has been a main thrust of this book—that an Ed Hastings or anyone else can make a better organizational or occupational choice once he comes to grips with his own interests, abilities, and self-concept. That is the right start to a successful career. Whether that good start will continue through the other stages of his career will depend, at least in part, on whether the organization and other environments provide experiences that are conducive to psychological growth and success and whether the individual will continue to make the necessary analysis of the relations between self and career experiences.

In Ed's case, the decision made some sense to him—as our decisions always do, at least at the time we make them. He approached the job market with an awareness of what he would like to *do* (not *be*): work with people, meet and talk with them in a business setting. Those activities, as Ed realized, can be satisfied in a variety of roles, and a sales position was as good as any other role.

Since their actual business experience is wanting, new hires tend to base their decision on the kinds of things they know best: their relationships and experiences with people. And when the people they come in contact with seem to be "their kind of people," they know at least that there won't be an immediate conflict in the job setting.

Will I be able to get along with these people? Do they do things that seem to be in keeping with my interests and abilities? Does their behavior suggest a climate that will make it possible for me to use my talents? Will I be accepted as a person? If these questions get affirmative answers, the new recruit is likely to be attracted to that setting, especially when the financial rewards are competitive.

Ed had already made up his mind that he wanted a job in a business setting. We don't know to what extent he considered size of company an important factor. We don't know the variety of industries he may have visited, so selection of an insurance company cannot be evaluated. We do know that he studied many companies and had many offers. It is interesting to note here that salary was not a determining factor so long as it was in line with Ed's expectations; apparently the highest salary bid did not come from Excelsior.

This tells us something about Ed's value systems—and, as we have seen, he is not an isolated case in this respect: people are exhibiting a greater concern for personal growth opportunities, for a chance to utilize their talents, and a lesser concern for salary and fringe benefits. These latter items are now more readily available and comparable among business organizations. Differences in positions are now more apparent in their response to higher-level needs for ego satisfaction.

Edgar H. Schein's summary of factors important to students in choosing their first jobs includes the following: advancement opportunities, doing something important and getting recognition for it, responsibility, using one's special abilities, challenge, opportunities for creativity, and high salary.*

We cannot ignore the careful preparation that Ed apparently carried out in studying the companies by which he was interviewed. The fact that he studied the organizations prior to the visit indicates a planful analytic approach to problems, even though his studies led him to see no real differences.

Undoubtedly, some companies are more progressive or more responsive than others, but recruits are hard pressed to see these differences from reading the recruiting literature; all the graphs go up, all salaries are "competitive and based on merit," and all companies claim to provide opportunities for "those who seek to work in an organization that encourages the creative use of one's unique talents." Since the differences are not apparent, the applicants will typically resort to their experiences in the interviews and the visits to the offices to make the necessary distinctions.

Ed's Selection of a College

At this early stage of our introduction to Ed Hastings, if we are not careful, we may impart motives to him that will not survive after we get to know him better. Nevertheless, let us develop some hypotheses regarding this man's motives; we simply have to keep in mind that they are hypotheses, to be tested against the accumulation and interpretation of more information as it becomes available.

* "How to Break In the College Graduate," *Harvard Business Review*, November–December 1964, pp. 68–76.

This is, of course, what we recommend for analysis of any behavior, including our own: an open-mindedness to change our interpretation as new evidence comes in through new experiences.

Ed's choice of college could have stemmed from a variety of motives. He may have chosen Dickinson College because he wanted to be close to home, because it is a good school and he wanted the best education he could get at reasonable cost, or because he wanted to please his parents, who wanted him to go to Dickinson. Or perhaps he chose Dickinson because it had more status than the local community college or because he wanted to live away from home. We could go on and on, but the message is clear: just looking at a bit of behavior does not give us clues as to why it occurred. The answer must come from a careful study of those preconditions that probably made certain values and needs more dominant for Ed than for others.

What are those preconditions? Ed knew that his parents were making a financial sacrifice; he wanted to minimize that, so he used his own funds to finance his college education as much as possible. It seems reasonable to assume, then, that (1) Ed has a concern for his parents; (2) he is willing to make personal sacrifices in the short run for some possible later and greater payoff.

Apparently his parents and he discussed the matter and agreed that going to Dickinson would provide a better education and that a sacrifice now would have a payoff in some "greater dividends later." This gives us some clues about the values held by Ed and his family: (1) a "good" education; (2) concern about longer-range goals rather than immediate pay-out; (3) open communications within the family; and (4) willingness to work and sacrifice for a worthwhile goal.

We do have evidence that Ed's homelife was enriched. There was an interest in intellectual development, as evidenced by the father's reading interests and the decision to seek a quality education rather than just any education. There is also evidence that association with and service to others was an important value (both mother and father support that) and that Ed learned the "value" of hard work and sacrifice to achieve financial goals, which were means to personal growth rather than ends in themselves.

There may be some question here about the parental influence. Some would view Ed's behavior as exhibiting too much dependency on his parents to make the major decisions for him. But this view need not be correct. Parents will undoubtedly have an influence on the behavior and the value and need systems of their children, but we cannot assume that this influence is permanent (to say so would deny the value of learning and new experiences) or that it is more important than the influence of other key people (teachers, friends, other adults) in a person's life.

Furthermore, there is quite a difference between asking parents (or other adults, for that matter) for their opinions and asking them to make the decision. We have no real evidence that Ed's parents made the decision or that Ed solicited their advice in order to do what they thought was best. Our clues for an answer to that must wait for a further look at how Ed relates to other authority figures and the extent to which he is influenced by them.

Ed's Parents and Their Values

We can get clues about Ed's value systems from this brief glimpse at his parents. However, any conclusion regarding this must be tentative because the more critical variable in assigning values to Ed is not so much what the parents did as how Ed interpreted those parental behaviors. Nonetheless, the parents' behavior gives us some indication of the kind of climate in which Ed grew up and therefore of the value systems to which he was exposed.

Both parents are people-oriented; the father, for the sake of social contact and discussion of current issues, the mother, for social service. Ed's interest in people and his (unconscious?) selection of a service industry may well be related to the value systems imparted by his parents. In any case, it appears that Ed's choice of a job was less a function of his concern for money than it was a result of his people-orientation.

There are those who will raise some question about Ed's desire to go into business. Does he have the proper value system? After all, if he, like his father, lacks a profit orientation, one might predict some difficulties and conflicts for Ed in a profit-oriented environment.

We cannot deny that certain interest patterns seem to be more compatible with some roles than with others. However, whether those patterns guarantee success in those roles can be questioned. Throughout this book, our emphasis has been on *activities* rather than on roles or positions. To what extent are Ed's values, needs, and beliefs in keeping with what he is *doing*?

Clearly, people in sales positions may behave in a variety of ways to achieve acceptable ends. Will Ed's value systems permit him to behave in ways that will achieve appropriate ends for him in his job? That is a matter of fit between job demands and person. At this point, conflict is not readily apparent.

Ed's College Performance

There is no doubt that Ed achieved much in college, and that gives us clues about the kind of person he is. We can assume that he is intellectually bright. Evidence for this comes from several sources. First, his acceptance by a highly selective college suggests that he competed successfully with many others of high mental ability. Second, his election to Phi Beta Kappa indicates high-quality academic performance—and this at a school where the competition is keen. Third, this performance was not the result of his being a "book grind" but was achieved while he carried on many extracurricular activities and held part-time jobs.

Also, it appears that he is well organized and has a high energy level. This is supported by our last statement indicating his ability to carry on a variety of tasks and do them well—so well, in fact, that he was named an outstanding member of the campus. His willingness to work in order to save money for college also indicates a high energy level and good organizational abilities, as does his approach to job hunting.

Furthermore, he seems to have a strong need to achieve. Although his outstanding achievements do not in themselves suggest that he values achievement for its own sake, there is much to be said for the argument that achievement thrives on itself; it is its own reward. When achievement gives indications of competency, it enhances our self-esteem and tends to drive us into situations that provide further opportunities to experience an even greater sense of competency. But an achiever is more than that—he has a keen sense of his strengths and is willing to set medium-risk goals that he thinks he can reach through the effective use of his own talents. He is not a gambler; rather, he sets challenging goals based on his own evaluation of his strengths, and he will strive to achieve those goals in the most effective way.

There are those who would fault Ed for not going out for sports. "He should have gritted his teeth and tried it. Nothing ventured, nothing gained!" they might say. True, not enough people venture far enough to test the outer limits of their abilities. But we see neither withdrawal nor defensiveness by Ed. On the contrary, what we see is a strong desire to succeed and a willingness to set challenging goals that are in keeping with his perceived strengths and talents. To reach an easy goal does not bring a feeling of competency. To reach a chancy goal is not rewarding either; it simply brings a sigh of relief and a word of thanks to all the luck bestowed on us. A sense of competency comes when individuals achieve goals that are accepted by them as challenging but realistic.

Finally, it appears that Ed is broad-gauged. We have written previously about the value of a broad perspective and a desire to have a variety of experiences. Ed gives us clues that he is people-oriented (his own self-perception, rap sessions, volunteer work, dramatics); that he is highly verbal (debating, dramatics, rap sessions, his high performance in a liberal arts college); and that he picks different media in which to express his interests and abilities. In short, we get a picture not of a narrow, limited individual but of an expansive person with broad interests in people, the arts, his parents, and himself.

Ed's Early Years at Excelsior

We turn now to a brief account of Ed's early years in his first full-time job. As we analyze the events of this period, we should try to determine whether they corroborate or deny previous hypotheses. What do the new data tell us about Ed Hastings and the kinds of issues of concern to him as his career continues to unfold?

In making our analysis, we should be looking for *patterns of behavior* (see Chapter 8 on learning). The isolated event in school or at work tells us very little. It is the series of events of a similar nature that gives us an indication of those aspects that are really core to the person. If Ed Hastings behaves in similar ways at work, school, home, and play, then we can be fairly certain that we are beginning to tap a pattern that permits prediction of behavior in the future in similar circumstances.

When Ed joined the company, Excelsior had about 10,000 employees scattered in 40 offices throughout the United States. The company's home office was in Boston. Sales were at the 700 million dollar mark. The past five years showed an almost phenomenal growth. The number of offices were now at 50; Excelsior had opened an operation in Canada and was reaching out some feelers into Europe. Sales were close to 1.2 billion dollars, even though earnings were down. New markets were opening up. Variable annuities, mutual funds, portable pensions, mass marketing concepts, new acquisitions, and government intervention were changing the face of the business and were putting new and different pressures on Ed's boss. The need for talented human resources was acute.

To keep pace with the rapid expansion, Excelsior had reorganized into five major geographical regions, each with its own regional vice president, who had a fair amount of autonomy to establish procedures within broad guidelines set down by the home office. Each region was hooked into a vast computer system. New information systems and procedures were being introduced to ease the paperwork, to provide the offices with information necessary to keep the company growing, and particularly to determine ways to reduce costs.

At the same time, the company had established a corporate planning division that was responsible for assisting Excelsior in the development of a five-year plan. Organizational and regional plans were formulated annually through a participative process between upper and middle management and ultimately submitted to appropriate personnel for implementation.

In those same five years, Ed felt that his own growth was keeping pace with the company's. After joining Excelsior in Philadelphia and spending two years there as a staff representative, he moved to Los Angeles. The move came at the time of the reorganization and seemed to offer the right kind of opportunity to him. The company assured him that the move did indeed mean a step up in his career, even though at the time there was no change in title. There was, however, a generous increase in salary.

In fact, as Ed looks back on that move, the salary increase was the saving grace. His wife wasn't too happy about leaving all her lifelong Philadelphia friends, and she wasn't sure in her own mind that Ed had made the kind of progress at Excelsior that was fitting to his talents and ambitions. He had been saying for a long time that he wanted to move into a job with more responsibility and had convinced himself and his wife that he could and should. Just before the move, his progress at Excelsior seemed so slow. Ed felt that he had learned a lot in two years but that he was beginning to level off. The job seemed less challenging, more routine.

The move to Los Angeles brought with it the excitement of new people and new problems. Los Angeles was a much larger office, with a greater variety of markets to serve and a marketing system that, according to the company, had to be renovated. It led to all kinds of problems for Ed's manager—problems that seemed to keep management incessantly busy just keeping their heads above water.

It was into this kind of environment that Ed moved. He couldn't say that he wasn't busy, because he was. The days were hectic; the hours were long. Weeks went by fast, and at the end of them, Ed felt he had very little to show for them. Working nights and Saturdays didn't exactly make his wife and family—or Ed, for that matter—happy, but it seemed to be the only way to keep up with things. "The hard work will pay off eventually," he thought.

When Ed got his promotion to staff supervisor just seven months ago, his boss was most complimentary. "Keep up the good work, Ed, and you'll go places with Excelsior. I know you've been working hard and long hours, and it's that kind of dedication that doesn't go unnoticed. I'm glad you're on my team."

Nevertheless, Ed had a gnawing sense of frustration about his job. He couldn't put his finger on it, but he felt he wasn't moving ahead fast enough. Many of his college classmates who never accomplished close to what Ed's record showed—Dean's List, an impressive list of extracurricular activities, positions of leadership—seemed to be making a lot more money and enjoying greater responsibilities in their positions. Surely he should be doing as well as, or even better, than they!

Information about the company and about Ed's reactions to his job provide opportunities for some interesting commentary on a career strategy for Ed.

Too frequently, individuals are oblivious to the changes that are occurring in their companies. Some of the changes—such as organizational shifts, budget and financial crises, shifts in products or markets—are dramatic. Others—for example, changes in the demands made on key executives, which may reflect shifts in policy, and changes in the work load, which again may reflect shifts in emphasis—are more subtle. Dramatic or subtle, the changes go unrecognized by the best of new recruits who seem hell-bent on "learning the business" and "doing my job so I impress the boss."

But these shifts can portend significant forces for the person who is sensitive to environmental changes and recognizes their potential impact on career strategy. Change is inevitable, and being aware of change permits shifts in strategy so that it remains an active process rather than a reactive one.

Take Excelsior, for example. It is expanding in size, and this signifies more job opportunities and probably more formal control mechanisms. It is opening up new markets and offering new products. New demands are being made on the company for talented people—always a good sign for the individual who is well-endowed with talents and who is aggressive in using them effectively. It is reorganizing, so opportunities at the line and staff levels are opening up. There is a growing need for the professionally and technically competent (note the reference to systems, data processing, and actuarial needs). There are new avenues for progress in management because of the shift toward decentralization and corporate planning.

Are they opportunities for Ed Hastings? The answer, of course, depends on, first, whether he is aware that these shifts are going on and, second, whether he has a clear idea of his own strengths and needs so that he can determine whether he should view them as opportunities or as threats. But to ignore them is potentially dangerous. The virtues of hard work and of good work have limited rewards, even for the new recruit.

Within this context, the company has "rewarded" Ed with salary increases, a shift to a larger office, and a job with more responsibility. And yet Ed feels a "gnawing sense of frustration." Apparently the rewards are not sufficient to bring about need satisfaction. As we try to explain why, we must take into account several different factors.

First, consider our "virtue of a better fertilizer." Most people approach new positions with expectations and attitudes that lead to some dissatisfaction after two to five years on the job. This seems to happen almost inevitably after the initial training, when bosses begin to accept and count on a certain level of performance from the recruit. When the honeymoon is over, people see the job more for what it actually is, and they naturally wonder: "What next?" If it is inevitable, then just knowing that makes a lot of difference, because people are prepared for it and accept it or try to minimize it.

But there are other explanations. Ed Hastings had had four years of successful performance at Dickinson College. The climate at college was for the most part well-structured, and feedback was precise and regular. The college student knows how many courses he must take, and often which courses he must take when. He knows what the reward system is like and figures out ways to achieve within that system to the college's satisfaction and his own advantage.

Ed worked within that structure, and feedback was positive and very ego-satisfying. He received awards that gave him a special sense of competency.

But there is more. The college system also allows a freedom of choice and of self-expression. How to spend one's time out of class and how to organize and plan to express one's individuality are stumbling blocks for many a first-year student. But the process forces some adjustment to this, and those who adjust well can point to growing experiences during their college years. Those who fail at this kind of self-expression struggle for ego-survival.

For Ed Hastings, the adjustment was magnificent. He had put it all together—studies, work, and play all meshed into an outstanding performance. Ego satisfactions for Ed were, to say the least, high.

Enter the world of work. Unfortunately perhaps, most young people find it highly structured initially. From an open flexible college environment Ed probably entered a training program complete with manuals, precise calendars for when to do what with whom, and precise rotation from one function to the next—all in the name of "learning the business." This precision has the advantage of providing some benchmarks for the trainee; he can see what progress he makes. It may be slower than he thinks it should be (many trainees complain that they really don't earn their pay); but at least he's learning, and that has some satisfaction to it.

But what happens when the job is stabilized, when days come and go and there are no longer any signs of progress? This is the situation in which Ed now finds himself. His move to Los Angeles brought no change in title but more money. In a business setting, salary increments are frequently used as indications of merit. While we in no way want to de-emphasize the value of money as a reward, there remains the question of when a reward is actually a reward: is it when it is *given* by an organization or when it is *perceived* as such by the receiver? Clearly, the latter is the important factor.

We have already indicated that more people of Ed's training see money as a less important incentive than those related to ego satisfactions. We begin to see why generous increases in salary for Ed will not compensate for a job that "seemed less challenging and more routine."

This may well explain why Ed is becoming overly concerned with having a job with more responsibility. At times like these we get others involved with our frustrations. Hence Ed and his wife both are caught in a spiral of increasing frustration.

When the job remains the same—or gets worse, as it did with Ed when he moved to Los Angeles (a lot more of the same routine and the same amount of time to do it in, and there were no signs of greater ego satisfactions)—we can predict that people will revert to other needs in order to maintain some sense of satisfaction. Salary now becomes more important; peers and social structures are more carefully surveyed; issues outside the job take on greater meaning.

Under such circumstances, does the promotion to staff supervisor really help? Probably not. Status does not necessarily provide ego satisfaction; feelings of competence and achievement are more important. Therefore, when an individual moves into a position that does not provide a sense of achievement, frustration inevitably results.

The Course of Frustration

Our observations still do not fully explain Ed's sense of frustration. Frustration results whenever an individual is thwarted in his effort to satisfy a goal. Typically in such situations, we find a barrier between the individual and the goal. That barrier may be physical and real; more frequently, it is psychological and imagined.

But is such the case with Ed? He's told by his supervisor that he's doing well and that he'll "go places." Frustration can also occur not because of barriers that prevent the individual from reaching his goal but because the goal attained is the wrong one. It is sad but true that many people strive most of their working lives for a certain goal only to find that there is no need satisfaction in its attainment. The outcome in such cases is not related to the need.

In addition, if we don't know what it is we're trying to achieve, then it's possible to perform well without understanding how or whether our performance is related to outcomes. This may well be Ed's problem.

Ed Hastings' is a classic case. He's working hard but had "very little to show" for all the hard work. What does his boss mean when he tells Ed that he's doing "good work," that he'll "go places"? Are the boss's goals for Ed the same as Ed's goals? Does Ed really know what he's doing that leads to these accolades from his boss?

As the work gets more harrying, communications are likely to break down because everybody's working harder to "get out the work." As bosses see less of their subordinates, there is even less feedback, and the consequence is more frustration. Closed systems, in short, hinder personal growth.

To add to this cycle, the frustration creates more issues on the home front. Apparently Ed and his wife have had discussions about his concerns, and apparently his wife had reservations about their transfer to the West Coast. We have evidence that Ed is family-oriented, and this will create more concerns for him when things "don't go right" at home. The pressures of settling into a new community, making new friends, and getting to a level of comfortableness comparable to the one he and his wife experienced prior to their move add extra burdens on Ed.

While Ed has outlets through his job for some of his needs, his wife will not readily find the same satisfaction. It is a perfect setting for what the behavioral scientists have labeled a double approach-avoidance conflict.

His wife has both negative and positive value to Ed; so does his job. Ed wants to be with his wife (positive value); but when he's with her, he is not at his job, which is demanding more of his time (negative value: "she's keeping me from my work"). When he's at work, getting things done has value to him (positive: "I'm responding to demands"); at the same time, the job makes him feel bad because he's not with his wife (now the job has negative value).

It's a kind of "damned if you do and damned if you don't" situation. It is not easily resolved and may tear a person apart; it creates a sense of not getting done all that he feels he must accomplish.

During this trial phase in one's career, many young people have similar critical choices to make. These choices center around work, education, family, and the self. In the following we list some of the major dimensions of each of these areas.

1. *Work.* How far is up for me? Do I really want to have upward mobility? Will others accept my decision on this? And if so, do I want to be a manager or a technician? Do I want my growth to be in depth of skill and knowledge in one area or in breadth of skill and understanding in a variety of areas? Is this the company for me, or should I look elsewhere?

What is really important in a job—security and enough time to live the "good life" or what? How important is it that I have a "good" boss or that I work in a "good" organization? What do I mean by a "good" boss and organization? How important is my work anyway?

2. *Education.* What's more important at this stage of my career-skill acquisition: professional courses for upgrading of present job or some formal education toward a degree? Is it more important to spend my time doing the present job well or taking some of that time for course work? If I do some formal course work, in what direction should I move: to job-related courses or to a "broadening" type of exposure?

3. *Family.* How do I portion out my time between job, family, and self-development? Is time with the family at this stage of my career important for them and for me? Do I dare consider a job that may lead to geographic relocation?

What impact will that have on my family or on my spouse's career? Is there a way that I can set up my job activities so that they don't compete with family goals but are convergent with them? How much of my work—its frustrations and problems—do I take home with me and share with my family? What's really most important to me: family or job?

4. *Self.* How do I take the best advantage of all my interests? Can I find a job that combines them all? Do I really want to broaden my interests? Must I compete with my peers in order to grow personally—is it a win-lose situation? How do I change to have a better impact on people? What can I do about my shortcomings so that I can be a better person? Do I really want to share my feelings with others or get them to be closer to me?

Central to all these areas is the ultimate question that you must face: Do you really want to change? A good many people (primarily those who are not sure of their own sense of self-esteem) seem willing to verbalize the nature of their career conflicts but are not quite sure that change is worth all the effort. They have not yet come to accept, or even to understand, what is important to them. That, in essence, is what this period of uncertainty is all about: trial-and-error learning before establishing any career roots.

Therefore, until Ed makes some decisions about the priority and timing of his goals and until there is some personal *commitment* to those priorities and acceptance of them by others, particularly his boss and his wife, Ed (and maybe his wife and his boss too) will remain in conflict.

An Aborted Attempt at Change

It was at this point in time that Ed began to reflect on his life-style and became convinced that time was passing him by without his accomplishing much except the daily demands of his job.

"Planning is the key," he said to a friend. "Time control is a big problem for me. Every Monday morning I make out my schedule for the entire week—who I'm going to see and when. But because of cancellations, emergency situations, and the like, it seems that the work schedule I actually follow for a week and the one I plan to follow are two different things. Although I'm never without things to do, it seems I never end up doing exactly what I planned. What I've got to do is plan better the use of my time."

With that in mind, Ed thought hard about himself and about his job and its requirements. He thought about his strengths and weaknesses and then listed the following goals for the next twelve months:

1. Hire three new agents and get them to a reasonable level of productivity.
2. Give better service to my agents.
3. Recruit one new staff representative.
4. Gain a better knowledge of the problems and changes in the insurance business.
5. Read at least one good book each month.
6. Be more effective in the scheduling of my work.
7. Become more involved in community affairs.
8. Spend more time with my family.

Ed's approach is insightful; he is aware that he must do planning. More important, he is aware that plans must be translated into objectives—some statements of what is to be accomplished.

But we predict frustration for Ed Hastings. He has thought hard about what to do, but in the doing has failed. His objectives do not meet the many criteria he might have used to lay out an effective action plan.

As Chapter 6 on implementing strategy suggests, Ed has failed on several counts. First, he has not indicated any sense of priority for his goals, either in terms of importance or of timing; neither has he established subactivities for his longer-range goals. For example, if by "becoming more involved in community affairs" Ed Hastings means that he will try to become a member of the Environmental Control Commission of his community, then there are probably some action steps on his part over a period of time that will require his attention. These action steps can be identified and time deadlines posted:

By September 1: Express interest in political party involvement to party chairperson.

By December 1: Make contact with commission chairperson; be involved in party activities.

By February 1: Read all past minutes of commission proceedings.

By March 1: Contact chairperson and indicate what he thinks his contributions can be; volunteer services.

By June 1: At least one public letter or report—in newspaper, journal, or other relevant publication—expressing concerns over major environmental issues.

By September 1: Actively seek commission vacancy.
By November 1: Be appointed to commission.

Establishment of these subactivities will help Ed monitor his progress and direct his activities as these deadlines come up. In the
meantime, other objectives can also be accomplished, and, indeed,
more important areas can still receive prime attention.

Second, Ed has not established measurable and verifiable standards for his goals; neither has he made certain that he can get the
appropriate feedback on how well he is accomplishing his objectives. For example, what does Ed mean by his desire to get his new
agents "to a reasonable level of productivity"? Productivity might
be measured in terms of commissions received, number of policies
written, amount of premiums received, or face amount of insurance
written. What will be considered "reasonable"? That is for Ed and
his production manager to decide, along with his agents. All are
involved in that particular objective, and all must agree that the
standard for "reasonable" is meaningful and acceptable to all, especially to Ed, who must judge his own sense of competence against
his own standard of achievement.

Whatever the standard, the feedback process should be direct
and nonjudgmental so that Ed can have information about his performance as soon as possible. To rely on someone else for feedback
on the accomplishment of his objectives may introduce an emotional element and a delay in the reinforcement process. Feedback
immediately following behavior increases the likelihood of effective learning and change. Delayed or distorted feedback makes it
less possible for an individual to assess the real consequences of his
behavior.

But that's the rub! Many of the key needs and value systems that
are the basis of an effective career strategy are rewarded primarily
through the actions of others. Higher-level needs require reactions
from others. The more open and trusting the relationship, the more
valid the feedback will be.

Third, Ed Hastings should consider the extent to which the objectives he has set are "stretch" goals for him. Are they challenging,
or are they just accomplishing the same thing he's done in the past?
Or has he stretched too far, to the point where the objectives are
unrealistic?

The likelihood is that the goals are not very challenging; many of
them, even in their general nature, are not stated in demanding
ways. "Reasonable level," "more effective," "one new staff

representative"—these terms suggest the usual performance expected of an individual in a job.

What is a realistic challenge? One possible way to strike a balance is to set three different standards—pessimistic, expected, and optimistic—and then, whenever possible, to make plans to reach the optimistic levels, with planned contingencies for the pessimistic, in the event that negative trends occur.

Fourth, there is no indication that Ed Hastings has thought through his involvement with others, either as valuable resources for the accomplishment of his purpose or for commitment purposes. For example, his agents must cooperate with him to achieve his purpose of increased productivity; better service will require help from his clerical staff.

Similarly, if Ed Hastings had announced to his family that he was going to spend more time with them, then that announced commitment in and of itself would have made it more difficult for him to retract. And if he did, his family would have been there to remind him of that commitment. As it happened, he kept that objective to himself, and if he falters, the only person who will know is he.

Commitment to his family would also mean that they could help Ed achieve his goals. By planning their own time, by thinking of activities that are acceptable to them and to Ed, both parties would receive some satisfaction. And that's the real payoff: when there can be congruence of objectives so that one's behavior can prove satisfying to oneself and to the others involved as well.

No wonder, then, that Ed's actions had little probability of a payoff for him. As it turned out, his frustrations were not lessened, and he thought more and more about leaving his job.

"It just isn't working out, Mr. Peterson, and I'm sorry," Ed heard himself saying to his boss. "Six months ago I set certain things I wanted to accomplish, and I just don't seem to be able to do all that I want to. Oh, sure, I hired five new agents, and they're doing O.K., I guess. And the agents I work with seem to like me, and we get things done together. But look at all that's not being accomplished. That's why I think I'm misplaced and should think about leaving Excelsior—or at least be transferred. That will be better for me and for the company all the way round."

Ed's manager was surprised and disturbed to hear these words. He meant it when he said, "Ed, you have been doing an absolutely superb job for us, and I think you'd be making a mistake to leave Excelsior. I just don't understand it. Your salary progress has been good, and your recent promotion shows you how highly we at Excelsior think of you.

"Sure, none of us accomplishes all that he'd like to, but we make dents in our plans, and that's the important thing. You can count on me to help you in any way I can. Let's sit down this afternoon for as long as you like and see what we can do to make this job a better one for you."

As Mr. Peterson thought about the meeting coming up, he tried to piece together some of his own ideas about Ed. Certain descriptive traits seemed to stand out as he thought about the kind of person Ed is: ambitious, intelligent, poised, self-assured, energetic, productive, enterprising and innovative, clear-thinking, verbally fluent, dependable, sensitive to others, with high social values.

He felt that Ed had not really gone out of his way to learn more about other jobs in the company and that, in fact, he was probably overdevoted to the demands of the present job. Ed didn't seem to be upward-oriented. He had to admit to himself that he hadn't spent as much time as he should have with Ed, but the pressures of the job had prevented that lately. Besides, he had assumed that Ed, because he was such a highly capable young man, needed little or no supervision.

Ed's reaction is not atypical. In matters of frustration, it is a rather common mechanism to withdraw physically from the source of the frustration—or at least from what appears to be the source. It happens most frequently with young, highly ambitious people. They typically see the source of their frustrations in a boss who does not recognize their talents, in a lack of reward by the company for a job well done, or in a lack of challenge in a job that has become boring and routine. So they withdraw from the job, the boss, or the company and try again somewhere else. But this generally fails to solve the problem because the cause of the frustration typically rests within the young employee himself.

A healthier approach is either to circumvent the source of the frustration or, better yet, to overcome it and thereby learn effective behaviors for dealing with similar situations in the future. That is the essence of Chapters 10, 11, and 12 in particular and of the entire book in general.

Ed is also falling victim to inconsistent and delayed reinforcement (see Chapter 12 for a detailed discussion of this problem). Organizations typically have expectations for quality job performance, but, particularly in times of rapid growth or of crises, they often do not provide the reinforcements, especially the positive types, at the time of positive behavior. Because reinforcement is delayed, learning and hence people's sense of personal growth are diminished.

Again, not all of this is the boss's doing. The responsibility for an appropriate learning environment is as much the learner's as it is the teacher's : In Ed's case, it appears that he had not kept in touch with his boss and had not done much to orient his own activities to the boss's needs. Does not the subordinate have some responsibility to alleviate, if possible, the pressure the boss feels from his job? Does not Ed have a responsibility to communicate to his boss just how much supervision he needs and wants and just how he feels about the job?

A Period of Analysis

Ed and his boss had not spent much time talking with each other. Ed thought doing a good job would be enough; Mr. Peterson thought that occasional promotions and verbal rewards would be sufficient. Luckily, in this situation, they started to talk.

The boss sensed Ed's hesitancy and his uncertainty about what the next step should be. And he was sensitive enough to know that Ed needed encouragement and time to think through the problems before making a decision.

Being achievement-oriented, Ed had moved so fast, been exposed to so much new information, and been required to develop new skills and professional expertise at such a rate that he had little time to ask, "Is this right for me?" His feelings of discomfort were now forcing him to address this question.

As a first step, Ed took a closer look at where he had been. Specifically, he completed a biographical analysis along the lines of the career planning worksheet shown at the end of Chapter 8. From this, some of his key attitudes and values became clearer.

Ed, it appeared from his self-evaluation, likes to be and gets involved in whatever he does. He is interested in the development of his total self—physically and psychologically—in education, in the community, and in his family. An enlarging lifestyle is an important objective for him. There is an underlying need for stability and security but at the same time a dislike for structure and detail in his working environment.

He is more a helper, a doer, an individual who serves well in a staff capacity. As such, he responds well to people who display similar qualities—who are helpful, thoughtful, analytical, bright, supportive, and articulate.

He raises questions about needing direction in his career and wants to get on with being as productive and creative as he was in his college years. He wants bosses who are sounding boards and yet admits to avoiding possible confrontation. He needs help in learning how to "face up" to some of his problems.

Through the company, Peterson also arranged for Ed to take some self-evaluation inventories that might provide additional insights. We describe them here to inform the reader of some of the instruments available to assist in the process of career strategy formulation.

The Strong-Campbell Interest Inventory* is based on a theory of John Holland.† Holland suggests that there is a strong positive relationship between personality and the environments to which people are attracted. He proposes six personality types and six matching occupational environments:

1. Realistic: involves behavior that is rugged, robust, strong; with emphasis on working with things rather than with people and feelings. Occupational areas include agriculture, biology, military, and mechanical activities.
2. Investigative: involves behavior that emphasizes thinking, analyzing, and understanding rather than feeling or doing; implies an enjoyment of ambiguous challenges. Related occupational areas are science, mathematics, medical science, and medical service.
3. Artistic: involves self-expression and behavior that reflects artistic creativity and individuality. Related occupational areas include music, drama, art, and writing.
4. Social: involves humanistic and interpersonal behavior. Teaching, social service, athletics, and religious activities are examples of the corresponding occupational areas.
5. Enterprising: involves verbal facility and a desire to lead, dominate, or persuade. Related occupational activities include law, politics, public speaking, merchandising, sales, and business management.
6. Conventional: involves structured, detailed, regulated behavior and a subordinate rather than leadership position.

Ed Hastings scores high on *social* and *enterprising* and moderately high on *artistic*. His *realistic* score is low; all others are average.

* Edward K. Strong, Jr., and David P. Campbell, *Strong-Campbell Interest Inventory*, Stanford, Cal.: Stanford University Press, 1974.
† *Making Vocational Choices: A Theory of Careers*, Englewood Cliffs, N.J.: Prentice-Hall, 1973.

The Allport-Vernon-Lindzey inventory* is based on the classification of six values described in Chapter 4: theoretical, economic, esthetic, social, and religious. Ed Hastings scores high on the theoretical, economic, and social values, in that order, with the other three being average.

The Guilford-Zimmerman Temperament Survey† measures the following personality characteristics: high/low activity level, restraint/impulsiveness, submissiveness/aggressiveness, shyness/sociability, moodiness/emotional stability, hypersensitiveness/objectivity, hostility/friendliness, unreflectiveness/thoughtfulness, and criticalness/cooperativeness. This is a relatively complicated instrument and (like all better psychological inventories) takes an experienced counselor to analyze for meaningfulness of the data generated.

In general terms, Ed's scores showed him to have a high activity level, with a social aggressiveness that puts him at ease with others and readily permits him to establish rapport. He is tolerant and understanding of others' feelings and approaches issues with a relatively objective (not egoistic) point of view.

The Personnel Relations Survey‡ measures two aspects of interpersonal relations: exposure and feedback. Exposure is a conscious attempt to share and to provide an open and candid expression of one's feelings. Feedback is an active solicitation by the individual of information that others may have and the solicitor does not. (See Chapter 9 for a discussion of how these factors relate to the Johari window.)

Exposure and feedback behavior can be measured in relation to peers, subordinates, and bosses. The author indicates that lack of balance in both scores predicts difficulties in communicating. The ideal is to have a high exposure score and a high feedback score.

Ed's scores indicate the following: high exposure and low feedback with subordinates; high exposure and high feedback with peers; and low exposure and low feedback with bosses. The first tends to signal to subordinates a lack of interest in their feelings and contributions; this will lead to the withholding of information and to highly selective feedback. The third (low scores in both exposure

* Gordon W. Allport, Philip E. Vernon, and Gardner Lindzey, *Study of Values,* third edition, Boston: Houghton Mifflin, 1960.

† Jay P. Guilford and Wayne S. Zimmerman, *Guilford-Zimmerman Temperament Survey,* Beverly Hills, Cal.: Sheridan Supply Co., 1949.

‡ Jay Hall, *Personnel Relations Survey,* Conroe, Texas: Teleometrics International, 1967.

and feedback with bosses) suggests an impersonal approach, a tendency to withdraw, and a security orientation.

The Work Motivation Inventory* measures certain needs that the individual feels must be satisfied in the work setting. The system follows the classification into physiological, safety, social, self-esteem, and self-actualization needs. You will recall that these are discussed in detail in Chapter 7.

Ed Hastings scores high on the needs for self-esteem, self-actualization, and safety and is more typical of the work population in the other two need areas.

A Summary Analysis of Ed Hastings

When all of the test data and biographical information were integrated, we came out with a good descriptive statement of the main forces directing Ed's behavior.†

He places substantial emphasis on digging into things, finding out about things; he likes to observe, analyze, and understand. His approach is cognitive, rational, and critical. He may try to solve issues through feelings and interpersonal behaviors and will emphasize the spoken word as a dominant communications device. All this is associated with a bent to be utilitarian and practical; even his learning needs to be perceived by him as useful and applicable.

He is also interested in people, and his concern for them leans toward altruism, helping others, and being sympathetic toward their needs and concerns. His verbal skills tend to be used for selling, promoting, dominating, and leading. He will avoid long periods of intellectual effort, preferring instead an interpersonal approach to problem solving. He avoids detail and structure. And although he indicates an interest in using his imagination, he prefers to apply it to situations where he has a sense of direction and can check out his progress with people in authority.

In this sense, then, he seeks working conditions that are predictable, secure, and relatively risk-free. He may therefore be overly compliant, lack resiliency and flexibility, and be somewhat dependent. At the same time, he desires situations in which he can display his competence so as to gain the concomitant rewards. Advancement, if tied to his strong need for security, may be desirable.

* Jay Hall, *Work Motivation Inventory*, Conroe, Texas: Teleometrics International, 1974.

† Parts of this analysis were contributed by Dr. Karl Springob, Stevens Institute of Technology, Hoboken, New Jersey.

While he enjoys interpersonal relationships, he is more likely to share feelings with peers and subordinates than with bosses. Information about himself, therefore, is most likely to be sought from peers, by whom he probably feels less threatened.

Ed has a high energy level and gives indications of being outgoing and willing to work and cooperate with others. He is socially aggressive and assertive and knows the right things to say. He seeks to maintain good human relations but may not always be sensitive to the feelings of others. The combination of high energy and social orientation leads him to want to perform well in a variety of social situations—at work, at home, and in the community. This may put him in conflict because he wants to behave effectively in all areas. Without some direction, he may flounder and become frustrated.

Occupations (specific roles) that are suggested by his talents and interests include teacher, director of social agency, psychologist, counselor, business manager, consultant, social worker, industrial relations manager, hotel manager, salesman, and political campaign manager.

The Action

As the data kept coming in to Ed, he sought out advice from many different sources: his boss, professionals, managers within and outside the company. Over a period of about six months, Ed tried to develop a strategy for his career that would balance out the many different facets of his interests, values, and needs and tie them to some of the trends evident in the company and elsewhere.

The result was a transfer to the home office, in the same department, but in a staff function that combined his interests in working with people, in analysis, in constructive work, and in using his verbal skills. Staying with the same company solved his security need, and his move back to the East and closer to his old friends and his family supported this and his desire for greater stability. The new job was in the human resources area and involved in-house consulting work for human resources planning and development.

There are, of course, a lot of Ed Hastings in this world. Many of them are still floundering, still trying to overcome their sense of frustration in their careers. Whether or not they resolve their tensions depends largely on them—on how they approach the analysis and implementation of their careers.

That's what this book has been all about.

14

The Results

Examples of Payoff

WHAT happens when people get involved in the process of trying to formulate and implement a career strategy? I asked individuals who had gone through a career planning process to establish some short-range objectives (see Figure 24). The individual kept a copy of this form for his own use; I retained a copy that the individual knew would be kept confidential. My copy served as feedback to me on how well I had gotten across some concepts and as the basis for further communications with the individuals.

At the end of six months I mailed my copy of the individual's plan back to the individual with an accompanying letter (Figure 25) requesting feedback. The responses were then compiled and returned with a covering letter.

The following are representative excerpts from the many responses I received, categorized around major career themes. *Comment* refers to observations made after reviewing the responses.

Career Issues Revolving around the Job and the Organization

Example: "It seems that everything's falling into place all of a sudden. Realistically, the change has been so subtle that I've just

Figure 24. Career growth activities worksheet.

5 major career growth activities (in priority order) over the next 5 years	Specific tasks to be completed within the next 6 months in support of one or more of these career growth activities (with planned date of completion)	Standards and feedback systems to be used for measuring achievement of these 6-month objectives	Commitment made to whom (spouse, boss, peers, subordinates, self)?

Comments on:

(a) achievements to date:

(b) difficulties in setting or achieving objectives:

(c) reasons for successes:

(d) behavior of those to whom commitment was made:

Any other observations:

Figure 25

Greetings! Six months ago we were all together trying to
figure out what the next six months should bring for us.
Well, the future is now.

You will recall that one of the major concepts all of us
kept pushing when we were together was the desirability
to make plans and also to develop some kind of a feedback mechanism to provide information on how well these
plans are being accomplished. Toward that end, on our
last day together, you wrote a note to yourself suggesting possible projects for the next few months that may
move you along toward your career objectives.

The time for feedback is at hand. Enclosed is the letter
that you wrote to yourself. We hope that you'll read it,
bring back into conscious memory the context in which it
was written, and reflect on how well you are progressing
toward the goals mentioned in the letter. We recognize
that not all of us make the same progress. Some of us,
because of other pressures, quickly forget some of the
goals we set; others are partially successful; and still
others set forth on a program of action that brings quick
achievement. Whatever your stage of progress, we hope
you'll take time to reflect on your letter and to give
yourself some feedback on what's been going on since you
completed the form.

To the extent that you discuss some or all of the content with your manager, peers, family--those who are
involved with your career--you will be getting more
feedback. And the greater the feedback, the better
you'll be able to evaluate your career plans and growth.

After you have done all this, will you please do us a
favor; a favor which we think will benefit you as well
as us.

Will you please take time to write us a letter, telling
us (1) how far you got in accomplishing the goals out-
lined in your first letter, (2) what difficulties you may
have had in achieving those goals and why, (3) to what
you attribute any of your successes since you returned
from the conference, (4) what problems you see in the
setting and achievement of goals in the next few months
and (5) what you plan to do over the next year. We'll
try to compile the information (protecting your anonym-
ity, of course) and share ideas and comments from others
with you.

now started to see it. My manager and I have had some frank discussions. I'm honestly not sure which of us was more startled, but a two-way conversation is now going on. I am now asked for advice on matters outside my job, and an element of trust/understanding seems to be growing. I'm doing well at my job and I know it. This is a statement that has taken me quite a while to write or say publicly."

Comment: This, it seems to me, is a beautiful example of the value of open communications and of taking the initiative in one's relationship with his boss. Just recently I was party to the following scene: in a manager's office, a subordinate and a manager were going over some data provided by a research firm regarding the internal operations for which the manager was responsible.

> Manager (as he looked over the data with some concern): "I'm absolutely amazed! I had no idea that these conditions existed!"
> Subordinate: "I could have told you that a long time ago."
> Manager: "But you didn't! Why not?"

What may be obvious to you may not be as apparent to your boss. You owe him the benefit of your observations; and they should be communicated to him in a manner that will permit both of you to deal with problems in constructive ways.

Example: "My big goal was to get a transfer to the _____ office. I have not gotten too far in that area, as my continued presence in _____ will attest. I feel satisfied, at least, that I made a determined effort to gain the promotion transfer. My ambitions have been made known to my superior. The reason given for no progress is that appropriate openings were not available. It sounds plausible. . . ."

Comment: Discussing your ambitions with your boss provides you with an opportunity to learn something about the realities of the promotion market and to determine just how your boss assesses your potential.

But there is another ingredient frequently overlooked: if you plan these discussions well, they will also provide you with a forum for planning a specific set of activities in which you should engage in order to improve the probabilities of promotion or transfer. In short, you should ask not only what your boss is doing about your promotion but also what kinds of things you should accomplish in your job to increase the odds of your getting what you want.

Note, too, that there is some satisfaction to be gained simply by trying to accomplish some goal, even if it fails. There's potentially more satisfaction in that than in not trying at all, because the feedback gives you a clearer picture of the realities in which you must function.

Example: "I have made progress in accomplishing both immediate and long-range goals. I have become more involved with the administrative functions within the unit. This has been possible mostly *because of the time I have spent training my supervisors in the clerical operations of the area.*" (italics mine)

Comment: Here's an example of delegation of those items that are best done by others. A good career plan uses all the resources available. We accomplish more when we have people working with us who know what needs to be done and how to do it. Frequently, our goal is not to do their work but to train them so they can do their work themselves!

This same person continues: "I really believe that having had the opportunity to look at the functions that I am now performing and at the setting of functions in a priority order has had much to do with the success I have achieved. To be truthful, the first time I had thought about this as a career was at our sessions together. Once the goals have been set, you have a direction to follow—you take the steps necessary to achieve those goals."

Comment: Right on! Our experience has been that setting goals is a prerequisite to any sense of achievement. You don't know if you're succeeding if you don't know what it is you're trying to succeed at!

Example: "So things are better all around. . . . The irony is: I do not have what I thought I required—a stable, concretely described position. It changes daily. . . ."

Comment: You'll recall our saying that all of us make our own jobs. This person thought he could not progress because his job was "hectic, ever-changing, at the whim of the organization." He wanted a job description and a clearly structured career path.

We may think we need job descriptions and precise statements regarding career paths, but the fact of the matter is that our greatest satisfactions and developments come from an intrinsic motivation generated by our own sense of direction. This is not to suggest that we don't need to know what is expected of us ,on our jobs. It is to suggest that things get better when we give direction to our own careers, with some realistic awareness of who we are and what the environment is like in which we function.

Example: In response to the question in the form about difficulties in achieving goals, one woman wrote: "Contrary to what I anticipated, the company has not really been a problem; if anything, I've found it supportive of me as an individual. What I am feeling, though, is that it's hard to be a woman now; I feel a special responsibility. . . ."

Comment: Isn't this what career growth is all about: the willingness to shift the responsibility for what happens from the organization, your superiors, and your subordinates to yourself? When you do that, the responsibility is awesome and somewhat frightening. But it's also very rewarding when you begin to see growth and know that it is due to your own efforts.

Example: "I have spoken to my manager and the regional vice president on how they feel my chances are for a promotion to manager. I even went as far as getting a time commitment out of my regional vice president on how long I should wait for that promotion."

Comment: Please don't think that we included this quote as propaganda. It simply points up again the very real value of initiating conversation about you, your job, and your career with those who are in a position to help. And, of course, it also emphasizes the value of doing some soul-searching first to give yourself a sense of direction.

But don't expect every manager to be definite about career timing. It is frequently difficult to know precisely when opportunities will arise for employees. This particular person was fortunate in talking about his career with his manager at a time when a more definite time schedule could be discussed. Nevertheless, most managers will be willing to talk with you about your potential and the plans you'll have to make for your own career growth.

Example: But it's not all roses. Here's another observation from a conferee: "Do you know that none of my bosses up the line sat down and asked me about my experience? Do you realize that I have tried to talk, and the majority of times they look at their watches—and that tells it all! Well, fortunately for me there are two or three around who still think of people as persons and not as 'things' that should be put to work for them."

Comment: There are all kinds of bosses—some good, some not so good. But good or not, they play a vital role in our careers. Our job is to learn how to work with them, how to use our strengths effectively, and how to utilize *their* strengths for our common good. It's not an easy task, but it is *essential.* If we don't do that, we withdraw from giving direction and purpose to our own careers— and that's when the environment and the organization will start shaping us.

Example: "Personal timetables are established. However, we are doomed by a variety of distractions. . . . My personal devil is the telephone. It rings every five minutes. It not only disturbs the continuity of the project at hand but creates new projects of the moment which apparently, from the whining tones wafting from the receiver apparatus, need immediate attention as well. If I could have an hour, two hours, guaranteed each day when the phones did not ring, I believe that I, my peers, my superiors, my subordinates would produce a breathtaking amount of work. . . ."

Comment: Isn't this problem really a motivation for personal planning? We frequently hide behind telephone calls, details, or office visits to delay projects, to help us feel "important," to play the martyr, or whatever. A serious look at some of the excellent materials on time management (and even delegation) would be a place to start in conquering the enemy telephone. For example, see Drucker's chapter on this subject in his book *The Effective Executive* or Alec Mackenzie's book on the same theme.

Career Issues Revolving around the Family and Other Interpersonal Issues

Example: "Home vs. career vs. family—I've been devoting more attention to the quality of time spent with my husband and find that our lives are richer as a result. Plans for starting a family are still in abeyance, but John has become more favorably inclined to the idea of it. If we do have a family, he is the logical one of us to be home; his career is far less established and less lucrative than mine; and he has expressed a willingness to play that role when the time comes."

Comment: If you (especially the males) find yourself questioning your spouse and his or her career needs, check your value systems carefully. We spent some time discussing the shifting values in our working force. These shifts offer options to us that we couldn't consider even a decade ago. It is exciting to consider the many different roles that husbands and wives may now play to establish enriching careers for both; those alternatives should be a part of your career strategy considerations.

Example: "I find myself daydreaming every once in a while about building a sumptuous house on the shore in San Diego . . . rather than scratching for a top-level executive position in the home office. Although I am stimulated by the thought of the pace of an executive life, I am also stimulated by the thought of that good life in Southern California. . . . Perhaps I should concentrate more on my medium-range goals in a West Coast environment and then see how I feel about things from there."

Comment: When we do our career planning, we should not dismiss our daydreams. They tell us a lot about what's important to us, what we'd *really* like to do. Of course, reality testing is also a key to sound personal development, so daydreams must be analyzed within that context.

The short- and medium-range goals are more effectively and more readily tested against reality. Dreams about the distant future are usually hazy and ambiguous. The more immediate goals can be described in more specific terms, with clearly delineated standards. That's why we should develop them first and work toward them in very specific ways—but always with the idea in mind that they are really means to some longer-range end. Career planning is a means-ends chain where the achievement of one end gives us the experience necessary to decide whether it should be the means toward some new goal.

So go ahead and daydream—and wait and see what real experiences will tell you about the validity of that dream!

Career Issues Centering on Self

Example: "I've changed my ideas about fate control and have come to realize that *my* control is critical. That's led to a new way of looking at my job—I got rid of a lot of things that were bothering me and have delegated a lot of the operations. I spend most of my time on control. In doing this, I've used some of my friends and new employees to help me sort it all out. This takes time, but I've learned that it takes time to bring yourself into some organized, controlled plan of action that can work toward the achievement of your goals."

Example: "Causes of my success since we were together: mainly, *a change in attitude* (italics mine). I feel freer to act, make decisions, be assertive, be expressive. If I'm more relaxed (which I am), it's because I feel I can be, and in fact *must* be, to function more effectively. My boss says I'm 'acting more like a manager' (whatever that means). I have noticed some improvement in my ability to determine priorities and to delegate tasks."

Example: "I never went back, as I said I would, to discuss such things as my strengths and weaknesses, how I fit into the department, or possible opportunities in other departments. . . . I haven't attempted to satisfy some of my other needs outside my work. . . . I've not been as involved with my wife and her activities as I wanted to."

Comment: Why not? The clue comes just a few words later, when this person writes: "I still do not know what I really want to do as far as my actual job goes."

Remember our discussion of the career wheel? The hub of that wheel is self-understanding: knowing one's self and understanding how the self-concept relates to all aspects of career—job, family, community. That comes first. Without it, setting priorities is difficult. And without priorities, it's difficult to know what to do when. As a result, there will be floundering, frustration, and inactivity. Granted, in trying to understand ourselves, there will be mistakes, wrong decisions, and misdirections. But we learn from those experiences; they give us clearer insights into who we are and what we need. Learning comes from doing. If we do nothing, we don't learn.

So, if you've been inactive in your own career planning ("I don't have the time"; "The job makes so many demands on my time, I can't afford the luxury of just thinking and planning"; "I'll have time later on to worry about other things such as doing things for me and my family"), sit back and ask yourself why. What does the answer tell you about what's important to you? Does it suggest that you really are doing those things that have priority for you, that you are really not willing to risk a change in those priorities?

Perhaps some of the experiences of your peers related here will suggest some possibilities for action.

15

Summary

The Basic Principles of Career Strategy

1. A career is more than a job. It is a series of roles which a person plays. The nature of each role and the manner and the situation in which it is played have some bearing on the next role in the series.

2. A career strategy formulates the various roles an individual plans to play at various stages, or at any given time, in his career and indicates the objectives necessary to implement that strategy, the resources needed to achieve those objectives, and the guidelines or policies for that achievement.

3. A career strategy requires flexibility, clarity, and specificity, a broad and imaginative perspective, a focus on purpose, action, and roles, an orientation to reality as well as to the future, and a willingness to deal with conflict and ambiguity and to take risks.

4. In formulating a career strategy, one should consider what might be done, what can be done, what should be done, and what one

wants to do. This requires an analysis of self and of the various environments in which the self is and will be functioning.

5. The environment influences the individual's career strategy through his perceptions of his job, of the environments created by his superiors, his peers, and his subordinates, of the broader cultural and socioeconomic environments, and of his family.

6. Individuals tend to resist thinking strategically about their careers. Barriers include the pressures of daily routine and the discomfort of change and of thinking too closely about oneself. Factors that encourage strategic planning of one's career include consistent performance below one's expectations, pressure from others to do it, predictions about an unsettled future, and the perceived success of others who have done it.

7. Some general career strategies include doing nothing (maintaining the status quo), broadening the base for utilizing one's strengths, complementing one's strengths with the strengths of others, diversifying into new fields by developing additional strengths, and accommodating one's own style to blend with conflicting styles of others.

8. Implementing one's career strategy requires first the identification of key tasks, followed by the organization of resources necessary to achieve these key tasks, the development of the necessary control (feedback) systems, and the creation of standards against which to judge one's results.

9. Career strategy objectives must have a stated priority in terms of importance and timing and be tied to measurable and meaningful standards. They should provide a sense of challenge and newness, hold a promise of longer-range payoff, and be clearly related to the total career. Finally a commitment should be made to others regarding schedules and performance standards for each objective.

10. Behavior is motivated. A person initiates behavior based on an expectation that he will be able to behave in appropriate ways to reach a desired outcome and that effective behavior will in fact lead to the desired results.

11. Desired outcomes are related to certain need states of the individual. A given need state may be satisfied in a variety of ways,

which are determined by experience. One outcome may satisfy many different needs.

12. Needs can be classified into certain levels or categories. When an individual is deprived of satisfaction of a felt need, fixation may occur at that need level in an attempt to satisfy the need. Continued frustration may lead to regression to lower-level needs in order to gain satisfaction.

13. For the mature adult, career satisfaction seems to be anchored primarily in higher-level needs related to ego status and self-actualization.

14. Human beings are primarily learning animals. Learning how to learn is fundamental to the implementation of one's career strategy.

15. Individuals learn best when the direction for change comes from them rather than from someone else, when their self-esteem is heightened, and when they commit themselves to a goal. Good career strategies take this into account.

16. There are a variety of ways by which an individual can learn, and an individual tends to develop his own learning style. That style has an impact on how he sees and approaches life in general. Hence learning style literally influences who we are.

17. Learning requires behavior and therefore interfaces with motivation. The process of learning takes on certain predictable forms—either early rapid change and gradual plateauing or early slow change followed by more rapid change and again gradual plateauing. The course of progress depends on such factors as the nature of the material to be learned, the motivation and skills of the learner, and the specific learning situation. Individuals can exercise some control over their learning process by influencing certain of these factors.

18. Career objectives cannot be achieved by an individual alone, no matter how well they're formulated. Implementation of a career strategy requires interaction with others. Thus the effectiveness of one's interpersonal relations is highly important in career planning and achievement.

19. We communicate through our total behavior pattern, verbal and nonverbal, and primarily for our own satisfaction. There are risks

inherent in communicating as well as in not communicating; both should receive consideration.

20. Mutual trust is a significant factor in effective communications. Adequate exposure of one's information and feelings and willingness to seek feedback from others are significant factors in establishing trust. Inadequate exposure and failure to seek feedback can cause frustration, hostility, and withdrawal in others and in oneself.

21. An individual's interpersonal behavior is generally the result of his self-concept and his perception of the interpersonal behavior of others. Each individual is the greatest single factor in improving his interpersonal behavior, and such improvement can have a beneficial effect on the interpersonal behavior of others.

22. Effective communication involves the ability to analyze people, the desired response, supporting data, and possible methods of approach. Effective listening and effective confrontation are two skills needed for effective communications.

23. Organizational/environmental factors may support good or poor interpersonal behavior. Organizational factors lead people to perceive environments and careers in ways that may enhance or frustrate career planning and goals.

24. Next to managing oneself, the most important thing in implementing a career strategy is to learn how to manage the boss.

25. The power a boss exercises over an individual rests largely with the individual's own set of needs, attitudes, and value systems.

26. The boss will most likely change (a) when he has internalized the need for change, (b) when he feels he has some acceptable options, (c) when the risk of failure is minimized, (d) when he can experience a sense of competence with the resulting change, and (e) when he can identify with the source of the proposed change.

27. An individual can develop effective strategies when the boss shows resistance to proposed change. These strategies are based on principles for managing conflict and on an awareness of individual differences among bosses.

28. What an individual is doing now, and how he feels about it, has crucial importance for his planning for the future. Part of what an individual is doing on his present job should be concerned with developmental needs and future functions as well as with present job demands.

29. How an individual defines his ideal job and how he evaluates his current job experiences will provide significant indications of the type of planning he should be doing for developmental experiences in the short- and long-range future.

30. Job designs can and should be related to the dominant need patterns of individuals in those jobs. Therefore, individuals who are aware of their dominant needs can identify jobs with characteristics that relate to those needs.

31. Based on predominant worker values present in today's society, characteristics of a good job can be described, and jobs can be analyzed with regard to those characteristics. They are direct feedback, a client relationship, a natural module of work, personal accountability, control of resources, and the opportunity to use a unique expertise.

32. The climate of an organization can be measured along various dimensions: conformity, responsibility, standards, rewards, clarity, and team spirit. Individuals can detect these characteristics and can personally do things to change each of them.

33. Every organization has personnel practices and policies and characteristic management philosophies that influence the direction of one's career. Awareness and understanding of those practices and policies is essential to the formulation and implementation of an effective career strategy.

34. Without behavior there can be no change. Without change there can be no growth. Without growth there can be no living.

Bibliography

Adams, Edward L., Jr. *Career Advancement Guide.* New York: McGraw-Hill, second edition, 1975.

Alderfer, Clayton P. *Existence, Relatedness, and Growth: Human Needs in Organizational Settings.* New York: Free Press, 1972.

Allport, Gordon W. *The Person in Psychology.* Boston: Beacon Press, 1968.

Anderson, Nels. *Work and Leisure.* New York: The Free Press, 1961.

Andrews, Kenneth R. *The Concept of Corporate Strategy.* Homewood, Ill.: Dow Jones-Irwin, 1971.

Argyris, Chris. *Integrating the Individual and the Organization.* New York: Wiley, 1964.

———. *Increasing Leadership Effectiveness.* New York: Wiley-Interscience, 1976.

———. *Interpersonal Competence and Organizational Effectiveness.* Homewood, Ill.: Dorsey Press, 1962.

Bardwick, Judith M. *Psychology of Women: A Study of Biocultural Conflicts.* New York: Harper & Row, 1971.

Beckhard, Richard. *Organizational Development: Strategies and Models.* Reading, Mass.: Addison-Wesley, 1969.

Bennis, Warren G. *Changing Organizations.* New York: McGraw-Hill, 1966.

———, Edgar H. Schein, David E. Berlow, and F. I. Steele (eds.). *Interpersonal Dynamics.* Homewood, Ill.: Dorsey Press, 1964; revised edition, Dorsey Press, 1968.

———, Kenneth D. Benne, and Robert Chin (eds.). *The Planning of Change.* New York: Holt, Rinehart and Winston, second edition, 1969.

Berlew, David E., and Douglas T. Hall. "The Socialization of Managers: Effects of Expectations on Performance." *Administrative Science Quarterly,* 11, pp. 207–223.

———, and Douglas T. Hall. "Some Determinants of Early Managerial Success." Working Paper No. 81–64, Sloan School of Management, M.I.T., Cambridge, Mass., 1964.

Bolles, Richard N. *What Color Is Your Parachute? A Practical Manual for Job-Hunters and Career Changers.* Berkeley, Calif.: Ten Speed Press, revised edition, 1975.

Borow, Henry (ed.). *Man in a World at Work.* Boston: Houghton Mifflin, 1964.

Bray, Douglas W., Richard J. Campbell, and Donald L. Grant. *Formative Years in Business.* New York: Wiley, 1974.

Calvert, Robert N., and John E. Steele. *Planning Your Career.* New York: McGraw-Hill, 1963.

Cartwright, Dorwin, and Alvin Zander (eds.). *Group Dynamics.* New York: Harper & Row, third edition, 1967.

Christensen, C. Roland, Kenneth R. Andrews, and Joseph L. Bower. *Business Policy: Text and Cases.* Homewood, Ill.: Irwin, fourth edition, 1977.

Cook, Paul W., and George von Peterfy. *Problems of Corporate Power.* Homewood, Ill.: Irwin, 1968.

Crites, John O. *Career Maturity Inventory.* Monterey, Calif.: McGraw-Hill, 1973.

————. *Theory and Research Handbook, Career Maturity Inventory.* Monterey, Calif.: McGraw-Hill, 1973.

Dalton, Gene W., Louis B. Barnes, and Abraham Zaleznik. *The Distribution of Authority in Formal Organizations.* Boston: Division of Research, Harvard Business School, 1968.

Deutsch, Morton. *The Resolution of Conflict: Constructive and Destructive Processes.* New Haven: Yale University Press, 1973.

Drucker, Peter F. *The Age of Discontinuity.* New York: Harper & Row, 1969.

Eiduson, Bernice T. *Scientists: Their Psychological World.* New York: Basic Books, 1962.

Filley, Allan C. *Interpersonal Conflict Resolution.* New York: Scott Foresman & Co., 1975.

Fogarty, Michael P., Rhona Rapoport, and Robert N. Rapoport. *Sex, Career, and Family.* Beverly Hills, Calif.: Sage, 1971.

Ghiselli, Edwin E. *Explorations in Managerial Talent.* Pacific Palisades, Calif.: Goodyear, 1971.

Golembiewski, Robert T., and Arthur Blumberg (eds.). *Sensitivity Training and the Laboratory Approach.* Itasca, Ill.: Peacock Publishers, 1970.

Guth, William. *Organizational Strategy: Analysis, Commitment, Implementation.* Homewood, Ill.: Irwin, 1974.

Hall, Calvin S., and Gardner Lindzey. *Theories of Personality.* New York: Wiley, second edition, 1970.

Hall, Douglas T., and Francine E. Gordon. "Career Choices of Married Women: Effects on Conflict, Role Behavior, and Satisfaction." *Journal of Applied Psychology,* 58, pp. 42–48.

Hall, Douglas T. *Careers in Organizations.* Pacific Palisades, Calif.: Goodyear, 1976.

Hall, Douglas T., and Khalil Nougaim. "An Examination of Maslow's Need Hierarchy in an Organizational Setting." *Organizational Behavior and Human Performance*, 3, pp. 12–35.

Hegarty, Edward J. *How to Succeed in Company Politics*. New York: McGraw-Hill, second edition, 1976.

Henning, Margaret, and Anne Jardin. *The Managerial Woman*. Garden City, N.Y.: Anchor Press/Doubleday, 1977.

Hilgard, Ernest R. *Theories of Learning*. New York: Appleton-Century-Crofts, 1956.

Hinrichs, John. *The Motivation Crisis*. New York: AMACOM, 1974.

Holland, John L. *Making Vocational Choices: A Theory of Careers*. Englewood Cliffs, N.J.: Prentice-Hall, 1973.

Jennings, Eugene E. "Mobicentric Man." *Psychology Today*, July 1970, pp. 35–40.

———. *The Mobile Manager*. Ann Arbor, Michigan: Bureau of Industrial Relations, Graduate School of Business Administration, University of Michigan, 1967.

———. *Routes to the Executive Suite*. New York: McGraw-Hill, 1971.

Katz, Daniel, and Robert L. Kahn. *The Social Psychology of Organizations*. New York: Wiley, 1966.

Kaufman, Harold G. *Obsolescence and Professional Career Development*. New York: AMACOM, 1974.

Kellogg, Marvin S. *Career Management*. New York: AMACOM, 1972.

Kindall, Alva F., and James Gaza. "Positive Program for Performance Appraisal." *Harvard Business Review*, November–December 1963, pp. 153–167.

Knowles, Henry P., and Borje O. Saxberg. *Personality and Leadership Behavior*. Reading, Mass.: Addison-Wesley, 1971.

Knowles, Malcolm S. *The Adult Learner: A Neglected Species*. Houston, Texas: Gulf Publishing Co., 1973.

Lawler, Edward E., III. *Motivation in Work Organizations*. Monterey, Calif.: Brooks/Cole Publishing Co., 1973.

Leavitt, Harold J. *Managerial Psychology*. Chicago: University of Chicago Press, third edition, 1972.

Levinson, Harry. *The Exceptional Executive*. Cambridge, Mass.: Harvard University Press, 1968.

———. *Executive Stress*. New York: Harper & Row, 1969.

———. "What an Executive Should Know about His Boss." *Think*, Vol. 34, No. 2, pp. 51–60.

Likert, Rensis, and Jane Gibson. *New Ways of Managing Conflict*. New York: McGraw-Hill, 1976.

Litwin, George H., and Robert A. Stringer, Jr. *A Brief Scoring Manual for Achievement, Affiliation, and Power Motivation*. Boston: McBer & Co., 1970.

Lorsch, Jay William, and Louis B. Barnes. *Managers and Their Careers: Cases and Readings*. Homewood, Ill.: Irwin-Dorsey, 1972.

Mackenzie, R. Alec. *The Time Trap: How to Get More Done in Less Time.*
New York: AMACOM, 1972.

Mager, Robert F. *Developing Attitude toward Learning.* Palo Alto, Calif.:
Fearn Publishers, 1968.

Mahler, Walter H. *Structure, Power, and Results.* Homewood, Ill.: Dow
Jones-Irwin, 1975.

Maslow, Abraham H. *Motivation and Personality.* New York: Harper, 1954.

———. *Toward a Psychology of Being.* Princeton, N.J.: Van Nostrand, 1962.
1962.

May, Rollo. *Psychology and the Human Dilemma.* Princeton, N.J.: Van
Nostrand, 1967.

McBer & Co. *Organizational Climate Survey Questionnaire: Scale Definitions and Profile.* Boston, Mass., revised edition, 1975.

McClelland, David C. *The Achieving Society.* New York: Free Press, 1967.

Miller, Delbert C., and William H. Form. *Industrial Sociology.* New York:
Harper, 1951.

Newman, William H., and James P. Logan. *Strategy, Policy, and Central
Management.* Cincinnati, Ohio: Southwestern Publishing Co., 7th edition, 1976.

Osipow, Samuel. *Theories of Career Development.* New York: Appleton-
Century-Crofts, 1968.

Peters, Herman, and James C. Hansen (eds.). *Vocational Guidance and
Career Development.* New York: Macmillan Co., second edition, 1971.

Rittl, R. Richard, and G. Ray Funkhouser. *The Ropes to Skip and the Ropes
to Know: Studies in Organizational Behavior.* Columbus, Ohio: Grid,
Inc., 1977.

Roe, Anne, and M. Siegelman. *The Origin of Interests.* Washington, D.C.:
American Personnel and Guidance Association, 1964.

Rogers, Carl. *Freedom to Learn.* Columbus, Ohio: Merrill, 1969.

———. *On Becoming a Person.* Boston: Houghton Mifflin, 1961.

Schein, Edgar H. "The Individual, the Organization, and the Career: A
Conceptual Scheme." *Journal of Applied Behavioral Science,* 7, pp.
401–426.

———. *Organizational Psychology.* Englewood Cliffs, N.J.: Prentice-Hall,
1965.

Schmidt, Warren H., and Robert Tannenbaum. "The Management of Differences." *Harvard Business Review,* November–December 1960, pp.
107–116.

Schoonmaker, Alan N. *Anxiety and the Executive.* New York: AMACOM,
1969.

Sheehy, Gail. *Passages: Predictable Crises of Adult Life.* New York: Dutton
& Co., 1976.

Skinner, B. F. *Beyond Freedom and Dignity.* New York: Bantam/Vintage,
1972.

Sofer, Cyril. *Men in Mid-Career.* London: Cambridge University Press,
1970.

Steiner, Gary A. (ed.) *The Creative Organization*. Chicago: University of Chicago Press, 1965.

Stoner, J. A. F., T. P. Ference, E. K. Warren, and H. K. Christensen. "Patterns and Plateaus in Managerial Careers: An Exploratory Study." Research Paper No. 66, Graduate School of Business, Columbia University, 1974.

Super, Donald E. (ed.) *Career Development: Self-Concept Theory*. New York: CEEB, 1963.

———. *The Psychology of Careers*. New York: Harper, 1957.

Toffler, Alvin. *Future Shock*. New York: Random House, 1970.

Warga, Richard. *Personal Awareness: A Psychology of Adjustment*. Boston: Houghton Mifflin, 1974.

White, Robert W. *Lives in Progress*. New York: Holt, Rinehart and Winston, third edition, 1975.

Winter, David G. *The Power Motive*. New York: Free Press, 1973.

Woodward, Joan. *Industrial Organization: Theory and Practice*. London: Oxford University Press, 1967.

Wrapp, Edward H. "Good Managers Don't Make Policy Decisions." *Harvard Business Review*, September–October 1967, pp. 91–99.

Zalenik, Abraham, and David Moment. *The Dynamics of Interpersonal Behavior*. New York: Wiley, 1964.

Zaleznik, Abraham, and David Moment. *The Dynamics of Interpersonal Orientation and Conflict in Career*. Boston: Division of Research, Harvard Business School, 1970.

Index

DATE DUE			
MR 3 '83	MAR 14 '83		
AP 26 '85	APR 28 '85		
NO 26 '85	NOV 26 '85		

DEMCO 38-297